Franc Exchange

Coursebook

FRANC EXCHANGE

Effective Business Communication in France

Juri Gladkow Cranfield School of Management

Carol Sanders University of Surrey

Colin Gordon Cranfield School of Management

Grammar kit contributed by **Minou Reeves**
Southern LX Consortium, IBEX and International Briefing Centre, Farnham Castle

Produced by BBC Milton Keynes, supported by Eurotunnel,
the Department for Trade and Industry and
Open University and published by Pitman Publishing

Pitman Publishing
128 Long Acre, London WC2E 9AN

A Division of Longman Group UK Limited

First published in 1991

Language material © Juri Gladkow and Carol Sanders 1991
Business material © Colin Gordon 1991
Grammar kit © Minou Reeves 1991

A CIP catalogue record for this book is available from the British Library.

ISBN 0 273 03300 X

All rights reserved; no part of this publication may be reproduced, stored in a retrieval system, or transmitted in any form or by any other means, electronic, mechanical, photocopying, recording, or otherwise without either the prior written permission of the Publishers or a licence permitting restricted copying in the United Kingdom issued by the Copyright Licensing Agency, 33–34 Alfred Place, London WC1E 7DP. This book may not be lent, resold, hired out or otherwise disposed of by way of trade in any form of binding or cover other than that in which it is published, without the prior consent of the Publishers.

Typeset by Tek Art Ltd, Addiscombe, Croydon, Surrey
Printed in Great Britain by The Bath Press, Avon

Further copies of this coursebook and the complete
Franc Exchange package (video, video transcript, coursebook and four audio cassettes) are available from:
The Sales Department,
Pitman Publishing
128 Long Acre,
London, WC2E 9AN.

Any information provided by Eurotunnel in this package reflects the views of those participants as at the time of production. The design, development and construction of the Fixed Link and the operation of the System are all subject to change before the planned commencement of operations in 1993.

Contents

Preface ix

Project team xi

Introduction to the pack xiii

Part one Setting the business scene

Chapter 1 The business environment in France 3
Introduction – Facts and figures – Land area – Population – Main cities – Climate – Weights and measures – Holidays – Currency – Time – Political environment – Political parties – Central government – Economic environment – Macro-economic scene – Structure – Foreign trade – Anglo-French trade – Social environment – The law – Business education – Affluence – Leisure

Chapter 2 The regional environment 13
Regional profiles – Alsace – Aquitaine – Auvergne – Bourgogne – Bretagne – Centre – Champagne-Ardenne – Franche-Comté – Ile-de-France – Languedoc-Roussillon – Limousin – Lorraine – Midi-Pyrénées – Nord-Pas-de-Calais – Basse-Normandie – Haute-Normandie – Pays de la Loire – Picardie – Poitou-Charentes – Provence-Alpes-Côte d'Azur – Rhône-Alpes

Chapter 3 French market entry strategies 28
Direct exporting – Direct selling – Agents – Distributors – Branch offices – Forming a French company – SARL – SA – Acquisitions – Establishment of a manufacturing plant – Business magazine: introduction

Part two The language of business

Introduction to the language sequences 41
Introduction – The organisation of each sequence – The sections in detail – Preparation – A. Listen and understand – B. Develop your skills – C. Extend your vocabulary – D. Make your language work – E. Dialogues – Business notes – How to organise your learning – Video and audio references – Pronunciation and intonation

Chapter 1 The trade fair 45
Introduction – Key words and phrases – Faux amis – A. Listen and understand – A1. Getting the gist – A2. Getting the detail – B. Develop your skills – B1. The present indicative: how to assert and affirm – B2. Using negative expressions correctly with the present – B3. The use of **il** with verbs – B4. French adjectives and past principles – C. Extend your vocabulary – C1 Masculin or feminin? – C2. The -age suffix – C3. Compound expressions – D. Make your language work – D1. Presenting your company – E. Dialogues – E1. The Unipart representative – E2. The satellite dish – Language comment – Formal and informal – Modes of address – Sketch: La France aux Français – Business notes – Trade fair check-list – Business magazine 1

Chapter 2 Direct selling 75
Introduction – Key words and phrases – Faux amis – A. Listen and understand – A1. Getting the gist – A2. Getting the detail – A3. Summing up the scene – A4. Equivalents – B. Develop your skills – B1. The present revisited – B2. Reflexive

v

verbs – B3. Expressions with **on** and **se** – B4. The present subjunctive – B5. Negative expressions in comparisons – B6. Emphasising what you are saying with **ce qui/ce que, c'est** – B7. Talking about the future – C. Extend your vocabulary – C1. Some expressions of time – C2. A few prefixes – D. Make your language work – D1. How to win orders and influence people – D2. Describe your product – E. Dialogues – E1. Greeting people – E2. Interview with M. Duvauchelle – Language comment – Sketch: De la confiture avec tout – Business notes – Home-based sales staff – Terms of payment – Discounts – Dealing with buyers – Business magazine 2

Chapter 3 Working with an agent 102
Introduction – Key words and phrases – Faux amis – A. Listen and understand – A1. Getting the gist – A2. Getting the detail – A3. Summing up the scene – B. Develop your skills – B1. The present subjunctive – encore! – B2. Direct and indirect object pronouns – B3. How to talk about the past – B4. Verbs taking the auxiliary **être** – B5. Further into the past – C. Extend your vocabulary – C1. More ways of expressing time – C2. From verb to noun – C3. Nouns expressing qualities – D. Make your language work – D1. Publicising your product – D2. Getting people to meet their obligations – E. Dialogue – Language comment – Sketch: Un produit européen – Business notes – Establishing a company – Agents – Distributors – Business magazine 3

Chapter 4 Business at a local level 143
Introduction – Key words and phrases – Faux amis – A. Listen and understand – A1. Getting the gist – A2. Getting the detail – A3. Summing up the scene – B. Develop your skills – B1. The imperfect tense – B2. Habitual/repeated actions in the past – B3. Description in the past – B4. Imperfect in 'if' clauses – B5. Imperfect and perfect – B6. Immediate past – B7. Disjunctive pronouns – B8. Demonstrative pronouns – B9. Possessive pronouns – B10. Indefinite pronouns and indefinite adjective – B11. Indefinite pronouns – C. Extend your vocabulary – C1. Expressions with **avoir** – C2. Expressing disagreement – C3. Problems, problems – D. Make your language work – D1. Contrat de bail commercial – E. Dialogue – E1. Arguing your case – E2. Putting across your point of view – Language comment – Sketch: Mesures impériales – Business notes – Business magazine 4

Chapter 5 The Tunnel and beyond 179
Introduction – Key words and phrases – Faux amis – A. Listen and understand – A1. Getting the gist – A2. Getting the detail – A3. Summing up the scene – B. Develop your skills – B1. Direct object pronouns – B2. The pronoun **y** – B3. The pronoun **en** – B4. Prepositions with geographical names – B5. How to express the passive – C. Extend your vocabulary – C1. Prefixes **dé-** and **re-** – C2. The suffix **-able** – C3. Compound expressions – C4. More compounds – D. Make your language work – D1. How to talk about . . . – D2. Comment le dire en quelques phrases – D3. A presentation – D4. Instructions – E. Dialogue – Language comment – Sketch: Routes sans frontières – Business notes – Business magazine 5

Chapter 6 Establishing a bridgehead 217
Introduction – Key words and phrases – Faux amis – A. Listen and understand – A1. Getting the gist – A2. Getting the detail – A3. Summing up the scene – A4. Equivalents – B. Develop your skills – B1. The conditional tense – B2. Who's who and who's what – B3. Making comparisons – C. Extend your vocabulary – C1. **Faire** with measurements, distances and time – C2. Cela fait hollandais – C3. Expressions with **faire** –C4. How to get things done – D. Make your language work – D1. Comparisons – E. Dialogue – Sketch: Les Anglais – Business notes – Establishing a bridgehead – Business magazine 6

Chapter 7 Conducting meetings 250
Introduction – Key words and phrases – Faux amis – A. Listen and understand – A1. Getting the gist – A2. Getting the detail – B. Develop your skills – B1. The subjunctive once more – B2. The perfect tense: conversational past – B3. Infinitives in English and French – B4. Verbs, adjectives and their prepositions – C. Extend your vocabulary – C1. Au niveau de

prepositions – D. Make your language work –
D1. Comparisons – E. Dialogue – Sketch: La
bise – Business notes – Business magazine 7

The Grammar Kit

Vocabulary list

Where-to-go guide

Preface

Franc Exchange is a communication course designed to help businesses operate more effectively in the French market. Communication calls in this respect for two important elements; first the ability to speak in French, and secondly a knowledge of the people and their business environment.

Franc Exchange bases its teaching and distance learning programme on seven authentic business situations, where French is being spoken in the course of transacting business. Because the situations are authentic, the issues and the language used to cope with these issues are real too. There are inevitably occasions where a better way exists of making the point or expressing a view, but the emphasis in this course is not on perfectionism, but on getting you, the exporter or representative, into the French market and helping you to communicate effectively with French colleagues. Perfection and fluency will come with practice. They will come less easily if you don't venture into the market.

It has often been said that English is the international language of business and that native speakers of English have a lesser need to learn other people's languages. This, however, misses the point entirely. The British business person travelling in Europe without language skills is put at an immediate disadvantage. Too easily the impression can be given that we do not care sufficiently about the market or do not have the long-term commitment. We are often in competition with other Europeans who do have language skills and who are therefore better able to gain an advantage. It is hard to be fully professional if you cannot even read a trade journal! Also, one of the great pleasures of international business is the forging of new friendships which create the trust that underlines successful new partnerships. In France the ability to speak some French will be greatly appreciated and reap rewards both in business and in friendship.

The single market transforms France into an integral part of the UK's domestic market. As the Channel Tunnel opens, important business centres are but a train journey away and doing business in mainland Europe is set to become increasingly challenging and increasingly demanding. France offers enormous opportunities for those businesses prepared to rise to the challenge. Recognising this the BBC, DTI, Eurotunnel, OU (Open University) and Pitman have collaborated to make *Franc Exchange* available as a vital ingredient in your European strategy.

May we wish you every success. Bonne chance!

Project team

Series consultants:

Nigel Reeves OBE MA DPhil FIL FRSA CIEX is Head of Modern Languages at Aston University. He is former Chairman of the Institute of Linguists Council, President of the Association of Teachers of German and President of the National Association of Language Advisers. Professor Reeves is the author of a number of books, his latest being 'The Invisible Economy', a profile of Britain's invisible exports, which he co-authored with Professor David Liston. It was published by Pitman in 1988.

David Liston OBE MA CIEX FRSA
Sadly Professor Liston died in May 1989, whilst working on this, his last, project. For 30 years he worked with the Metal Box Company before becoming the first Assistant Director of The Manchester Business School. His other academic appointments included, Pro-Rector and Visiting Professor of the Polytechnic of Central London; Professor at the European Business School; Visiting Fellow, Henley School of Management and External Assessor for The Open University course in International Marketing. For three years he was industrial adviser to the Government and led UK teams to EEC seminars on East-West Trade. Professors Reeves and Liston collaborated as consultants on *Making Your Mark* – the first communication pack in this series – published in 1988 by Pitman Publishing.

BBC production team:

Roger Penfound
Jenny Moore
Colette Thomson
The project has been organised by the BBC Milton Keynes production centre. From this centre the BBC works in partnership with the Open University to produce a wide range of distance-taught courses.

Business author:

Colin Gordon BA
Senior Lecturer in European Management, Cranfield School of Management (also a co-author of The Handy Report on Management Education).

Language authors:

Carol Sanders MA DU PGCE FIL Chev. Palmes Acad.
Professor of French at the University of Surrey. Also a contributor to a number of other language courses including some produced by the BBC.

Juri Gladkow Licencié traducteur
Cranfield School of Management (Head of French, Spanish and Russian in the European Languages Unit).

PROJECT TEAM

Grammar Kit:

Minou Reeves DBA MA
Teaches French and German for the Southern LX Consortium, IBEX, and at the International Briefing Centre at Farnham Castle.

Critical reader:

Lucinda Campbell-Gray
Eurotunnel Consortium

Acknowledgement

Thanks to Marianne Howarth of Brighton Polytechnic and Michael Woodhall of Dorset Institute, authors of *Making Your Mark*, for their help and work on the original teaching concept.

Introduction to the pack

The pack consists of

- a video cassette
- a course book
- a video transcript
- four audio cassettes

Video

The video contains seven sequences, each showing an authentic business situation where British business people are seen to be dealing effectively with the French market.

The course book

Part One of the book provides you with a general background to France and its business environment.

The language chapters in Part Two run parallel to the video sequences. In order to be able to do the exercises you need to have watched the relevant video sequence.

The appendices contain a Grammar Kit, with more detailed information and essential grammatical points, a vocabulary list, and a Where-to-go guide with sources of further information and advice.

Video transcript

This booklet provides a full transcript of the video sequences. You can use it to help you understand what is said on the video and once you have progressed a little, to analyse the language in more depth.

INTRODUCTION TO THE PACK

Audio cassettes

The pack contains four audio cassettes

- a travel cassette
- a study cassette
- two business magazines cassettes.

On the travel cassette you will find selected extracts from the video sound track and some useful pointers to improve comprehension. You can listen to this cassette while travelling to and from work, on the way to visit customers, while mowing the lawn, in short: whenever you find yourself with some spare time on your hands.

The study cassette contains exercise material for active speaking exercises and some possible answers to some of the exercises in the book.

The remaining two cassettes contain an introductory and seven further Business magazines. The seven magazines tie in with the seven language chapters and tackle the business issues raised in these chapters. You will hear a variety of people talking about their experiences in the French market.

In addition to these four cassettes, you will need a blank cassette to record your answers to some of the exercises.

Part 1

Setting the business scene

by Colin Gordon

Chapter 1

The business environment in France

Introduction

France is a country on the crest of a wave, its economy surging forward after several years languishing in the doldrums. Growth is strong, capital investment is at peak levels again and inflation is low and moving even lower. It is a country, too, which is vigorously gearing up in all sectors for the single European market. This has been adopted as the nation's rallying cry and is seen as one of the main elements of its macro-economic strategy. To gain maximum advantage of the single market all its resources are being mobilised. Overseas investment has never been higher (FF65 bn of acquisitions in the first half of 1989 alone) but at the same time France is throwing open its domestic markets and welcoming new foreign investment, both to stimulate its own growth and technology, and to create the jobs it so badly needs. Helping to lead the charge, there is a growing breed of young and fiercely competitive entrepreneurial managers capable of financial wizardry on the capital markets who are taking over from the retiring founders of many small and medium sized companies. As they do so, they are rapidly breaking away from the cloistered élitism of the *grandes écoles* management and technical education system, still prevalent in some of the large indigenous French companies.

The face of France is also changing with this new leap forward. The Xth economic plan has as one of its platforms, the renewal and extension of the country's basic infrastructure – particularly motorways and high-speed train links – in the firm conviction that more must be done to help the 'depths' of France (*la France profonde*) benefit from the greater European movement. So, Lille, Marseille, Nice and a number of other towns are to be redeveloped as '*Eurométropoles*' with an emphasis on service industries and facilities, following the example of many regional towns in West Germany and the United Kingdom. Tourism, too, has been identified as a major target for development.

And the French consumer reflects some of this dynamism. Shopping is fun, and the French are stimulated by colour, style, design and new, sophisticated gadgetry. They are prepared to pay a high price for high quality but also have a keen eye for a bargain. But they are harder to please, too, and will generally take much more time in making their purchases as they inspect every aspect of a product. Often, the entire family is consulted. Technical and design features are therefore important. 'In every Frenchman there lies a peasant' goes the saying, and his basic conservatism together with his love for flair and dazzle is just one of the paradoxes that make up his often highly individualistic personality.

Much of industry is booming, and the hypermarkets and supermarkets (*les grandes surfaces*) offer a glittering array of products to an avid, discerning public. This is the France which offers so many opportunities in all sectors to those British businesses which are prepared to take a long, hard look at the exciting potential of the

SETTING THE BUSINESS SCENE

French market and to understand the intricacies of its business practices.

Facts and figures

Land area

Metropolitan France, (as opposed to the DOM-TOM, *Départements* and *Territoires d'Outre Mer* – French overseas possessions) is the largest country in West Europe. It covers an area of 550,000 km^2, of which 61 per cent is agricultural land and 26 per cent forest.

Population

In 1988, the population was established at over 55.7 million people, including 4.5 million immigrants. The annual population growth rate was 0.4% (0.1% in the UK, −0.2% in West Germany) in 1987. With 14.1 births per 1,000 inhabitants annually, France has the second highest birthrate in the EC, behind the Republic of Ireland. Nevertheless, as in other West European countries, the population is ageing, albeit at a slower rate. In 1987, 10 million people were over 60, a figure due to rise to 12 million in the year 2000 and 15 million in 2020. In the year 2000, France will, however, also have more people in their 20s than any other European country. Nevertheless, the top item of expenditure by the year 2000 will be health.

Main cities

The major urban centres of population are:

Paris	8.7 million
Lyon	1.2 million
Marseille	1.1 million
Lille	0.9 million
Bordeaux	0.7 million
Toulouse	0.6 million
Nantes	0.5 million
Nice	0.5 million
Toulon	0.4 million
Grenoble	0.4 million
Rouen	0.4 million
Strasbourg	0.4 million

Source: INSEE

Population by region is approximately:

Ile-de-France	10.2 million
Nord-Pas-de-Calais	3.9 million
Picardie	1.7 million
Champagne-Ardenne	1.3 million
Lorraine	2.3 million
Alsace	1.5 million
Franche-Comté	1.0 million
Haute-Normandie	1.6 million
Basse-Normandie	1.4 million
Bretagne	2.7 million
Pays de la Loire	2.5 million
Poitou-Charentes	1.5 million
Aquitaine	2.7 million
Midi-Pyrénées	2.3 million
Languedoc-Roussillon	1.9 million
Provence-Alpes-Côte-d'Azur	4.0 million
Rhône-Alpes	5.1 million
Bourgogne	1.6 million
Centre	2.3 million
Auvergne	1.3 million
Limousin	0.7 million
Corse	0.2 million

Source: INSEE

Climate

France has a temperate climate, with some considerable variation of temperatures and rainfall between the Atlantic and Channel coasts and the Mediterranean area.

Weights and measures

Weights and measures are expressed in the metric system.

Holidays

There are 11 bank holidays in France, one of which is statutory, the remainder are recognised by collective bargaining agreements. They are as follows:

1 January,
Easter Monday,
1 May (Labour Day – statutory),
8 May,

Whit Monday,
Ascension Thursday,
14 July,
15 August (Assumption),
1 November (All Saints Day),
11 November (Armistice Day) and
25 December.

When a bank holiday falls on a Thursday or Tuesday, it is customary in France to take the intervening Friday or Monday off, too (a practice known as *faire le pont*)! For this reason in May it may be particularly difficult to contact businesses in France.

Annual paid leave (the legal entitlement is 5 weeks) is often split between a winter holiday in January–March and a sacrosanct summer holiday in July–August. Holidays taken by businessmen are, therefore, less staggered than in the UK, and every effort should be made to avoid doing urgent business during those two summer months (particularly August).

School holidays vary somewhat according to region, but are generally speaking as follows: *Summer* – 6/8 July to 9/10 September, *All Saints* – 24/27 October to 2/5 November, *Christmas* – 19/22 December to 4/7 January, *Winter* – either 13/14 February to 1/4 March *or* 20/21 February to 8/11 March, *Spring* – either 17/20 April to 4/6 May *or* 25/27 April to 10/13 May.

Currency

French Franc (FF) = 100 centimes. There is sometimes still a confusing tendency, however, to refer to *anciens francs*, particularly when talking of houses or cars, eg: 10 millions de francs *might* be 100,000 new francs (divide by 100).

Time

One hour ahead of the United Kingdom (for two weeks or so in October no time difference exists!). Most French managers start work between 8–9.00 am and some finish quite late in the evening between 7–8.00 pm. The best time to make phone calls to France is, therefore, between 9–11.00 am and 1–5.00 pm (UK time). Long lunches are becoming somewhat of a myth, particularly in Paris, but less so further South. Breakfast meetings are now quite common in Paris.

Political environment

For administrative purposes France consists of 22 *régions* each comprising two to five *départements*, of which there are 95 in Metropolitan France. The *départements* in turn comprise a number of much smaller units called *communes* (some can have as few as 20–30 inhabitants!). At each level there are elected representatives, grouped in councils (*conseils*). In the regions these councils are lead by a council *président* and in *communes* by a mayor (*maire*). Their power and influence either on local or national terms should never be underestimated in business, since quite frequently they have been in their posts for many years (up to 25–30 years in many cases) and they double up their duties by being either *député* (Member of Parliament in the lower chamber, the *Assemblée Nationale*) or *sénateur* (in the *Sénat*, the upper chamber). They can and do use their influence to bring major investment and improvements to their areas. Knowing them could be rewarding! Also very important are State-*appointed* representatives, such as the *préfet de région* and the *préfet* at département level. Over the last decade there has been a general tendency to move away from the highly centralised administration France had known for centuries, to a situation where local authorities at *commune*, *département* and *région* level, are much freer to make key decisions. As sources of investment grants and incentives, therefore, they are as significant as the State development agency, DATAR (*Délégation à l'Aménagement du Territoire et à l'Action Régionale*) More of this later.

Political parties

The major parties in France are the Socialist Party (PS – *Parti Socialiste*), the Gaullist Party

(RPR – *Rassemblement pour la République*), a federation of parties (Republicans, Radicals) called the *Union pour la Démocratie Française* (UDF), the *Union du Centre* (UDC) centred around Raymond Barre, the ex-finance minister under the ex-president, Giscard d'Estaing, the Communist Party (PC – *Parti Communiste*) and the National Front (FN – *Front National*).

Central government

The era of the right of centre one-party rule which had lasted virtually unbroken since 1958, came to an end in 1981. The new socialist Government elected in that year was ousted by the Right in 1986, only to be returned to power in 1988, this time without an overall majority, however. After the mistakes made by the Socialists in 1981–83, the present political climate is characterised by moderation and caution of a Social Democratic hue which no longer frightens anyone, including business. The Communist Party being the most orthodox and hard-line of the Western communist parties is generally seen to be out of step with present trends. The National Front party gives rise to some concern, however, particularly over racist issues. It continues to benefit in elections from the vacuum created by the right and left-wing parties who do not wish to be too damagingly dogmatic on this highly inflammatory question. With this exception, however, there are no longer the great political conflicts witnessed in the 1960s and 1970s. Companies wishing to invest in France can be assured of a level of political stability which is likely to last into the foreseeable future, whatever the party in power.

Economic environment

Macro-economic scene

The French proudly refer to the years 1945–1975 as *les Trente Glorieuses* because they correspond to a period of virtually continuous growth. Vital factors were a series of indicative five-year national plans; a strong, technocratic civil service; a strong and unifying head of state in the person of General de Gaulle; and the insistence on an industrial policy which stressed national independence and defence, and which generated many of the high-tech industries (aerospace, nuclear energy) of which the French are fiercely proud. Following the first oil shock the economy faltered, however, and entered a period of crisis (the French still refer to this continuing process of greater global economic instability as *la crise*). Individual purchasing power was maintained through indexed wages and comfortable social security benefits, at the expense of corporate profits and hence investment.

The Socialist experiment with reflation, and extensive nationalisation and job creation programme in 1981–82 only exacerbated a worsening situation, particularly in terms of inflation and unemployment. Reflation let in a flood of imports at a time of deep world recession; indexed wages and higher social security charges sucked the lifeblood out of companies unable to respond competitively to increased demand; and hence profits nosedived. In 1983 the government was forced to make a complete U-turn, introducing a policy of 'rigour' (*politique de rigueur*), which involved a prices and incomes policy, strict exchange controls and extra taxation and compulsory loans levied on individuals. This policy has gradually been softened, although there is keen pressure to keep the lid on wages.

It is vital to understand this background to appreciate the sea change in the economy, as France has made up for the fact that it had failed to gain as much advantage from increasing buoyancy in world markets as other OECD countries. Since 1986, both growth (3.5% – 1988, 3% forecast for 1990) and profits have picked up dramatically, leading to the biggest surge in investment (8%) since 1973. Growth has been engendered more by industrial investment than a high street boom. After a surplus in 1986, the trade balance has slipped back into deficit (FF 40bn in 1989) but there is nevertheless an air of optimism and confidence, particularly with inflation at around 3% (9.7% in 1982). This low rate of inflation is attributable to both France's membership of the European Monetary System and continuing wage restraint (unit labour costs are actually rising more slowly than in West Germany) although this restraint has relaxed a little since the law allowed in 1986 the introduction of widespread, flexible profit-sharing schemes (*intéressement*). Both modernisation and investment in new capacity mean that the French feel capable of increasing their exports and stemming the flow of imports over the next two to three years.

Unemployment at just over 10 per cent (2.5 million) is, however, a major source of concern. The figure is particularly high amongst the 16–25 year olds (23 per cent), a fact linked to the number of young people leaving the education system with few or no qualifications, and could well climb more sharply if France fails to maintain its present growth rates or, as seems unlikely, in spite of recent industrial unrest, wage demands become excessive as workers seek to grab their share of rising profits.

Structure

Although agriculture still plays an important role in the French economy (France is the main agricultural power in the EC), only 7 per cent of the working population are engaged in this sector, as opposed to over 30 per cent in 1945. Indeed, it is the belated industrialisation of France and the move away from over-reliance on agriculture which has been an important factor behind the surge of the French economy since the War. In 1988 agriculture, fisheries and forestry together accounted for 3.3 per cent of GDP. Services, both government and private, account for 50.5 per cent, industry 19.5 per cent, transport and telecommunications 5.8 per cent, construction 5.4 per cent and energy 4 per cent. (In 1986 70 per cent of electricity was generated by nuclear power, because France has virtually no coal or natural gas left and thus relies heavily on oil imports and substitute forms of energy. It now has a surplus of cheap electrical power which it exports, notably to the UK.)

Industry does not cover the wide spectrum of specialities to be found in West Germany. In general, there has been a tendency to specialise more in high technology sectors to the detriment of medium and low technology. A familiar complaint in France is that it is impossible to buy products 'made in France' ranging from simple garden implements to basic tooling and machinery used in industry. The worsening trade deficit underlines this trend. For this reason, France must be considered as an open market, full of opportunity and not a country where 'the French only buy French'. Every sector should be examined carefully to detect the many profitable niches open to suppliers of specially tailored high quality equipment. The main strengths of French industry are vehicle and transport engineering (cars, railway rolling stock, etc.), aerospace (Ariane satellite launcher, Airbus), telecommunications (CGE – Compagnie Générale d'Electricité), defence electronics (Thomson CSF) and software (Cap Gemini Sogeti). In many other sectors, although there are companies which are strong individually, France has hitherto failed to gain an important position. Examples of such companies are Rhône-Poulenc (chemicals), BSN (food), Elf-Aquitaine (oil) and Thomson (electronic consumer goods). One outstanding feature of the present industrial scene in France, however, is the frantic dash for growth by acquisitions in the run-up to the Single Market. Many French companies are aware that they are some way behind their major competitors in terms of size and international presence and are avidly acquiring companies both at home and overseas. Banking, insurance, chemicals, defence electronics and tyres are just some of the areas involved. At present, size is of more importance to companies than return on capital.

Luxury goods is one of the sectors which continue to shine and it has undergone a veritable explosion (increase in turnover of 18 per cent in 1988, positive trade balance of FF 36bn). This sector (clothing and accessories, perfumes, wine, food, etc.) is a rich patchwork of dynamic small and medium sized companies, many of which are becoming objects of consider-

SETTING THE BUSINESS SCENE

able attention by overseas investors, a fact not overlooked by the French government (there is a monthly meeting of a Treasury committee to discuss investments by overseas companies).

Companies in France are classified according to the number of employees: below 500 they are known as PME – *Petites et Moyennes Entreprises*, above 500 they are large companies. Few companies fall in the latter category, some 918 (2.8 per cent), whereas 82 per cent fall in the 10–100 band. A large number are privately owned, with many examples of companies (62 out of the top 200) which are still firmly controlled by the founding families (e.g. Peugeot, Michelin, Carrefour, Casino, Matra, L'Oréal, Pernod, LVMH). However, France also has one of the largest nationalised sectors in Western Europe, ranging from banking (Crédit Lyonnais, Banque Nationale de Paris) and insurance (UAP, GAN, AGP) to competitive industrial areas such as computers (Bull), defence equipment (Thomson), telecommunications (CGE), aluminium (Péchiney), chemicals (Rhône-Poulenc, Orkem) oil (Elf-Aquitaine, CFP), aerospace (Aérospatiale [SNIAS], SNECMA, Dassault), air transport (Air France), rail transport (SNCF, RATP), electricity and gas (EDF-GDF), and cars (Renault). A process of privatisation (there are now 7.5 million private investors as a result) was started under the right-wing Chirac government in 1986, but was halted by the October 1987 stock market crash and the incoming Socialist government in 1988. Mitterand is on record as favouring a policy of '*ni-ni*' (*ni privatisation, ni nationalisation* – neither privatisation nor nationalisation).

In spite of more liberal sounding pronouncements, it would be a mistake to believe that the French do not retain certain interventionist reflexes, since some of the biggest institutional investors – *les zinzins* – are precisely the nationalised banks and insurance companies that have seats on the boards of many major French companies.

The main industrial areas are in the Paris Basin, the Rhône-Alpes region centred around Lyon and Grenoble, Toulouse (aerospace industry) and the Nord-Pas-de-Calais region (textiles, cars, steel). With the demise of the smoke-stack industries, particularly in the latter region, there is the growing importance of a 'sun-belt' stretching from the Pyrenees to the Alps, with Toulouse, Montpellier and Nice as its focal points and with a concentration of high technology and innovative industry.

Other areas are of significance, however, and will be dealt with in the next chapter.

Foreign trade

After current balance deficits in 1982–83, France recovered rapidly to show a small surplus of FF 21bn in 1986. The next year, 1987, saw another considerable deficit (FF 24bn), however, which set a pattern for the following years (1988 – FF 34bn, 1989 – FF 37bn, 1990 (projection) – FF 32bn). The terms of trade improved (due to a weaker dollar and lower raw materials prices) but the main problem was caused by the trade balance, with imports of goods continuing to exceed exports particularly in industrial sectors for reasons already explained. Main exports are road vehicles, railway equipment, aerospace (but fewer sales of Airbus have a dramatic effect on the trade balance!), business equipment, food and agricultural products. Energy alone accounts for 22 per cent of imports with business equipment (18 per cent) and chemical products (14 per cent) being the next most important items.

France has traditionally enjoyed comfortable surpluses on services. Tourism and services relating to major civil engineering contracts are the main areas of strength both of which have suffered since 1986, however; the first because of the depreciation of the dollar and the second because of the drop in demand for large contracts from developing and oil-rich countries.

Anglo-French trade

France is Great Britain's third largest export market, whereas Great Britain is France's fifth largest. Until 1986, the UK had a small trade surplus which has since been turned into a deficit as its share (percentage value) of France's import market has gradually been eroded. This has been principally due to the drop in oil prices, as non-oil exports rose by 23 per cent in 1987 and 14 per cent in 1988. Oil still constitutes our largest export item, followed by food (particularly meat and fish products), office machinery, road vehicles, electrical machinery and special purpose machinery. The Department of Trade and Industry has drawn up the following list of priority sectors:

- car components and accessories,
- medical equipment (electro-medical and aids for the disabled),
- aerospace and defence components,
- designer clothing,
- gardening equipment,
- golf equipment,
- giftware and jewellery,
- electronic measuring and testing equipment,
- security equipment,
- information technology for financial institutions,
- water supply and pollution control equipment (as France becomes increasingly "greener"),
- domestic electrical appliances,
- building materials,
- synchotron project (Grenoble),
- mail order sector (although a long postal strike and the constant competitive pressure from the *grandes surfaces* have progressively made this sector more vulnerable),
- printing machinery and tools.

In overall terms, it should be remembered that with the strong surge in investment, France holds out many excellent opportunities for capital equipment suppliers and it is also highly attractive for manufacturers of consumer goods, being the world's fourth largest importer of such goods.

Further information on British goods and services exported to France can be obtained from the DTI (Department of Trade and Industry – see Where-to-go guide.)

Social environment

The law

In all aspects of business and social life, the French are highly legalistic and used to confronting a whole battery of often complex, contradictory and incomprehensible laws. The paradox is, however, that having formulated such a system, the French tend to show some considerable delight in flouting it! Seat-belts and crash helmets are often not worn (particularly in the South), red traffic lights tend to be ignored and in business, contracts are often scrutinized for ways round them and loopholes. The law also regulates many internal company operations and structures: works committees (*comités d'entreprise*), trade union representation, training budgets and social 'balance sheets' (*bilan social*) are all rigorously determined according to company size. The number of hours worked per week, overtime, nightwork, temporary jobs and minimum wages are also subject to detailed legislation. British businessmen should therefore be aware that seemingly over-bureaucratic and legal procedures are necessary, even for relatively simple matters, and that time and patience are required. (Failure to do so can cost money: delayed payments, for example, can often be the result of not getting the right signatories to authorise payment.)

Business education

Managers in France, particularly in the large companies, may come across as competitive and intellectually tough. Much of this results from the unique system of higher education which lays stress on the rigid selection of a narrow élite for France's top engineers and managers.

The process of selection begins at a fairly early age, with pre-eminence in mathematics being

SETTING THE BUSINESS SCENE

all-important. The baccalauréat is the equivalent of our 'A' levels, but has a much wider basis, with groups of six to seven subjects taken. *Baccalauréat C* with Mathematics, Physics and Chemistry as the main core subjects is the most highly regarded group. To ensure their children stay in the mainstream of education, which leads to the *baccalauréat*, parents increasingly insist that they repeat a year at the age of 13. For those not making the grade, this is to avoid what is considered to be very much a socially inferior alternative, a two-year course leading to the CAP (*Certificat d'Aptitude Professionnelle*), a craft qualification which allows specialisation in a wide range of manual skills. Nevertheless, as we saw earlier, the youth unemployment rate is high, since many leave school with no qualifications at all.

The ultimate prize, in terms of both future salary and status, is a place in one of France's *grandes écoles*, the highly prestigious engineering and business schools (*école d'ingénieurs, école de commerce*) which exist side by side with universities, but do not form part of the same system. To enter the latter, success at the baccalauréat will suffice. A place at a grande école, however, requires two more years of intensive studies (called *classes préparatoires*) leading to a tough entrance examination (the *concours*). Those who manage to pass this exam are virtually guaranteed several lucrative job offers at the end of their studies and will immediately acquire the rank of *cadre*. This is roughly the equivalent of 'manager' in the UK, but much more hierarchically defined, both in terms of qualification and experience, in collective bargaining agreements. Nearly all senior managers in France's leading companies will be ex-students of *grandes écoles* and there is hence, not without some justification, often talk of an old-boy 'mafia'. Top civil servants will also have been to the same colleges and often end up as heads of private companies, particularly in the financial sector.

When doing business, it is important to understand this system for a number of reasons. Firstly, in large state and private companies, and in the civil service and government, there are many close links and relationships arising from the *grandes écoles* and this network can be used to great advantage when recruiting and appointing for specific functions. This is particularly true when setting up in France or acquiring or merging with a French company. Secondly, the pride and occasional superior aloofness of some French managers (but by no means all!) must be seen in the context of this competitive education system, which sometimes leads those lucky enough to benefit from it to believe absolutely in their own intellectual and technical superiority. They are made to believe they are the best and are proud of the prestige and status they have achieved. They are the new aristocrats, predominantly from middle class backgrounds (fewer managers are from working class backgrounds than in the UK, West Germany and USA). Thirdly, when doing business with them, you should remember they are highly trained professionals (arts graduates rarely make the grade as managers without further qualifications).

Affluence

France is the fourth largest economy of the OECD countries and has a per capita GDP which considerably exceeds that of the UK. The French are thus reasonably well-off, as exemplified by the range of consumer goods in French households, even those in the lower socio-professional categories: 94 per cent have telephones (85.7 per cent in UK), 92 per cent have washing machines (80.1 per cent), 69 per cent have freezers (38.3 per cent) and 83 per cent have cars (66.3 per cent). Although all classes have benefited from the strong post-war growth, the distribution of wealth is far less equal in France than in other European countries such as the UK, West Germany and Italy. The present socialist government has restored the wealth tax scrapped by the previous Chirac government, but it does little to close the gap between the rich who are often very rich and the poor, who, on average, may be poorer than their counterparts in the UK, in spite of a statutory minimum wage, the SMIC (*salaire minimum inter croiss-*

ance). This is partially due to rates of income tax being relatively low by UK standards and to the fact that tax evasion is rife, particularly amongst the self-employed. The luxury goods sector could, therefore, prove to be highly profitable to British manufacturers, remembering, of course, that this is a sector in which the French themselves excel and competition is therefore keen.

The attitude towards wealth, profits and even companies, which were once taboo subjects, has changed completely in France. The image of the company and profit have gained a new respect. There is a new generation of young dynamic entrepreneurs prepared to take advantage of a rejuvenated Stock exchange, leveraged management buyouts and all forms of risk capital and financial engineering. The company is now seen in a positive light; it no longer allegedly exploits its workers but is a source of wealth and personal development at a time when other institutions (trade unions – with a membership of below 10 per cent of the working population – the law, the government, the administration, etc) are seriously being questioned.

In spite of the general level of consumer affluence, the French savings rate is a healthy 11.5 per cent of disposable income and beginning to rise again after many years of gradual decline (a trend which is particularly encouraged by the government in its efforts to stem imports). Property represents a major investment, as 51% of the French own their own home and France boasts more second homes than any other country in the world, apart from the USA.

Leisure

The French have traditionally been viewed as a nation enjoying such pleasures in life as long meal-times spent talking, but leisure in its more organised manifestations is more recent. The number of second homes points to one abiding obsession of the French, the weekend, particularly away from Paris. This means the Do-It-Yourself sector (*le bricolage*) is flourishing (present annual growth of 14 per cent; growth of 44.3 per cent between July 1985 and July 1988 – 3,277 points of sale) and is being given even more of a boost by the number of British snapping up and renovating old farmhouses and barns from Calais to Biarritz.

The French work hard, but in a different way and hence prefer longer holidays (taken in longer blocks) to shorter working hours. The official working week is 39 hours, but there is some pressure to reduce this. Many work much longer than this, however, by way of overtime. Employees are expected to work Saturdays in many manufacturing industries and in spite of already long opening hours (hypermarkets regularly close at 9.00 pm) there is increasing demand for shops to stay open on Sundays. In the leisure field, teenagers (15–20 yr olds) are a particularly important group and with average monthly expenditure of FF 445 on small regular purchases, they represent a veritable gold mine in the clothing, shoes, records, books, magazines and cinema sectors. As in other countries, France is developing its own 'society of the ego' with the emphasis on individualism rather than on the collective solidarity of the past.

At the other end of the age scale, more leisure time is being enjoyed by France's senior citizens (*le troisième âge*) since the Socialists brought down the retirement age to 60.

Chapter 2

The regional environment

In 1947, Jean-François Gravier wrote the book *Paris et le désert français* (Flammarion, Paris) and although much has changed since then, there is still much evidence as to the dominance of Paris in economic, industrial, financial and even educational terms. It has 77 per cent of all top management posts in the services sector and 83.5 per cent of the head offices of the top 200 French companies. In terms of investment, the greater Paris region (Ile-de-France) accounts for 59 per cent across all sectors, 66 per cent of loans to the service sector, 84 per cent to transport and 91 per cent to energy. Unemployment remains at 8.4 per cent, below the national average of 10.1 per cent and the region's contribution to national added value has remained at a steady 22 per cent. Paris houses 34 per cent of France's university population and the region's share of private sector R&D has remained virtually unchanged since 1973 (61.7 per cent).

So there is no denying the importance of Paris but the national regional development agency (DATAR) has ensured over the last 30 years that the rest of France has gradually – albeit patchily – been endowed with a greater share of industrial growth. It would therefore, and for various other reasons, be wrong to concentrate business solely in the hands of an agent in Paris. Firstly, given the size of France, he or she may be unable to cover the length and breadth of the country. National exclusivity clauses should be avoided at all costs, for this reason alone. Secondly, a significant number of other areas, e.g. Lyon, Toulouse, Grenoble, have rapidly grown in size and importance and offer a whole range of industries and services which should not be ignored. An initial regional toe-hold could hence be more advantageous as a spring-board to a future network of agents nationally. Thirdly, various regions are important for different sectors: the east of France shows the strongest activity in the DIY sector; golf is flourishing everywhere but particularly along the South Coast between Marseille and Nice, with many new courses being planned; there is a greater preponderance of older and retired people on the South Coast; the aeronautics industry is based in Toulouse, etc. Rates of unemployment and growth, the age structure and density of population and communications are all important factors. A word of warning, however: the centre of activity may be in a particular region, but major *decisions*, particularly concerning new products, purchasing, etc., may still be made at the head office in Paris. In the retail sector, too, different hypermarket groups (whose headquarters and buying agencies are not *all* situated in Paris!) may operate either a centralised or regional, even store-by-store purchasing policy. Every effort must be made, therefore, to research markets not just on a national but on a region-by-region basis.

So where can help be found outside Paris when considering various regions? In a recent survey, French managers themselves ranked the various possible organisations offering help and

SETTING THE BUSINESS SCENE

advice in the following order of importance:

1. regional banks,
2. regional councils (*conseils régionaux*),
3. chambers of commerce (CCI – *Chambres de Commerce et d'Industrie*),
4. *comité d'expansion économique* (usually attached to CCI)
5. the French state development agency (DATAR),
6. ANVAR (*agence nationale pour la valorisation de la recherche* – an organisation dispensing R&D finance),
7. *Sociétés de Développement Régional* (regional venture-capital organisations),
8. trade and professional bodies (*union patronale*),
9. the council of the département (*conseil général*),
10. municipal councils and members of parliament.

DATAR's help is still important, particularly in terms of financial aid and grants in those depressed areas which have been earmarked for restructuring (the Nord-Pas-de-Calais is a good example of this). Regional councils have much more tax revenue at their disposal than hitherto, however, and these, together with many municipal and departmental councils, are at present fiercely competing with each other to create technopoles, quasi-technology parks which bring together research laboratories, a university or engineering/business school and a myriad of small start-ups. Consequently, a British company seeking to set up in France can gain considerable advantage in terms of finance, land and buildings from these technopoles. Many are, however, only in their infancy and care must be taken to ensure that the glossy brochures paint an accurate and realistic picture of the potential market, the supporting infrastructure and ease of access.

Some initial idea of the economic importance of the various regions is given by the development of growth rates between 1969 and 1984:

	GDP/-capita France = 100 1969	GDP/-capita France = 100 1984
Ile-de-France	131	144
Champagne-Ardenne	90	95
Picardie	102	87
Haute-Normandie	130	106
Centre	83	89
Basse-Normandie	82	83
Bourgogne	81	88
Nord-Pas-de-Calais	107	84
Lorraine	104	90
Alsace	100	107
Franche-Comté	96	89
Pays de la Loire	84	86
Bretagne	71	80
Poitou-Charentes	75	77
Aquitaine	94	93
Midi-Pyrénées	75	85
Limousin	78	74
Rhone-Alpes	105	105
Auvergne	83	80
Languedoc-Roussillon	85	75
Provence-Alpes-Cote d'Azur	92	93
Corsica		66
France	100	100

Source INSEE

In general terms, the Paris region still dominates the scene, but a number of regions have surged ahead quite dramatically, in particular Alsace (close to Germany), Bretagne (electronics and telecommunications), Midi-Pyrénées (aerospace). The effects of the demise of the steel, coal and textile industry on the Nord-Pas-de-Calais, Picardie and Lorraine can also be clearly seen.

In terms of French managers' perception of the dynamism of their regions, a recent survey listed the Rhone-Alpes in top position, followed by the Ile-de-France, Alsace, Midi-Pyrénées and Bretagne. Regions at the bottom of the scale were Auvergne, Poitou-Charentes, Limousin, Basse-Normandie and lastly Champagne-Ardenne. The most dynamic regional capitals were cited as Paris, followed by Toulouse, Lyon, Montpellier and Strasbourg.

THE REGIONAL ENVIRONMENT

SETTING THE BUSINESS SCENE

Regional profiles

Alsace	Regional capital:	Strasbourg
	Population:	1.6 m
	Population density per km²:	194
	Unemployment:	7%

In many ways, Alsace is a microcosm of the single European market with a high level of unhindered movement of both goods and people across the border with Germany. It has a highly trained workforce, many of whom are educated and trained in both French and German; a level of unemployment much lower than the national average, and the strongest growth rate in France. If to this are added a dense network of retail outlets, a high level of international investment (35 per cent of total, as opposed to 16 per cent average for the whole of France) and a TGV (*train à grande vitesse*) planned for Paris-Strasbourg, then it is clear that Alsace merits close attention, although hitherto British companies have been slower to invest than the Americans and Japanese.

Textiles, textile machinery, cars, beer, processed foods, general engineering, shoemaking, furniture manufacture and building materials manufacturing are amongst the most prominent activities of Alsace.

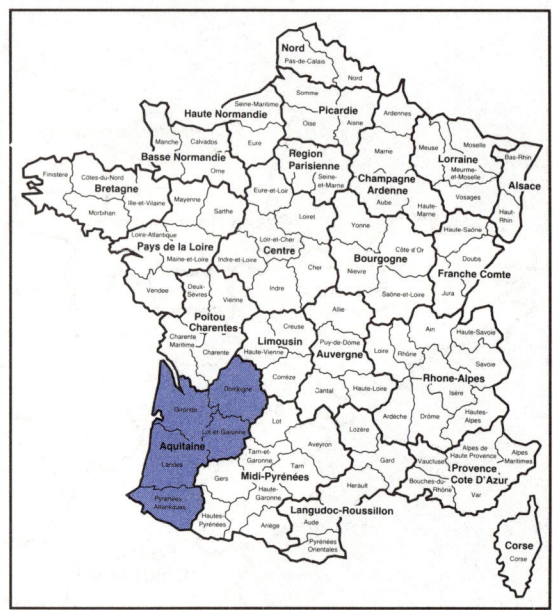

Aquitaine	Regional capital:	Bordeaux
	Population:	2.7 m
	Population density per km²:	66
	Unemployment:	11.6%

Growth has begun to pick up in Aquitaine, with pronounced investment in heavy industries, particularly the paper industry. It relies heavily on the aerospace industry and was hence relieved when the government decided to press ahead with building France's own independent fighter aircraft, the Rafale. The region is generally becoming much less isolated from the rest of France and also has close and developing links with Spain (35,000 Spaniards already live in Bordeaux). There is hope that the TGV from Paris will eventually link up with Spain, which is to build a high-speed network of its own.

THE REGIONAL ENVIRONMENT

Other important activities are food products, wine, composite materials, building materials, pharmaceuticals, general engineering and tourism. The region is furthermore markedly pro-British!

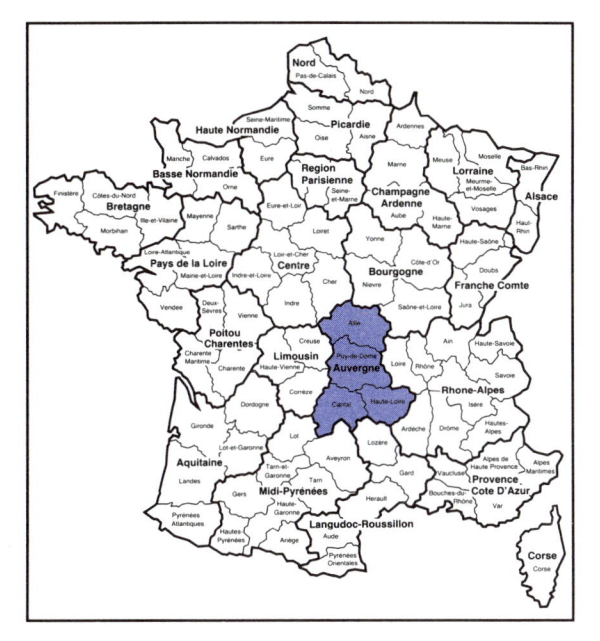

Auvergne	Regional capital:	Clermont-Ferrand
	Population:	1.3 m
	Population density per km^2:	51
	Unemployment:	10.4%

Auvergne is a region struggling to recover from the effects of the failure and restructuring of many of its largest employers (Michelin, Dunlop, Valéo). Nevertheless, the automotive industry is still important, together with plastics (in the Haute-Loire valley) and pharmaceuticals. Agriculture is strong, too, but it is felt that more could be made of food-processing industries.

In terms of communication, a new motorway links Clermont-Ferrand with Paris, but good East-West links and access to the South are sorely needed.

Bourgogne	Regional capital:	Dijon
	Population:	1.6 m
	Population density per km^2:	51
	Unemployment:	10.1%

In spite of its rural image and its reputation for wine, art and pleasant living, Burgundy does have its industrial side with electronics (Thomson), automotive industry (Peugeot and Renault), metallurgy (Ugine) and textiles (DIM tights and stockings) as major activities. The leisure industry is also of some significance, particularly around the canals, and Club Méditérranée has recently announced it will open a new prestige site in the region. The north around Le Creusot-Montceau (the only TGV stop between Lyon and Paris) was badly affected by the demise of the major engineering firm Creusot-Loire but, through Framatome (nuclear power industry) and Peugeot-Citroën, is fighting back in various high-tech areas (e.g. lasers). Chalon-sur-Saône is the main industrial centre and is experiencing its biggest investment and building surge for ten years.

SETTING THE BUSINESS SCENE

Bretagne	Regional capital:	Rennes
	Population:	2.7 m
	Population density per km^2:	102
	Unemployment:	10.5%

Centre	Regional capital:	Orléans
	Population:	2.3 m
	Population density per km^2:	60
	Unemployment:	9.3%

Brittany is still dominated by agriculture and the agro-food industry (which employs some 35 per cent of the region's working population). The region has a large number of specialist research centres in these sectors, including biotechnology, which are mainly located in Rennes. These centres have in turn, given rise to strengths in packaging, transport, associated services and mechanical engineering. Although Citroën is still a large employer in Brittany, the other most important industries, electronics and telecommunications, appear to be running out of steam.

In spite of its low unemployment rate, the Centre region shows considerable differences between its constituent *départements* in terms of growth and dynamism. In the Cher department, for example, there is a crisis in the clothing industry centred around Châteauroux, whereas in the Loiret, subcontractors are overwhelmed with orders as foreign investment pours into a wide range of industries (the West Germans, British and Benelux companies are the biggest investors). The new TGV-Atlantique and two motorways, one to the West and South-West and the other South, will undoubtedly be the spur for yet more growth in this 'jardin de la France'.

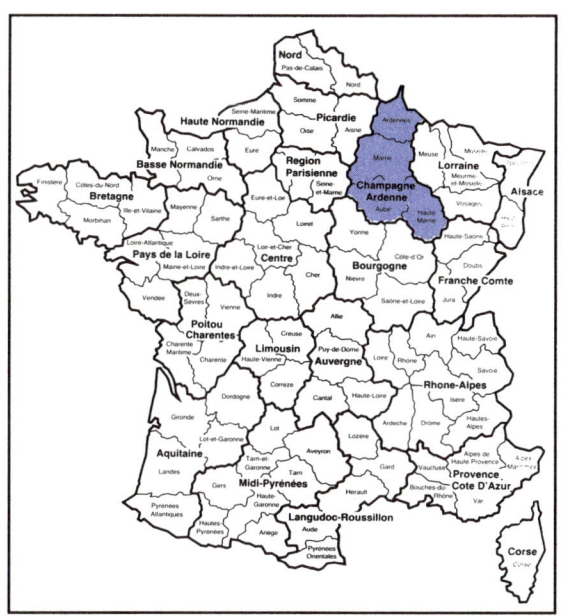

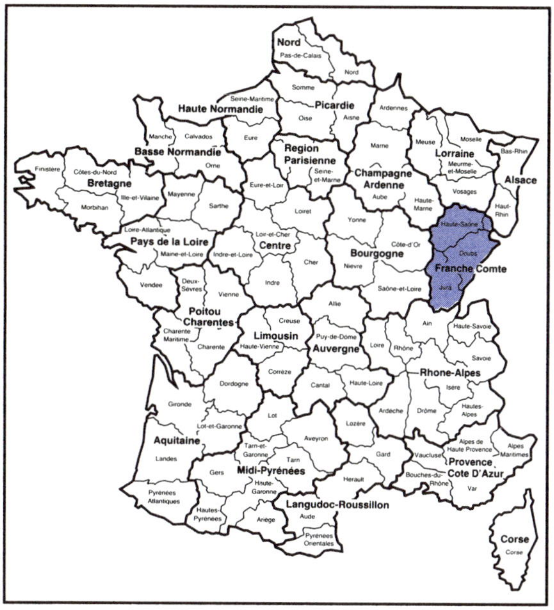

THE REGIONAL ENVIRONMENT

Champagne-Ardenne

Regional capital:	Chalons-sur-Marne
Population:	1.3 m
Population density per km²:	53
Unemployment:	11.3%

One of the most sparsely populated areas in France, this is a region experiencing some difficulty in regaining its former prosperity after the problems encountered in the metalworking industry in the Ardenne and in the textile industry around Troyes. The Marne is the most prosperous *département* around Reims and its main activities are champagne-bottling, cereals and sugar. The new motorway linking the Channel Tunnel with Dijon and the South via Reims and Troyes (with a spur off to Paris) creates the expectation that this will become a major European crossroads and hence important for distribution purposes.

Franche-Comté

Regional capital:	Besançon
Population:	1.09 m
Population density per km²:	68
Unemployment:	10%

Franche-Comté is made up of a host of small specialist and highly secretive companies (toys, furniture, spectacles, musical instruments) and larger companies in the automotive (Peugeot), computers (Bull) and locomotive engineering (Alsthom) sectors. Besançon, once famous for its watch industry, is depending more and more on precision engineering (*microtechniques*) for its future prosperity. In terms of access, it is a region hampered by poor communications.

SETTING THE BUSINESS SCENE

Ile-de-France	Regional capital:	Paris
	Population:	10.3 m
	Population density per km^2:	857
	Unemployment:	8.9%

Virtually all major manufacturing industries are represented in the Ile-de-France area, ranging from cars and aerospace, to chemicals, textiles and steel. Leisure and tourism are of obvious importance, a fact underlined by the siting of the Euro Disneyland close to Paris (and to be served by the Paris-London TGV link).

One notable characteristic is that increasingly jobs are being created in the West of the region and more housing being built in the East. This not only leads to increased commuting (up by 50 per cent over the last five years) but an imbalance in the distribution of wealth as the factories, shops and offices fill local councils' coffers in the West with their *taxe professionnelle* (a form of local business rates), leaving the East to make do with takings predominantly from taxes on private dwellings.

Finally, the huge development of Charles de Gaulle airport as a combined road, rail and air pivotal hub, the presence of the large warehousing and distribution centre at Garinor near the airport and the construction of the outer ring road, the A86, all combine to underline the major influence Paris will continue to exert in logistical terms.

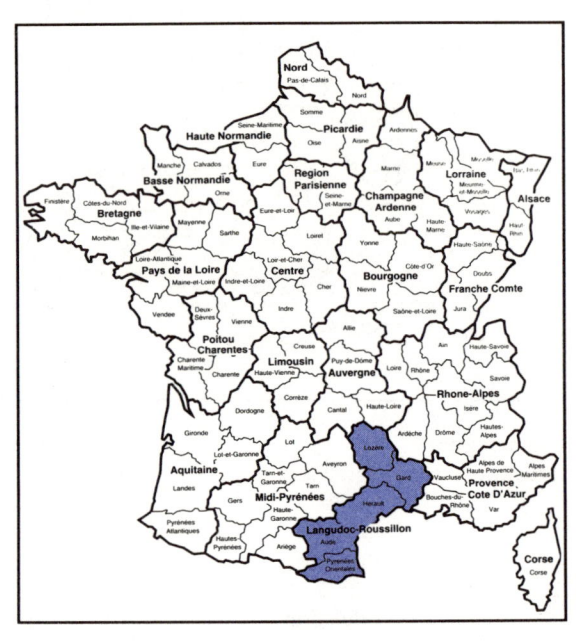

Languedoc-Roussillon	Regional capital:	Montpellier
	Population:	2.07 m
	Population density per km^2:	76
	Unemployment:	14%

This is a region of great contrasts, ranging from the comparatively underdeveloped and industrially languishing Western area around Perpignan and Béziers to the fantastic growth area of Montpellier and, more lately, Nîmes, with their activities in the bio-medical, pharmaceutical, data-processing and robotics sectors. The contrasts are most dramatically illustrated by the fact that the region has both the highest rate of unemployment in France and the greatest number of start-ups (11,000 annually). Only lasting dynamism and growth will prove that the area is indeed set to be a major centre in the burgeoning French sun-belt.

Tourism and leisure activities have long benefited from the development by the centralised planning authorities of the whole shoreline between Spain and the Camargue – an area highly popular with both French and foreign holiday-makers.

Limousin	Regional capital:	Limoges
	Population:	0.73 m
	Population density per km²:	43
	Unemployment:	8.5%

The Limousin region has been scarcely touched by the *crise* – its low unemployment rate is proof of this – but there are worries in the region about where future growth is to come from. It has a number of major handicaps: it is one of the poorest regions, it is the least efficient, its workforce is the least qualified and, lastly, it has an ageing managerial stock. Access to the region has also hitherto been difficult, but there are plans for a dual carriageway between Vierzon and Brive by 1993 and attempts are being made to get the TGV to pass through Limoges.

Agriculture is the basis of the region's economy and Limoges is world famous for its porcelain. Ceramics and biotechnology are just some of the high-tech areas which have been pin-pointed for future development.

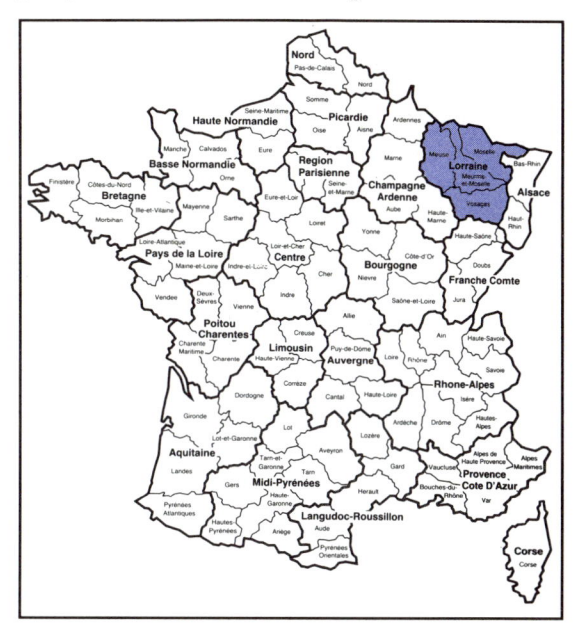

Lorraine	Regional capital:	Metz
	Population:	2.3 m
	Population density per km²:	99
	Unemployment:	10.8%

Despite the recent revival of the old traditional industries such as steel, coal and chemicals, the Lorraine has difficulty in attracting new companies and is indeed losing many of its existing companies. In the East, more jobs are likely to be lost in the textile industry of the Vosges and many young workers are leaving the region to work elsewhere. Being so close to the Belgian and Luxemburg borders creates problems, as many of its inhabitants cross these borders to shop in the two neighbour countries where products (cars, consumer goods generally) are cheaper.

SETTING THE BUSINESS SCENE

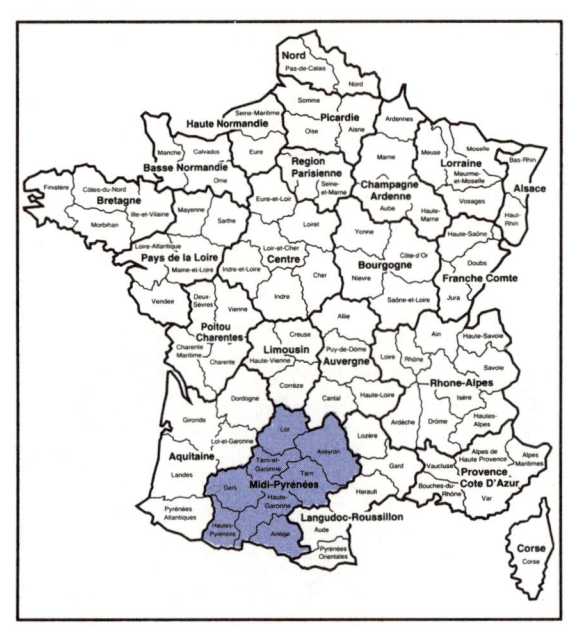

Midi-Pyrénées	Regional capital:	Toulouse
	Population:	2.73 m
	Population density per km²:	52
	Unemployment:	10%

This is the biggest of the French regions and still dominated by agriculture (16 per cent of the workforce). Toulouse is undoubtedly the star performer of the region with its vigorous start-up rate, its flourishing aerospace industry and the general reputation of being the second high-tech capital of France (after Grenoble). Plans for better communications (road, rail) between Toulouse and other towns in the region should ensure a more even distribution of the area's prosperity. To the south, the region is looking more and more towards Spain, with its strongest growth rate in Europe. To the North, the TGV and a new motorway through Brive and Bourges (1995) will ensure quicker access to the capital and elsewhere.

Nord Pas-de-Calais	Regional capital:	Lille
	Population:	3.9 m
	Population density per km²:	316
	Unemployment:	14.3%

The region has one of France's highest unemployment rates, but nevertheless is making steady progress on the road to recovery from the closure of its shipyards, coal-mines and textile factories. Its proximity to Paris and other European capitals, to which it will be linked by the TGV, and the building of the Channel Tunnel, with three new motorways converging on Calais, will undoubtedly make the area a major European crossroads. Warehousing facilities are already plentiful and expected to increase considerably and Coca-Cola's and Continental Can's new manufacturing site in Dunkirk are proof of the area's excellent geographical position close to the main concentrations of consumers in Europe.

The Nord-Pas-de-Calais region has a high birth-rate and a relatively young population – it is also after Paris, the most densely populated.

THE REGIONAL ENVIRONMENT

One of its main drawbacks is its poor image amongst French managers who are reluctant to settle and work here, and hence, considerable efforts are being made to improve the environment, particularly in Lille which is undergoing an extensive face-lift.

Its main industries are textiles in the Roubaix-Tourcoing area, steel at Dunkirk, metalworking in Valenciennes, glassware at the Cristallerie d'Arques and cars in Douai and Lens. The property and leisure markets are also of growing importance, particularly as an increasing number of British buy second homes in the area.

presence of many companies employing less than ten people (only 4,500 out of 75,000 exceed this figure). Agriculture is still a major activity but suffers from low productivity – plots are small – and the effect of EC quotas, particularly on milk. Tourism is of increasing importance, energised by a growing British presence in Cabourg, Honfleur and Deauville. A new motorway crossing the region through Caen is to be built within the next six years and may help solve the region's problem of attracting new companies.

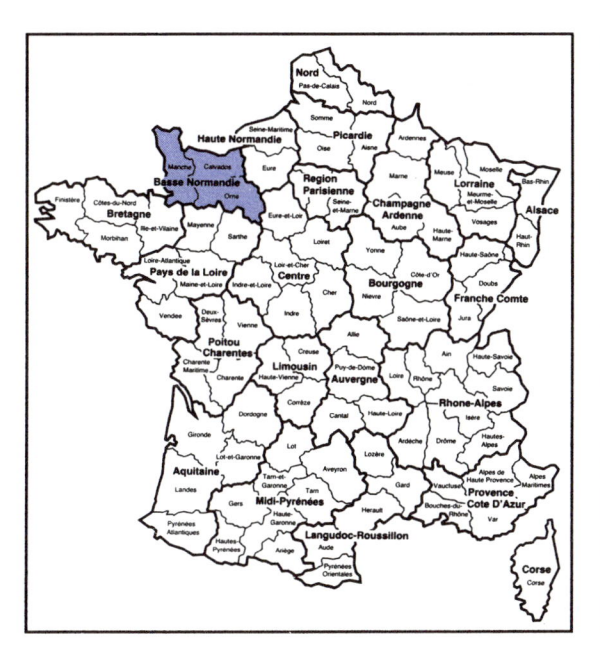

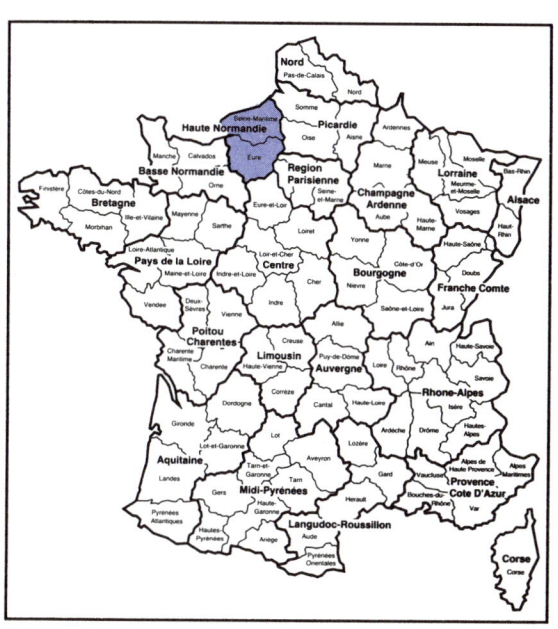

Basse-Normandie

	Regional capital:	Caen
	Population:	1.37 m
	Population density per km²:	75
	Unemployment:	10.2%

Many of the large companies, which once favoured Basse-Normandie in their quest for decentralisation and cheaper labour, have now gone and the region is characterised by the

Haute-Normandie

	Regional capital:	Rouen
	Population:	1.68 m
	Population density per km²:	137
	Unemployment:	12.7%

The *département* of Eure is proving to be the most flourishing of the region's two departments (the other is Seine-Maritime) as large companies gradually move out from Paris down the Seine.

SETTING THE BUSINESS SCENE

The cosmetics and pharmaceutical sectors are particularly active and provide work for a whole cluster of sub-contractors.

Le Havre is pinning its hopes on a new container port to rival the Dutch ports – it already is France's busiest port, ahead of Marseille. A new bridge linking Le Havre with Caen and the Northern Channel ports are important future developments, together with Dieppe's determination not to be overshadowed by the opening of the tunnel.

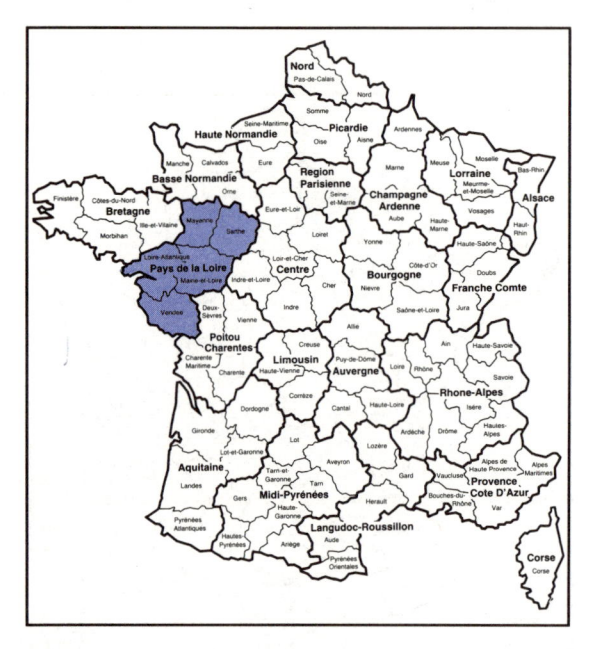

Pays de la Loire	Regional capital:	Nantes
	Population:	3.01 m
	Population density per km^2:	94
	Unemployment:	11.3%

Nantes, Angers and Le Mans are the main centres of activity in this region (cars, agro-food, computers, building materials, electrical household goods). The Japanese have recently decided to invest quite extensively in the area, no doubt partially inspired by the improving motorway and rail network (TGV and motorway from Nantes to Niort). It remains to be seen whether Nantes will succeed in its vowed intention to rival Rennes as the capital of Western France.

Picardie	Regional capital:	Amiens
	Population:	1.78 m
	Population density per km^2:	92
	Unemployment:	11.4%

Employment is still forecast to fall in Picardie as textiles and other traditional industries continue to shed labour which is amongst the most underqualified in France. High-tech industries are poorly represented in the region, and like its northern neighbour, Nord-Pas-de-Calais, it has difficulty in attracting high-calibre managers.

THE REGIONAL ENVIRONMENT

Poitou-Charentes	Regional capital:	Poitiers
	Population:	1.60 m
	Population density per km^2:	62
	Unemployment:	11.4%

Provence-Alpes-Côte d'Azur	Regional capital:	Marseille
	Population:	4.11 m
	Population density per km^2:	131
	Unemployment:	12.5%

A relaxed lifestyle typifies this region of cognac and oysters, but it has the reputation of being the least dynamic of all the French regions. A number of big factory closures, high unemployment and an ageing population all contribute to this image. La Rochelle, Poitiers and Niort are the main industrial centres on a small scale with the latter having the reputation of being the most extensively cabled town in France. It also houses the headquarters of all the main *sociétés mutuelles*, mutual societies catering for specific professions which offer a number of different services, e.g.: car and other insurance, to their members. Of considerable importance, is the fact that they run their own warehouses and offer members a wide range of goods at considerably reduced prices. Those situated in Niort are MAIF, MACIF, MAFF and CAMIF and British suppliers should be well aware of their existence.

The Marseille area is enjoying a modest revival of its fortunes after the failure of its traditional port activities. Aerospace, electronics and particularly petrochemicals are particularly buoyant in a mix of high-tech and heavy industry in Fos, Aix-en-Provence and around the Etang de Berre. Unemployment is still running high, however, particularly in such black spots as La Seyne and La Ciotat.

Much effort is being made to promote high technology around six major areas:
1. *Nice*, which has in Sophia Antipolis, the largest technology park in Europe with its 170 companies in the electronics and data-processing, fine chemicals and pharmaceuticals, energy, biomedical and biological engineering fields.
2. *Toulon-Var Technopole*, concentrating on robotics, instrumentation and aeronautics.

SETTING THE BUSINESS SCENE

3. *Marseille-Provence Technopole*, on a greenfield site at Chateau Gombert.
4. *Aix 2000*, micro-electronics, fine chemicals and new materials.
5. *Manosque-Cadarache*, robotics and electronics on an old Atomic Energy Authority site.
6. *Avignon Agroparc* – agrofood.

Generally speaking, the region comes second for high technology after the Rhône-Alpes region and is a popular choice with French managers if a move has to be made from Paris (Aix-en-Provence was recently voted to be their most popular town after Paris).

Tourism and leisure activities (particularly golf with five new courses planned for Cannes alone) are of obvious importance with large scale residential developments (popular with French holiday-makers) in evidence along most of the coastal areas.

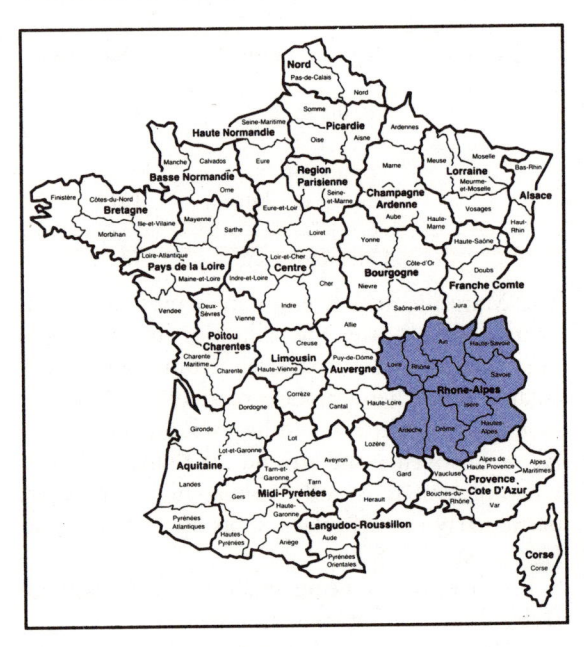

This is undoubtedly the number one region for dynamism and the quality of life, with most of the activity centred around Lyon and Grenoble. The smaller towns and areas of the region are not excluded from its prosperity, however, as witnessed by the flourishing textiles industry in Beaujolais, and plastics in Oyonnax. Plant modernisation is a key factor in both large and small family concerns, particularly in the silk and agro-food sectors. Rhône-Alpes is also the top region in research and development, boasting 12 universities, 30 *grandes écoles* and many research centres.

Lyon's main industries are mechanical engineering, chemicals, petrochemicals, pharmaceuticals, synthetic fibres and textiles. There are also official plans to further develop Lyon as a banking and financial centre.

Grenoble, the high-tech capital of France, manufactures electrical switch-gear, electronic devices, large turbines and measuring instruments and enjoys one of France's highest standards of living. Being so close to the ski-slopes greatly enhances its tourist and leisure activities.

St-Etienne is also starting to regain some of its former importance as the old industrial sites are rebuilt and developed. Particularly attractive investment incentives are on offer.

A major recurrent theme throughout this brief set of profiles is the massive public investment France is making in its road and rail infrastructure. This in itself represents an opportunity for British suppliers, particularly those working with or through French acquisitions, partners or subsidiaries (such as Emess and Thorn Lighting in the public lighting sector) but overall it points to the dramatic way in which distribution and logistics will evolve in the short term as more remote parts of France become accessible and the country makes a determined effort to become the distribution hub of Europe. Deregulation of road transport will also be a significant factor as, with the gradual phasing-in of *cabotage* (the ability to pick up and deliver loads within another country), loads will be bigger and transported over longer distances. The siting of

Rhône-Alpes	Regional capital:	Lyon
	Population:	5.17 m
	Population density per km^2:	118
	Unemployment:	8.6%

26

depots and warehouses will hence become a major strategic decision for companies with activities both in France and on the continent generally.

Whatever the region, key sources of information are the Conseil Régional situated in the regional capital and Chambers of Commerce in the main towns (*chef-lieu*) of individual départements.

The DTI also has commercial representatives in the consulates in Bordeaux, Lyon, Marseille and Lille from where detailed information about specific areas may be obtained.

Chapter 3

French market entry strategies

Direct exporting

When exporting directly to France it is important to make the initial distinction between selling directly into France using the company's own sales force working from the home base, and using a middleman located in France.

Before exploring these two possibilities more fully, it cannot be overstressed that a thorough survey and reconnaissance of the French market must be undertaken, together with the establishment of a policy to monitor the market constantly in order to detect any changes in regulations, fashions, trends and competition (from local and other overseas suppliers). Such a statement may well be dismissed as facile and obvious but time and again French agents, distributors and purchasing organisations point to the failure of British exporters to understand fully the nature of the French market and to respond to changes as the outstanding factors in any apparent resistance to British goods. As far as the product itself is concerned, scant regard is often paid to French taste, in particular such features as design and packaging (which is likely to require a higher quality with written instructions for use in appropriate French and adapted to French usage requirements).

It is with distribution channels and how they operate that most lack of proper understanding occurs. The British exporter particularly seems to have problems with the more fragmented nature of retail distribution ('France is too difficult a market because it's such a big country' is a frequent comment); the crucial positioning of goods in either the specialist or the *grandes surfaces* (hypermarkets, supermarkets) outlets; the complex system of *grandes surfaces*' purchasing organisations, their discount structure, delivery and payment conditions, etc. The regional, even local, nature of markets was stressed in the first chapter. As one French company summed it up in a recent influential British report on a sector of the automotive market: 'We feel that British companies have not understood that the French market is very strongly regionalised and that several distributors are necessary to service the market effectively'. This could well apply to many other products and markets in which British goods are not present. French protectionism cannot be blamed since suppliers from other major European countries are well represented, and the only solution to this problem must therefore be patient and detailed research. Persistence and commitment to the longer term are two other qualities which are often cited as lacking with British suppliers, who frequently turn to exporting in times of slack domestic demand, only to withdraw when demand picks up again at home.

There is obviously a price to be paid for good market surveys, but the Department of Trade and Industry operates an Export Marketing Research Scheme whereby eligible surveys, either in-house or by external consultancies may well qualify for payment of up to half the cost. Full details may be obtained from: Export Marketing Research Scheme, The Association of British Chambers of Commerce, 4 Westwood House, Westwood Business Park, Coventry, CV4 8HS, tel: 0203 694484.

Direct selling

Faster travel will increasingly enable more firms to develop their export sales by using their own staff working from Great Britain. The introduction of a vastly expanded TGV network with the creation of 'nodal' points of trade and commercial activity in towns such as Lille (as spotted by British property developers) should not be underestimated in this respect. The main advantages of such an approach are direct contact with customers, thus enabling more rapid appreciation of changes in the market and a greater degree of control. Companies often prefer direct sales to using an agent or distributor, firstly because the latter often require exclusivity for both products and regions and if they fail to develop sales well, it is extremely difficult to terminate a contract without paying a heavy financial penalty. Secondly, where agents represent other products, initially they make every effort to impress with sales to major clients but often after 2–3 years fail to maintain these efforts when faced with an offer to represent a new supplier. In the words of one direct salesman 'they are order-takers rather than order-makers' and may not use the sales techniques preferred particularly by subsidiaries of American companies. Care needs to be taken with the question of exclusivity, however, a point which will be discussed when dealing with intermediaries.

The French market is often very conservative in many respects and many customers will remain loyal to traditional suppliers. The *grandes surfaces*, particularly, which stock many thousands of products, are constantly solicited by suppliers of thousands more, and therefore must see good reasons for change. This means that complete professionalism is required and that a knowledge of French is crucial with a direct sales force (the chief buyer of the Casino chain of hypermarkets complains bitterly of the British habit of mail-shots in English). In addition, an intimate knowledge not only of how goods are sold in a particular sector but of French commercial practices in general is essential. For this reason, employees involved in direct sales should have spent some time living and working in France to achieve the right level of credibility and confidence.

Direct sales to France also have their drawbacks, however, and these will vary in degree of seriousness according to the particular sector, and even to particular customers within the same sector. Firstly, government departments, such as UGAP, the French Public Procurement Agency, will almost all only buy imported goods through French importers or other intermediaries. Secondly, certain private companies, such as Euromarché in the retail sector, prefer to deal directly with companies based in France or through an agent (*prestateur de service*). Such a local presence is considered vital to be able to meet with the requirements of a sophisticated distribution network, particularly where activities such as special promotions requiring a local representative are concerned. Reliable deliveries and quick, efficient after-sales service are also essential in many product sectors in France, and many companies would consider that these are only possible through an intermediary who can respond quickly and who will hold the necessary levels of stocks. The problem regarding stock can, however, be overcome by using warehousing facilities from which the exporting firm may sell direct to retailers or other customers. This is a particularly attractive solution for exporters of both capital and consumer goods which are heavy consumers of spare parts. Further information may be obtained from the French desk of the DTI.

As much will depend on individual circumstances, and particularly on the degree of concentration of a particular market, the importance of a thorough knowledge of the market must again be stressed.

One final point needs to be mentioned:

payment of VAT (TVA – *taxe sur la valeur ajoutée*). TVA can only be paid by a resident of France registered to do so, and not all customers are registered for this purpose. In such cases, a fiscal representative (the DTI French desk will help but a bank or an accountant in France will also do) needs to be used to arrange payment of TVA. Fundamental changes are expected, however, in 1992.

Agents (*L'agent commercial*)

Most small and medium sized companies use agents for their exports, largely because it enables some measure of control through the use of payment by commission related to turnover. In addition, for those companies lacking any experience of the French market, using an agent overcomes language, cultural and other practical barriers which might otherwise exist. Problems which may occur with agents have already been mentioned and therefore great care must be taken when appointing them. The most important factors covered in their contracts should include:

- the specific territory to be covered (crucial if more than one agent is employed);
- the clients to be visited, eg: wholesalers, retailers, etc.;
- the percentage of commission;
- duration of contract (to avoid later slackening of interest, it may be advisable in the first place to appoint on a trial basis).

Termination of the contract is often the cause of serious problems, since agents can claim compensation (*indemnité*) if termination is for no serious fault on the agent's part. If the written contract is registered with the Commercial Court (*Tribunal de Commerce*), it may be difficult to prove breach of contract and penalties can be severe for premature termination.

So what practical steps can be taken to find and appoint an agent? A considerable number of organisations can offer help:

- The DTI French desk, which will supply, through its various consulates, a report on a specific market and carry out status reports on any agents recommended. Banks or Dun & Bradstreet will provide credit-rating reports.
- British and French Chambers of Commerce (remember that the latter are very powerful and have considerably more clout and a bigger membership network than their British counterparts).
- The British consuls in Paris, Lille, Lyon, Marseille and Bordeaux.
- Trade associations.
- If you already know various customers and end-users, they may well know a good agent with whom they already deal.
- British accountants and lawyers operating in France. (The DTI has a list of both and you may well need one of the latter anyway to advise on precise contractual conditions. Remember at all times that French law can be very tricky and full of traps.)

When negotiating with an agent, the following points should be borne in mind:

- His experience in dealing with similar lines of products (agents who sell to *grandes surfaces* may not be appropriate for specialist shops).
- The number of competing lines he represents (there shouldn't be too many).
- His turnover and annual growth rate (but take care in interpreting his accounts (*les comptes*) which are for tax purposes only in France and therefore tend to understate profits. British accountants in France should be used to ascertain the precise position).
- His ability to carry stocks and carry out after-sales service (many agents will not keep stocks, however, and do not deal with invoicing and delivery).
- to what extent promotional and other advertising costs are to be shared (many agents expect these to be extensively covered by the

principal, and to do so demonstrates your commitment in their eyes).

- the precise nature of the agent's sales force. It may be important to establish whether the agent's sales force are single-product VRP (*Voyageur, Représentant, Placier*) or *multi-cartes* representing more than one principal. Many customers prefer *multi-cartes* VRP because they have a fuller range and might not therefore accept having to see a single-product VRP. Agents often prefer the *multi-cartes*, too, since they are paid on a commission basis only, and therefore cost less when trade is not good.
- Sales literature must be in French. The surprise and pleasure this creates in France should not be underestimated!
- The agent must be assured that no problems of communication will arise through lack of ability in the home sales staff to speak and/or understand French. Much frustration and a bad image for British goods may be otherwise created.

A vital part of the process of appointing an agent is the measure of future contact envisaged. The agent should be visited regularly, and there should be provisions for trips, at short notice. If the reason for one of these trips is technical sales support for a customer, it could be essential to send someone with good colloquial French. Visits to customers also provide excellent opportunity for both identification with the supplier and his products and provide knowledge of a customer base for future use if problems occur with the agent. This can be doubly advantageous in that it allows the supplier a greater degree of control and at the same time reassures the agent of the supplier's serious commitment to the market. This reassurance is vital to motivate the agent and hence stimulate sales.

Quotations also form part of the communication process and the ability to provide these quickly and accurately (always CIF and, adding an adequate percentage increase if necessary, remembering that payment can be up to 120 days) is also a sign to the agent of a supplier's professionalism. Remember that the French market can be tough and aggressive and much of this is due to both this professionalism and profit motivation. The latter quality in an agent can be to your advantage!

Distributors

The essential difference between *l'agent commercial* and the distributor (*le concessionnaire*) is that the latter buys and sells on his own account and actually owns the goods the supplier provides before he resells. He will often ask for exclusivity but care should be taken to distinguish between the different types of exclusive and non-exclusive agreement. In particular, agreements whereby a distributor claims sole national coverage should be avoided unless it is quite clear that he can actually service the whole country. More usual types of agreements are those which may grant exclusivity for one particular region and these have distinct advantages in cases where companies are based away from Paris, for example, Casino in St Etienne, and which have strong links with local distributors able to effect the best introductions. Such distributors might claim non-exclusivity, however, for the range of other goods they sell, and often represent several (often foreign) manufacturers at the same time. This means it is obviously vital to know your competitors and on which features you can compete most strongly (price, quality, etc). Much can be learnt, incidentally, by studying an example of a successful manufacturer using the distributor in whom you are interested, to see what the precise features of his success are.

Sole distribution agreements may fall foul of the fundamental rules of the EC regarding competition. Generally speaking, agreements with agents who negotiate on behalf of their principals without financial responsibility of goods are exempt from EC rulings. So-called 'parallel imports' pose the greatest problems: under EC law they cannot be prohibited and hence an exporter cannot prevent an end-user or other trader from buying goods, covered by an

SETTING THE BUSINESS SCENE

The distribution chain

exclusive contract, in *another* EC country (where prices are low). Only advertising goods for such buying or selling is prohibited. Advice on EC competition policy may be obtained from the Competition Policy Department, 1–19 Victoria Street, London SW1H 0NN, tel: 071–215 4546.

Distributor contracts are subject to the *Code Civil* and typically cover the following:
- minimum amount of goods the distributor will be committed to buy annually,
- the area covered,
- terms of termination of the agreement,
- specific margins and,
- whether the distributor must undertake to sell the goods using the manufacturer's brand name or whether he can use his own logo, which is often an important point.

The ability of a distributor to use his own name on the supplier's products, thus operating a form of franchise (*une franchise*), can be important if the target market is local authorities, hospitals, schools, etc., which may be highly lucrative but may practise a covert 'Buy French' policy. A French name from a French distributor could, therefore, open the right doors. Loss of brand identity for the manufacturer is a major risk, however, depending on the market sector, e.g., in the capital goods sector where a supplier might trade heavily on its names associated with technical excellence.

Choice of a distributor involves the same criteria as for an agent but it can sometimes be difficult to find a totally suitable distributor, mainly because of competing lines he may carry and the question of exclusivity. Again, the point about the need to appoint several distributors must be reiterated.

Branch offfice (*Succursale*)

If a supplier has determined to establish a more long-term presence in France (and this often happens after initially using an agent/distributor), many companies prefer simply to set up a branch of the parent company instead of a fully-fledged French company. This is often seen as an easier route since it seems to require less formalities (no minimum capital, etc.). In reality it may prove to be no easier than establishing a company since it does require certain formalities which are different but nonetheless just as onerous. For instance, the parent company's articles of association have to be translated into French and filed with the Clerk of the Commercial Court (*Greffe du Tribunal de Commerce*). A declaration of direct investment must be filed with the French Treasury, together with a list of names and addresses of shareholders and the existence of the brand must be declared to the local tax, social security and other authorities. Finally, the company's name, a commercial lease and translations of the birth certificates of the Président and Branch Manager must be filed with the Commercial Register (*Registre de Commerce*)!

The main advantage of a branch is that any losses generated in the first few years may be set off against the parent's profits. The main drawback, and this is a significant one, is that the head office is liable for all debts incurred and its accounts may be investigated by the French tax authorities in the event of financial irregularities occurring in the branch office.

In almost all cases it is necessary to appoint a French manager since he or she alone would be aware of current business practices in France. Sales should be in the hands of either a salaried employee (*un représentant*) responsible for a single product, or a VRP (*voyageur-représéntant-placier*) whose terms of contract can be quite draconian, particularly clauses covering severance payments including indemnity for goodwill and an *indemnité de clientèle*. VRP salaries are now usually part fixed, part variable with the latter being no more than 30 per cent of the total to avoid the situation where VRPs enjoy a *rente de situation* (guaranteed income) from the commission earned from a large network of customers. A number of textile firms have actually had to 'buy back' their clientèle from their former VRP! More attention is now being paid to merchandising, logistics and quality with the introduction of incentives for number of units made, new customers, etc. Only when a sufficient level of turnover can be guaranteed should this next step up from the agent be envisaged.

Forming a French company

Various forms of partnership are available; e.g. the *société en nom collectif* (SNC), a general partnership in which its partners are jointly and severally liable for all of its debts. The *groupement d'intérêt économique* is a form of joint venture and is used primarily for joint research and development, sales, exports, etc. Of interest in this context is a new form of business organisation called the 'European Economic Interest Grouping' which enables existing companies from more than one Member State of the EC to retain their independence but combine various non-profit making ancillary activities, such as R&D and marketing. It is mainly intended for small and medium size companies unable to take advantage of other forms of company.

The *Société à Responsabilité Limitée*

By far the most usual forms of company in France are the private SARL (*Société à Responsabilité Limitée*) and the public SA (*Société Anonyme*). The SARL is the most popular type and suitable for small businesses in that the legal requirements are less strict. A minimum of two and a maximum of 50 shareholders (*détenteurs de parts*) are possible, with a minimum share capital of FF 50,000. Shares (*parts sociales*) are freely transferable only amongst the shareholders; there is no Board of Directors but one or more managers (*gérants*). Since 1985, it has been possible for a single individual to form an *Entreprise Unipersonnelle à Responsabilité Limitée* (or transform an SARL into EURL) and this form of corporate entity is popular with foreign companies since it only has to have one share and can thus control all major decisions and shareholders' meetings!

The *Société Anonyme*

The SA, on the other hand, is more akin to the British plc and may be quoted (*cotée en Bourse*) or unquoted (*non cotée*). It needs a minimum of seven shareholders (*actionnaires*) with a legal share capital (*capital social*) of FF 250,000 (or FF 1.5m if offered to the public). Most shares (*actions*) are common shares, but preferred and non-voting shares are also available. Double votes are possible, as is a limit to the number of votes per shareholders holding the same class of share.

The conditions described above are considerably less tough if a company seeks a listing on the *Second Marché*, the equivalent of the Unlisted Securities Market in London. This approach has proved popular with over 250 companies as it requires only 10 per cent of a company's shares to be offered to the public for listing and auditing, and profitability and dividend policies are all considerably laxer. The largest of the *Petites et Moyennes Entreprises* (PME) – small and medium sized companies – are listed on the *Second Marché* in Paris and the rest on the regional *Bourses* in Lyon, Bordeaux, Lille, Marseille, Nancy and Nantes.

An SA may be directed by a PDG (*Président-Directeur-Général*) who is appointed by a board of directors (*un conseil d'administration*) whose members (between three and 12 shareholders) are called *administrateurs*. An alternative form of management would be to appoint a *directoire* (up to 5 members) to deal with day-to-day matters and appoint a *conseil de surveillance* (supervisory council) to deal with longer term strategy and finance. This form of management is however not very common in France except in State-run companies where trade unions are more powerful and workers' representatives sit on the *conseil de surveillance*.

The larger SARLs (over 50 employees, FF 10m assets or FF 20m turnover) must appoint an auditor (*un commissaire aux comptes*). All SAs have auditors, two if its accounts are consolidated (*bilan consolidé*) or if it is quoted. According to French commercial law all businesses must also maintain a *livre journal* for recording day-to-day operations, a *grand livre*, a general ledger and a *livre d'inventaire* which registers all annual financial statements.

All companies must recognise the establishment of a trade union branch. Companies cannot demand that their employees belong to one, single union and, according to its size, various representatives and committees must be appointed. These are:

- the *délégué syndical*, the trade union shop steward,
- the *délégué du personnel* (employees' representative) in companies employing more than ten people and
- the *comité d'entreprise* (works council) in companies of over 50 employees.

Companies have a duty (very specifically laid down in law – the *Code du Travail*) to recognise various rights and privileges according to the representative or committee.

Acquisitions (*Acquisitions*)

British companies are no exception when it comes to the international trend of building up market share by acquisitions. Establishing brands takes time and money, so in the run-up to the establishment of the Single European Market, companies are taking the short-cut to external growth and trying to buy established brands. It is, however, interesting to note that a number of companies, particularly in the food sector, do not seem prepared to spend the large sums of money involved in buying established brands, and are looking at the own-label market which remains less well developed in continental Europe.

Contrary to popular opinion, France is proving to be one of the most open markets for foreign buyers (with the UK leading the way) with 91 acquisitions being made in the first half of 1989. Much of this acquisition activity (77 per cent) did not take place on the Stock Market, however, since much of the focus has been on dynamic family-run companies set up just after the Second World War, whose proprietors are now retiring and where there is no obvious successor in the wings. In addition, the Bourse is far smaller than the Stock Market in London (approximately one-third of its capitalisation) which is historically due to the absence of the pension schemes which provide the bulk of London's liquidity.

The increasing number of foreign takeovers in France have however, caused some considerable debate over the last few years, as more and more of its well-known brands (Dim, Peaudouce, Chambourcy, Huiles Lesieur) disappear into foreign ownership. Hostile takeover bids (OPA – *offre publique d'achat*) were once almost unknown, but now even these are on the increase, although on nowhere near the scale of the United Kingdom and the USA.

Apart from the reasons already given, there are two others why France is becoming a favourite target for acquisitions. First, with its rapidly expanding rail and road network, France is being seen as the best bridge-head for Europe in terms of distribution and logistics.

Secondly, many of France's PME, although creating high value added and possessing incomparable know-how, are often too small and therefore vulnerable to takeover.

Their fellow French companies are unable to match the huge sums offered by UK and USA companies simply because many of them are not big enough and might well disappear themselves. Furthermore, as already explained in the previous chapters, many companies have not been making enough profit to invest until relatively recently. In a recent report by the Bain Consulting Group in Paris for the French Ministry of Industry it was calculated that the average turnover of the top 250 companies in the turnover range FF 1–35bn i.e. between the top 20 companies and the PME), is 35 per cent and 45 per cent less than that of comparable British and West German companies respectively. (Overall only 50 French companies figure in the top 500 companies in the world, with none in the top ten.)

So how is the British company to unearth companies of potential interest? The most effective way is through the company's normal business contacts in France, in particular through conversations with suppliers and customers. Local help is essential in order to be able to make a thorough search, to screen possible targets, to interpret information, even to negotiate and close the deal. Again, local banks and Chambers of Commerce provide this sort of service, as do the major merchant banks and consultancies in both the UK and France. If negotiations are to be held without the help of a third party, language is an important element, of course, but so too is a complete understanding of the French environment and of the need for trust.

The acquisition of a **listed** company would typically involve informing shareholders of that company of the intention to purchase either for cash through an *Offre Publique d'Achat* (OPA) or for securities via an *Offre Publique d'Echange (OPE)*. The offer must be for at least 10 per cent of the target company or 5 per cent in the event of the share capital exceeding FF 10m. The Stock Exchange Committee, followed by the Ministry of Economy, must receive all necessary documents and a successful bid is notified to the Stock Exchange and then to all shareholders concerned.

Because the Bourse is so much smaller in France, many target companies will be unlisted and special care must be taken to collect information from the sources described above. Confidentiality during negotiations is important and a breakdown in negotiations could involve penalties. Other points to watch are: the taxes to be paid (e.g. there is no longer any liability to stamp duty on the transfer of shares), the purchase price (without a determined price the sale may be revoked), and the drafting of the agreements (the words 'subject to contract', for example are meaningless in French).

Important sources of information on acquisitions:

'Ten Golden Rules for Acquiring an Unlisted Company in France', *Acquisitions Monthly*, December 1989, pp 50–53.

Terence E Cooke, *International Mergers and Acquisitions*, Blackwell, 1989.

Hill Samuel Bank Limited, *Mergers, Acquisitions and Alternative Strategies*, Mercury Books, 1989.

Important changes are being made in the law covering takeovers, not only in France but more particularly in directives coming from Brussels. For the present, however, potential investors in France are strongly advised to look at the capital structure of companies which may be acquired. Non-voting stock, investment certificates, double voting rights, different classes of share and rights of first refusal are often used in French companies to preserve a majority interest. By-laws and articles of incorporation, as well as specific agreements between shareholders (*concert parties*) should hence be examined carefully.

Another risk in these takeovers is undisclosed liability, particularly tax liabilities incurred as a result of a *contrôle fiscal*, the tax authorities' final year check on company accounts (there is no notional agreement on tax between tax-paying corporations and the tax authorities, as in the UK).

Finally, any acquisition in a French company by a non-resident of France, even if EC resident, must be submitted to the French Treasury which has up to one month to respond.

Establishment of manufacturing plant

Both central and local authorities provide incentives of one kind or another for investment in industrial and R&D operations.

At national level, DATAR provides grants (PAT – *prime d'aménagement du territoire*) of up to 25 per cent of an investment (land, buildings, equipment) depending on:

- the geographical location (particularly in western, south-western and central France),
- the number of jobs created (minimum of 20 within first three years or 10 if these jobs represent an increase of the existing work-force), and
- size of company (e.g. minimum worldwide sales of FF 300m or an investment of more than FF 20m).

A government committee decides on the amount which is paid locally by a Ministry of Finance representative.

Grants of 37.5 per cent of the total investment in North-Eastern France (Longwy) are available through a joint EC-French government programme.

There are also special grants for R&D centres meeting the following criteria:

1. they should be in engineering or software
2. they should not be located in the greater Paris area (there is in fact a development *charge* (*agrément*) for developments in Paris)
3. 30 jobs must be created over 3 years
4. worldwide sales of FF 300m.

The grants are worth FF 35,000 per new job or FF 50,000 in an urban area. Such grants are taxable in the first year but the depreciation of a fixed asset investment can be increased by 50 per cent of the PAT and consequently only 50 per cent of the grant is taxed. R&D project grants can be spread over ten years.

Local and Regional Grants and Subsidies. As seen in chapter 1, most local authorities, particularly chambers of commerce operate *technopoles* and industrial zones. Land is sold or leased and new buildings may be subsidised up to 25 per cent of the cost. In addition, in certain areas, local authorities may totally or partially exempt

FRENCH MARKET ENTRY STRATEGIES

new industrial or service companies from the business tax (*la taxe professionnelle*) for up to five years in the event of an investment totalling FF 800,000 in urban areas of more than 15,000 inhabitants and creating at least 30 new jobs.

At the regional level, there are regional employment grants (*prime régionale d'emploi*) of FF 10,000 per job created in towns of over 100,000 inhabitants and FF 20,000 if outside such towns (but within PAT areas). Regional grants for the establishment of new companies (*primes régionales de création d'entreprises*) are awarded up to FF 150,000 or FF 200,000 in priority areas.

In the old smoke-stack industry areas, particularly the North-East, *Conversion* aid is available, covering low interest loans and purchase of land, machinery, etc., from existing plant at little or no cost.

Sociétés de Développement Régional and *Instituts de Développement* are to be found in all regions and take equity in small and medium sized companies.

Enterprise Zones (*Zones d'entreprise*). These were set up in Dunkirk, La Ciotat and La Seyne (Toulon) and allow exemption from corporation tax for ten years (*impôt sur les sociétés* – in 1990, 40 per cent for those distributing dividends, 38 per cent for those not distributing dividends, to encourage investment). Only incorporated companies are eligible, they must employ at least ten persons after two years of operation, and no other government grants can be awarded in such areas. Exemption from corporation tax for up to three years is also available in many other areas, so any relative advantage of the enterprise zones is in reality limited to seven years. Dunkirk has been the most successful, with 16 new companies, including Coca-Cola. Its geographical position mainly explains this success.

One major problem concerning grants of any kind in France is their bewildering abundance and careful advice is therefore necessary from the British Consuls, accountants, lawyers, etc. In addition, DATAR has a London office, the French Industrial Board, 21–24 Grosvenor Place, London, SW1X 7HU, tel: 071–823 1895. Another important organisation is ANVAR (*l'agence nationale pour la valorisation de la recherche*), particularly for R&D grants and Hi-Tech companies.

Finally, whichever route you decide to take into France, it is worth reiterating the influence of regional banks (of which there are many), chambers of commerce, mayors of communes (*maires*) and other elected representatives (*sénateurs* and *députés*). Local notables are extremely powerful and well-connected in France and, although the price may be a covert diversion of funds for the funding of political parties, it could pay handsome dividends in terms of preferential treatment, but this is all part of getting to know France and its many distinct business practices and customs. They are as important as its language so take time to establish contacts, to talk and discover how each company and sector operates. Personal relationships can never be overrated in a French context.

Business magazine 0: Introduction: 'Getting to know you'

Many British companies are now looking across the few miles of Channel to our closest neighbour – France, and the lucrative market that awaits. An ability to speak the language undoubtedly gives British business people in France a big competitive edge. However, it is also important to understand the French themselves; the way they live, work and play. This first business magazine looks through the eyes of people who know France well at the people who make up the market.

Part 2

The language of business

Introduction to the language sequences

The language section of this coursebook consists of seven sequences which run parallel to the video and the travel cassettes. You are recommended to do the sequences in order, unless you are particularly advanced or have a pressing reason for doing a later sequence early on. The sequences are as follows:

1. The trade fair
2. Direct selling
3. Working with an agent
4. Business at a local level
5. The Tunnel – and beyond
6. Establishing a bridgehead
7. Conducting meetings.

The course is designed to cater for a variety of levels, so you should work at your own pace. On average it aims at a rusty O-level, but it may be used by those who need to relearn, the basic tenses of French, as well as by those for whom such basic knowledge will be the starting point from which to go on to more advanced work. If you are among the former, you should concentrate on practising the basic structures, if among the latter, then you can focus on acquiring the more advanced idioms which you will hear. Remember that you can always improve in a language: if you know the structure, listen to the pronunciation and intonation and so on. Learning a language is a bit similar to making an investment: a little is better than none at all, but the more you invest, the greater the rewards.

The organisation of each sequence

Within each sequence there are seven essential sections:

- Preparation for watching and listening to the video
- Exercises A – E:
  A Listen and understand
  B Develop your skills
  C Extend your vocabulary
  D Make your language work
  E Dialogues
- Language comment
- Sketch
- Business notes

The sections in detail

Preparation

Before watching the video, you should read the introduction to the sequence and look at the list of key words. Only words and expressions which are essential for understanding the video have been included. You should try to understand the **video sequences** with the help of the key words only, trying to guess what you do not know from the context, and from related words which you do know. The key to understanding is to listen to as much French as possible, so listen to the sequences on the video and on the

THE LANGUAGE OF BUSINESS

travel cassette (as well as to regular French radio programmes) as often as possible. You will learn more from listening several times than from listening once and stopping to look up words every few minutes. If, after having listened several times, you still have trouble understanding certain parts of the video, you can read through the transcript and look up the words in the glossary. (We have put in the glossary words which we think many people may not be familiar with.) To help you even further you can look at the left-hand column of *A1 Getting the gist*, as the questions there are intended not only as a test of your understanding, but also as signposts to the main points of the sequence.

A Listen and understand

In every sequence this section consists of three parts. In the first part (A1) you should try to get the gist of the story, the broad outline. The second exercise (A2) requires more detailed understanding, and in the third (A3) you are asked to produce more continuous French rather than just short sentences. For example, you may be asked to provide a summary of a part of the sequence.

You will find possible answers to the questions in parts A1 and A2 in italics in the right-hand column, so that you can cover them up while going through the questions. (Do bear in mind that these answers are just *suggestions*; they are by no means the only correct ones.) You may find it useful to repeat these answers, or to record them on a blank cassette. In some sequences, possible answers are given on your study cassette.

B Develop your skills and C Extend your vocabulary

These two sections contain some exercises in the traditional sense. Section B concentrates on grammar whereas section C deals with vocabul-

Extending your vocabulary

INTRODUCTION TO THE LANGUAGE SEQUENCES

ary. Grammar and vocabulary are to a language what foundations and bricks are to a house; both are vital elements. The main grammar points which you will need for effective communication are covered in the seven language chapters. For those of you with previous knowledge and experience of French, some of the grammar may be a revision and consolidation, and other parts may be new. For this reason, we give only a brief grammatical explanation in section B; more detail is given in the Grammar Kit for those who need it. In section C, we concentrate on common endings, ways of turning one part of speech into another, and words which have a large number of uses, rather than on vocabulary lists.

Sections B and C together represent quite a formidable array of exercises, covering various topics which you need in order to be able to handle the freer exercises of section D. It is therefore advisable to look at those sections before going on to section D. This does not mean that you should plough through them at one sitting – it is better not to – but to intersperse them with listening to the video or **travel cassette** again, or perhaps trying one of the dialogues in E. (See below: How to organise your work sessions.)

D Make your language work

This section is designed to make you use the skills you have acquired and apply them to communication situations relevant to business. You may be asked to describe a product, to introduce yourself, or to compare two documents. In this section you should not be too preoccupied with 'correctness'; say as much as you can, and try out some of the expressions you have learned.

E Dialogues

The dialogue section gives you a chance to practise participating in genuine dialogues, and sometimes you are even asked to invent one. Listen to the **study cassette** and try to perfect your own recordings as much as you can.

Business notes

At the end of each language chapter you will find a 'business notes' section. This section provides additional practical business information linked to the video sequence, which will help you to be more effective in your dealings with the French.

How to organise your learning

While it is advisable to check that you are thoroughly familiar with the structures and vocabulary of sections B and C before doing section D, this does not mean that you should go through them all in one session. On the contrary, it will probably be better to do two or three exercises a day, interspersed with looking at or listening to the sequence again. It is important to divide each sequence up into several sessions, and to watch the video, or take a break, between exercises. Depending on your level, each sequence requires anything upwards of five to six hours' work. How intensively you wish to work is a matter for individual preference and circumstance. Below we give a suggested pattern for those who wish to divide each sequence into six sessions each of an hour long:

Session 1: Follow the suggestions under Preparation, on p. 41–2, and view video at least twice; start section A.
Session 2: Review video, finish section A, try exercises 1 + 2 of section B. The travel cassette will also help you with this and perhaps also exercise 1 and 2 of section C.
Session 3: Do part of B3, 4 and 5, and C3, 4 and 5.
Session 4: Review video and do the remaining exercises in sections B and C.
Session 5: Review video and look at section D.
Session 6: Section E

Remember this is only a suggestion!

Video and audio references

Wherever you see this reference you will need to refer to the **video sequences**. The numbers will guide you to the correct point on the tape.

This symbol refers you to the **travel cassette**. Each language chapter has its own section on the cassette. The abstracts serve as a general aid to comprehension. Feel free to listen to it any time.

This symbol refers you to the **study cassette**. Each exercise with a reference to the study cassette will have some instructions on how to use it.

This symbol refers you to the **Business Magazines**. The number on the briefcase indicates which magazine is referred to.

Pronunciation and intonation

While this course does not contain any specific exercises on pronunciation and intonation, we do give some tips in the sequences, and again at the end of the Grammar Kit. Take note of these points and try to detect them in the recordings: they will help you to understand and be understood.

Remember that the French will appreciate it if you make the offer to speak even a little French. Of course they will appreciate it more if you speak fluently and correctly!

Bon travail et bonne chance.

Chapter 1

The trade fair
'Je voudrais vous présenter les produits de notre société'

Introduction

For many business people trade fairs are the way into a new market. They provide an opportunity to size up the competition and gauge reaction to different products. It is also a good opportunity to meet people, such as buyers, agents and distributors.

At a trade fair you will need to be able to present your company and product or service. Technical details may be contained in professionally translated literature, but your initial contacts will be much more fruitful if you can communicate in the language of the market.

THE LANGUAGE OF BUSINESS

In the video sequence which accompanies the chapter, you will:

- see a multi-national company, Unipart, with its highly developed approach to exhibiting;
- watch a French company, TMA, give a presentation;
- learn how the DTI may be able to help your company enter the French market;
- watch a product presentation being made by Graeme Harwood – who has his own small company, Davair.

You will also learn some of the language skills that you will need to communicate effectively at trade fairs or in any situation where you need to present your company or service, including:

- revising the present tense;
- preparing other tenses;
- using negatives;
- building up your vocabulary;
- describing your company.

Now watch the Trade Fair sequence (10 03 35).

The following words and phrases should give you some help in understanding the dialogues in this sequence.

Key words and phrases

Unipart

se lancer sur le marché français	to launch a product/company on the French market
une marque	a make, a brand name
la distribution/livraison des pièces	the supply/delivery of parts
les ruptures (f) de stock	break in supply, stock-out
réduire les délais (m)	to reduce the time span
les pièces (f) sont acheminées	the parts are dispatched, transported
compte tenu de la taille de la France	taking the size of France into account
développer une filiale	to set up a subsidiary

THE TRADE FAIR

La Société TMA

on fabrique des boîtes (f) de vitesse	we make gear-boxes
l'embrayage (m)	the clutch
tout ce qui est approvisionnement (m)	everything to do with supplies, stock
la gestion	management, administration
un local (pl. des locaux)	premises

Présentation d'un appareil

à quoi sert cet appareil?	What's this machine for?
chauffer un atelier	to heat a workshop
une grande gamme	a wide range
l'huile (f) de vidange	sump oil
un gicleur qui ne se bouchera jamais	a jet that will never get blocked
c'est breveté mondialement (un brevet = a patent)	it's patented worldwide
le service après-vente	after sales service
une pièce de rechange	a spare part
le prix de revient	the cost
une remise de vingt pour cent	a 20% discount
passer une commande (NB *not* placer)	to place an order
une petite entreprise de transport	a small transport business
envoyer un devis	to send a quote
je compte sur vous	I'm counting on you

Faux amis (pitfalls)

Beware of the following words. Their meaning is not necessarily the one that immediately springs to mind!

actuellement (= maintenant, de nos jours, en ce moment)	*not* 'actually'. It means: now, at present, at this very moment, these days
un délai	*not* necessarily a delay, simply a period of time.

THE LANGUAGE OF BUSINESS

Listen and understand

Have a look at the questions in the left-hand column before turning to the video. After having watched the Trade Fair video sequence you should be able to answer the questions in exercises A1 and A2. Try answering them on your own first, covering the answers in the right-hand column. Then look at the possible answers and compare them with your own. This should give you an idea of how well you have understood the video sequence.

A1. Getting the gist

1. Qu'est-ce qui préoccupe l'intervieweur de *Linéaire auto?*

   C'est la distribution de pièces qui le préoccupe.

2. Dans quel domaine d'activité s'est spécialisée la société TMA?

   Elle fabrique et reconditionne des pièces auto, telles que les boîtes de vitesse.

3. A quoi sert l'appareil?

   L'appareil sert à chauffer un atelier.

A2. Getting the detail

Unipart

1. Selon l'intervieweur, quel est le plus gros problème dans la distribution des pièces?

Le plus gros problème, ce sont les ruptures de stock.

2. Combien de temps faut-il pour livrer des pièces de Londres à Paris?

Il faut quarante-huit heures.

3. Qu'est-ce qu'il faudra faire pour améliorer la distribution de pièces dans toute la France?

Il faudra avoir des points de distribution dans d'autres régions de la France.

4. Est-ce que Unipart a l'intention de créer une filiale en France?

Non, pas en ce moment.

La Société TMA

5. De quoi s'occupe-t-elle, la dame qui est interviewée?

Elle s'occupe de la publicité, de la gestion et des clients; tout ce qui est des contacts, en somme.

THE LANGUAGE OF BUSINESS

6. Et son mari? *Son mari s'occupe de l'approvisionnement.*

7. Quels sont leurs projets d'avenir? *Ils envisagent la création d'un local mieux équipé.*

L'appareil

8. Quel est le métier du client qui s'intéresse à l'appareil? *Il est transporteur.*

9. Quels sont les avantages et les qualités de cet appareil? *C'est économique, c'est garanti pour deux ans, et il n'y a pas de problème pour les pièces de rechange.*

10. Est-ce que le client passe une commande sur place? *Non, il va attendre de recevoir un devis. (NB Not 'une quotation'!!!)*

A3 Summing up the scene

Listen again to the interview with the journalist from *Linéaire auto* (10 06 07) and give a full summary of what the European Sales Manager of Unipart says. You can either do it entirely in your own words, or you can use the expressions given below to help you. Try recording your summary on the blank cassette and listening to yourself.

Unipart – pas très connu – pourtant – se développer sur le marché français – effectivement nous avons fait des tests – pas de problème de rupture de stocks – car – une livraison de pièces dans 48 heures – en plus – l'intention de développer d'autres points de distribution – cependant – pas de filiale en France.

B Develop your skills

B1 The present indicative (*How to assert and affirm*)

The present tense in French has two moods:

- the indicative, to state or affirm something
- the subjunctive, for use in expressions of doubt, likelihood, desirability, rather than straight assertion.

In this sequence we will only concern ourselves with the present indicative. The subjunctive will be discussed later on.

The present indicative is the verb form which is used the most. It can indicate that something is *happening at present*, or that something is *a regular occurrence*. It also forms the basis of most other verb forms. This explains why you need to be thoroughly familiar with this tense.

When using the present indicative in French, it is good to keep the following in mind:

- The French present indicative expresses both the English simple present (I do – regularly, often, generally, etc.) and the progressive present (I am doing).

Compare, for instance:

Qu'est-ce que **vous faites** quand ils ne répondent pas?	What **do you do** when there is no reply?
En général, **j'envoie** une télécopie.	I usually **send** a fax.

and

Qu'est-ce que **vous faites** là?	What **are you doing** now?
J'essaie de les joindre par téléphone.	**I am** (in the process of) **trying** to get through to them on the phone.

THE LANGUAGE OF BUSINESS

If you want to stress the fact that you are in the process of doing something, you can use **être en train de**.

   Je **suis en train de** leur écrire.   I **am in the middle of** writing them.

• Pronunciation in French can make all the difference. It is therefore important to listen carefully to the video and audio cassettes. Two golden rules are:

1. Many final consonants (and groups of consonants) are silent. For instance, in all of the following examples the final consonant(s) are not pronounced.

   Tu va$\cancel{s}$
   Nous pouvon$\cancel{s}$
   Je prend$\cancel{s}$

The 's' of **nous, vous, ils, elles,** is only pronounced before a vowel (e.g. **vou$\cancel{s}$ voulez** *but* **vous‿avez**)

2. An 'e' without accent is a 'neutral' vowel. It is either barely pronounced or not at all.

J(e) parl(e) français not 'J(ay) parl(ai)' français (cf. j'ai parlé)
J(e) pai(e) par chèque not 'J(ay) pay(ai)' par chèque (cf. j'ai payé)

The exercises below allow you to check how well you know the present indicative. If you find that you get more than a few of the verbs wrong, you should use the Grammar Kit at the back of the book to revise the present tense.

A vous

Read the sentences below aloud to yourself and choose the correct present indicative form of the verb in brackets. Check the Grammar Kit if you are not sure of the present tense!
1. Ils (reconditionner) les boîtes de vitesse.
2. Nous (travailler) avec les particuliers.
3. On (fabriquer) des pièces de rechange.
4. Tu (poser) la question en français et ils (répondre) en anglais.
5. Ils (saisir) l'occasion pour présenter leur nouvel appareil.

6. Nous (commencer) par une mise au point de la situation actuelle, et nous (finir) avec les projets d'avenir.
7. Vous (croire) que c'est cher, cet appareil pour lequel ils (faire) de la promotion?
8. Elles (connaître) à fond le problème.
9. Nous (prendre) toutes les décisions dans notre conseil d'administration.
10. Ils (acheter) toujours nos produits car ceux-ci sont de bonne qualité.
11. La présidente (ouvrir) le débat en citant tous les avantages de l'OPA (une offre publique d'achat = a takeover bid).
12. C'est le PDG (président-directeur général) qui (venir) nous voir demain.
13. Avant de décoller, vous (éteindre) vos cigarettes.
14. Vous (conclure) donc qu'il n'y a pas de collaboration possible entre nos deux sociétés?
15. Du point de vue technique, ils (faire) beaucoup de progrès.
16. Vous (voir) ce que je (vouloir) dire?
17. Vous (pouvoir) passer une commande tout de suite.
18. Ce (être) des appareils japonais.
19. Je (vendre) des voitures d'occasion.
20. (Compter) sur nous! (to someone you don't know well).

Answers: *1. reconditionnent 2. travaillons 3. fabrique 4. poses, répondent 5. saisissez 6. commençons, finissons 7. croyez, font 8. connaissent 9. prenons 10. achètent 11. ouvre 12. vient 13. éteignez 14. concluez 15. font 16. voyez, veux 17. pouvez 18. sont 19. vends 20. comptez*

B2 Using negative expressions correctly with the present (*It ain't necessarily so.*)

As you probably already know, negative expressions in French consist of the word **ne** in combination with **pas** (or **plus, jamais, point,** etc). These two words, which together form the negative expression, should be placed either side of the verb.

Je **ne** fume **pas**.	I **don't** smoke.
je **ne** fume **plus**.	I **don't** smoke **any more**.
Je **ne** fume **jamais**.	I **never** smoke.
Je **ne** fume **ni** les cigarettes **ni** les cigares.	I smoke **neither** cigarettes **nor** cigars.
Il **n'a aucun** prétexte pour acheter une cigarette.	He has **(absolutely) no** excuse for buying cigarettes.

THE LANGUAGE OF BUSINESS

but

    Il n'y a personne qui fume ici.   There is no one here who smokes.

In the last example you can see that the two negative adverbs are not only separated by the verb, but also by **y**. For more information on the position of **y** and other object pronouns in negative expressions, check the Grammar Kit.

Two comments:

- in (colloquial) French, the **ne** is often dropped. However, it is best if you keep it in.
- following a negation, the articles **un, une, du, de la, des,** all become **de**.

    J'ai **une** pipe.   Je n'ai pas **de** pipe.

A vous

Now make the following sentences negative.

1. Nous avons du personnel technique. (ne - pas)

   Nous n'avons pas de personnel technique.

2. On a eu des ennuis avec cette machine. (ne - jamais)

   On n'a jamais eu d'ennuis avec cette machine.

3. Il y a une remise sur ce modèle. (ne – plus)

   Il n'y a plus de remise sur ce modèle.

4. Nous avons reçu le catalogue et l'échantillon. (ni – ni)

   Nous n'avons reçu ni le catalogue ni l'échantillon.

5. Il y a un risque de rupture de stock. (ne – aucun)

   Il n'y a aucun risque de rupture de stock.

B3 Il faut and other impersonal verbs

A number of French verbs, which you will need regularly, only occur in the form of the third person singular **(il)**. These are all either impersonal verbs or verbs used in the impersonal way. Examples of these verbs

THE TRADE FAIR

are **falloir – il faut, pleuvoir – il pleut, s'agir de – il s'agit de, valoir – il vaut**.

Il faut lui téléphoner tout de suite.	You/we must (it is necessary to) phone him immediately.
Il pleut tout le temps en Bretagne.	It rains all the time in Brittany.
De quoi s'agit-il?	What does he want? [annotated: ✗ what's it about?]
Il s'agit de la réunion de jeudi.	It's about Thursday's meeting.
Il s'agit de proposer un prix plus bas que celui de nos concurrents.	It's a matter of proposing a lower price than our competitors.
Il vaut la peine d'essayer; les enjeux sont importants.	It's worth trying, the stakes are high.

A vous

These verbs obviously occur in more than just the present tense. Below you find a number of the most common ones in a variety of tenses. Try to fit them in the following sentences.

pleuvra (future)   a plu (past)
vaut (present)   vaudrait (conditional)
s'agit (present)   s'agirait (conditional)

1. Bonjour, Monsieur. De quoi _____ -il?
2. A mon avis, cet appareil _____ bien le modèle précédant.
3. Il _____ hier et selon la météo il _____ encore demain.
4. Le PDG ne s'est pas prononcé en public, mais selon toutes les indications il _____ simplement d'une OPA lancée par un consortium britannique.
5. Je me demande s'il ne _____ pas mieux vendre les actions tout de suite.

Answers: *1. s'agit 2. vaut 3. a plu, pleuvra 4. s'agirait 5. vaudrait.*

The most common of these impersonal verbs is **falloir**. See if you can rephrase the following sentences, using the appropriate form of **falloir**.

Infinitive: falloir

present:	il faut	imperfect:	il fallait
future:	il faudra	conditional:	il faudrait
past:	il a fallu	past conditional:	il aurait fallu

THE LANGUAGE OF BUSINESS

Example: Il est nécessaire d'avoir un stand à la foire. *Il faut avoir un stand à la foire.*

Now cover up the right-hand column and try to rephrase the following sentences in the same way, matching the form of **falloir** to the verb in the left-hand column:

1. Il **sera préférable** de créer une filiale en France. *Il faudra créer une filiale en France.*

2. Il **serait judicieux** de faire de tests d'abord. *Il faudrait faire de tests d'abord.*

3. **Nous avons dû** trouver de nouveaux locaux. *Il a fallu trouver de nouveaux locaux.*

4. **De** combien de pièces **avez-vous besoin?** *Combien de pièces vous faut-il?*

5. **Nous aurions dû** traduire notre plaquette en français. *Il aurait fallu traduire notre plaquette en français.*

6. **Il était indispensable** d'avoir des renseignements précis. *Il fallait avoir des renseignements précis.*

7. **Il va être important** d'expédier la commande dans le plus bref délai possible. *Il va falloir expédier la commande dans le plus bref délai possible.*

B4 French adjectives and past participles (*Their agreement is needed.*)

> In French, adjectives and past participles used as adjectives agree with the noun they refer to, or qualify, in gender and number.
>   The most common sort of adjective agreement adds **-e** for the feminine, **-s** for masculine plural and mixed masculine and feminine plural, and **-es** for feminine plural.
>
> **la** situation actuell**e**   l'air comprim**é**
> **le** marché français   **une** marque connu**e**
> les petit**es** entreprises

THE TRADE FAIR

A vous

You are a representative of Unimax; the following are the notes you are preparing for a press interview.

In this exercise you are asked to add appropriate endings, where necessary, to the past participles and adjectives. Only few agreements can be heard but they are important for making things clear in written French. Write these words out first, and then read, and preferably record, the whole paragraph.

> Nos produits ne sont toujours pas connu*(1)* en France. Nous sommes une société allemand*(2)*, représenté*(3)* en France et en Belgique par Unimax, et en Espagne par deux agences récemment ouvert*(4)*. Des enquêtes ont été fait*(5)* en France et ailleurs avant de nous lancer sur le marché. Les pièces sont produit*(6)* en Chine et exporté*(7)* vers l'Allemagne. La remise est basé*(8)* sur la quantité de marchandise acheté*(9)*. Une nouvelle machine a été promis*(10)*, et une nouvelle filiale sera créé*(11)* dans le proche avenir.
>
> Answers: *1. connus 2. allemande 3. représentée 4. ouvertes 5. faites 6. produites 7. exportées 8. basée 9. achetée 10. promise 11. créée*

C Extend your vocabulary

The majority of French words are built up according to a fixed pattern, so extending your vocabulary becomes relatively easy once you know these patterns. In this section we shall be looking at some suffixes which are very common in business and technical French. These suffixes can also be very helpful in determining the gender of a word.

C1 Masculine or feminine?

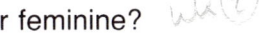

See if you can deduce any general rules by looking at the list below:

masculine	*feminine*
le développement	la distribution
le reconditionnement	la disparition
l'approvisionnement	la présentation
	la fabrication
le problème	la gestion
le système	la consommation

masculine	*feminine*
le tourisme	la publicité
l'importateur	la rupture
le spectateur	
le montage	
l'avantage	
l'assemblage	

You will probably have worked out that words ending in:

-ment	-isme
-ème	-eur

are usually masculine, as are polysyllabic words ending in **-age**.
   Words ending in:

-tion	-te
-aison	-ure

tend to be feminine.
   Beware, however! There are always exceptions, and many words ending in **-é** or **-e** are masculine.

le marché	le principe
le risque	le manque.

Furthermore, some words change meaning according to gender, e.g.:

le poste = a post, a job	**la** poste = the post office
le mode = way, mode	**la** mode = fashion

l'industrie de la mode est très développée en France	the fashion industry is highly developed in France
le micro-ordinateur est en mode conversationnel	the p.c. is in interactional mode

Always note the gender of a new word, and try to learn it in a phrase.

THE TRADE FAIR

A vous

Try to give a French equivalent for the English phrases below. Compare your answers to those in the right-hand column.

1. the Common Market — *le Marché Commun*
2. a financial problem — *un problème financier*
3. a very complete service — *un service très complet*
4. an immediate delivery — *une livraison immédiate*
5. a serious lack of money — *un manque sérieux d'argent*
6. an important principle — *un principe important*
7. a big risk — *un gros risque*
8. defective distribution — *une distribution défective*
9. the instruction manual (means of use) — *le mode d'emploi*

C2 The **-age** suffix

This masculine ending is very common in technical language, and indicates an action or an operation. With **-er** verbs, you simply take off the **-er** ending, and add **-age**. (With verbs ending on **-ir**, you add **-age** to the third person plural stem – **finir, finissage**).

assembler -> assemblage (=assembly)
usiner -> usinage (=manufacturing)
filtrer -> filtrage (=filtering)
lever -> levage (=lifting)

A vous

In the exercise below you should replace the verb in brackets with the appropriate noun.

Example: Un contrôle est nécessaire pour le (repérer) des défauts.
Un contrôle est nécessaire pour le repérage des défauts.

1. Le (débrayer) sur ce camion se fait automatiquement.
2. Le rayon de (braquer) de la R16TS est de 5 mètres.
3. Nous recommendons l'(équilibrer) des roues lors du remplacement des pneux.
4. Avant de passer à l'atelier de peinture, il faut procéder au (dégraisser) et au (rincer) de la carrosserie.

THE LANGUAGE OF BUSINESS

5. Après la première couche de peinture la pièce passe dans une étuve de (sécher).

6. Le niveau de (remplir) du réservoir est contrôlé par un système électronique.

Answers: *1. débrayage 2. braquage 3. équilibrage 4. dégraissage, rinçage 5. séchage 6. remplissage.*

A vous

In this exercise, we ask you to reply to the question as indicated, using a word in **-age** in your answer.

Example: Nettoyer les outils, c'est obligatoire? (Oui) — *Oui, le nettoyage des outils est obligatoire.*

1. Démonter la machine, c'est réalisable? (Non) — *Non, le démontage de la machine n'est pas réalisable.*

2. Découper le tunnelier, c'est une opération inévitable? (Oui) — *Oui, le découpage du tunnelier est une opération inévitable.*

3. Forer dans une couche de craie bleue, c'est plus facile que de forer dans un terrain perméable? (Oui) — *Oui, le forage dans une couche de craie bleue, c'est plus facile que de forer dans un terrain perméable.*

4. Démarrer le projet à la date prévue, c'était une tâche facile? (Non) — *Non, le démarrage du projet à la date prévue n'était pas une tâche facile.*

5. Régler les engins s'est avéré plus difficile que prévu? (Oui) — *Oui, le réglage des engins s'est avéré plus difficile que prévu.*

C3 Compound expressions

You can also extend your vocabulary by knowing that French joins up nouns with **de** or **à** to make compound nouns. Here we concentrate on nouns linked by **de**.

a visiting card – une carte **de** visite

As you can see, the word order in French is exactly the opposite of that in English. The qualifying word, which precedes the main word in English, follows the main word in French.

THE TRADE FAIR

A vous

Try to find the translation of the following English phrases. Do not look at the answers in the right-hand column until you have completed the exercise on your own.

1. a spare part　　　　　　　　　*une pièce de rechange*
2. the cost (or unit) price　　　　*le prix de revient*
3. a gear box　　　　　　　　　　*une boîte de vitesse*
4. a brake pad　　　　　　　　　*une plaquette de frein*
5. a meeting room　　　　　　　*une salle de réunion*
6. a business man　　　　　　　*un homme d'affaires*
7. a fuel pump　　　　　　　　　*une pompe d'alimentation*
8. the retail price　　　　　　　*le prix de détail*
9. a heating apparatus　　　　　*un appareil de chauffage*

D Make your language work

D1 Presenting your company

In this section you are going to practise giving information about your company. Just as an example we have reproduced an article from *Linéaire auto* in which you can see how one company, Hoppecke, presents itself.

HOPPECKE

Créée en 1982, la filiale française du fabricant allemand de batteries et d'accumulateurs bénéficie d'une longue expérience acquise par la maison-mère depuis 1927.

Largement impliquée sur le marché européen, Hoppecke est une des plus grandes marques de batteries : elle s'est d'ailleurs forgée une réputation internationale.

La qualité extrême de sa production et la diversité de ses applications conduit Hoppecke aussi bien dans les salles d'opération des cliniques que dans les centrales électriques.

La recherche intensive, une politique d'écoute des besoins du marché et une nette intégration des technologies de pointe se traduisent aussi par les batteries cadmium-nickel à structure fibreuse (FNC). De même, Hoppecke signe le démarrage des locomotives diesel et la batterie Duplex prend une longueur d'avance pour le démarrage des véhicules.

HOPPECKE: PARTENAIRE DES CONSTRUCTEURS

C'est grâce à ses recherches permanentes qu'Hoppecke fournit en première monte des constructeurs très exigeants tels que Daimler-Benz, Ford, VAG, Deutz, MAN. La marque est homologuée pour le rechange également par d'autres constructeurs et par de nombreuses Administrations (y compris en France).

Pas moins de 1100 personnes fabriquent dans 4 usines (dont une en France à Trémont-sur-Saulx, près de Bar-le-Duc), non seulement ses fameuses batteries mais aussi les machines et les outils nécessaires à leur production.

L'usine française produit à elle seule 250 000 batteries par an avec 75 employés. Près de la moitié de la production est exportée.

Hoppecke s'est mobilisée très tôt pour la protection de l'environnement. Le plomb et ses alliages sont en grande partie recyclés sur place. De 1980 à 1986, la société a dépensé 30 millions de francs pour la protection de l'environnement, soit 20% des investissements.

THE LANGUAGE OF BUSINESS

A vous

Below you find some details about *le Groupe Rubiroues*. Using these as your notes, expand them into a written paragraph presenting the company. Read this paragraph aloud, preferably recording on your blank casette and then listen to it. You will find one possible description on p. 64. Do not look at it until you have done the exercise!

Le groupe Rubiroues
Créé en 1940.
Siège social: 10 km de Paris.
1er groupe industriel français.
6ème constructeur d'automobiles du monde; dans 150 pays; 110 usines; 200,000 personnes (En France: 70 usines 130 000 personnes).
Chiffre d'affaires: plus de 100 milliards.
Production: plus de 2 000 000 de véhicules, dont la moitié produite/vendue à l'étranger.
Filiale: Rubiroues Véhicules Industriels
       70% des véhicules vendus en France.
Autres activités: Moteurs industriels, machines-outils.
Projets d'avenir: accroître investissements, 5 années.

A vous

Now, use what you have already learned to describe your own company. The checklist of phrases below can be used in this exercise as well as in your day-to-day work. You may find it useful to record your description on a blank cassette and listen to it again.

Describe your company

| Notre société est | une entreprise / un groupe | de | petit(e) taille / grand(e) taille / taille moyenne* |

| Nous | fabriquons / vendons | .... |

| Moi-même je m' / Mon secteur s' / Ma collègue s' | occupe de ... |

*cf. les PME – les petites et moyennes entreprises.

THE TRADE FAIR

La société emploie ... personnes.

Elle a été | créée / fondée / établie | en | 18.. / 19.. | par ...

Le siège social est situé ..., | à environ ... km de ... / près de ... / pas loin de ... / dans le nord

Nous avons / On a / X possède | ... usines | en France / implantées en Angleterre / dans ... pays différents

Nous sommes représentées en France par ...

Nos | produits / machines | se vendent principalement / sont distribuées | en ... / sur le marché international / par l'intermédiaire de ... / sous la marque ...

Nous exportons / Nous essayons d'exporter | peu / beaucoup | vers | l'Europe / la France / le continent africain / les Etats-Unis

X | a / a réalisé | un chiffre d'affaires annuel de plus de ... | francs / livres / dollars

Bien sûr, notre activité ne se limite pas à ...

Nous sommes également présents | sur le marché de ... / dans le secteur de ...

X, ce n'est pas seulement | l'automobile / l'ordinateur | mais également des produits tels que ...

THE LANGUAGE OF BUSINESS

Suggested answer to exercise D2

Mesdames et Messieurs,

On m'a demandé / Je me propose de vous présenter notre groupe en quelques mots.

Le groupe a été créé en 1940, par M J Rubiroues. Son siège social est situé à environ 10 km de Paris. Sixième constructeur d'automobiles mondial, Rubiroues est également le premier groupe industriel français, un groupe à l'échelle internationale qui est implanté dans 150 pays. Ce groupe possède plus de cent dix usines dont soixante-dix en France. Il emploie deux cent mille personnes à travers le monde (cent trente mille personnes en France).

L'année dernière le groupe a réalisé un chiffre d'affaires de plus de cent milliards.

L'automobile reste l'activité dominante car elle représente soixante-dix pour cent du chiffre d'affaires global. En 199X, plus de deux cent mille véhicules (y compris Rubiroues Véhicules Industriels) sont sortis des chaînes de montage. Plus de cent mille sont vendus ou produits à l'étranger.

Le poids lourd fait partie de la tradition Rubiroues depuis la première guerre mondiale. Une filiale, Rubiroues Véhicules Industriels, assure l'essentiel de la production française: soixante-dix pour cent des camions, des automobiles et des autocars.

Le groupe Rubiroues est également présent à travers ses filiales, dans de nombreux autres secteurs de l'économie tels que les moteurs industriels, les machines-outils, etc.

Au cours des cinq prochaines années, le Groupe Rubiroues va accroître ses investissements.

E Dialogues

To communicate effectively, you will have to be able to produce a certain flow of French, as opposed to short phrases. The dialogue section of the language chapters gives you an opportunity to acquire and practise this skill.

THE TRADE FAIR

E1 Dialogue 1 The Unipart representative

A vous

Listen to this dialogue on the study cassette. Rewind the cassette and listen to it again, this time reading the part of the Unipart representative. Use the pause button when its your turn to speak!

REC.

Rep: Et bien, écoutez, la gamme Unipart est scindée en deux groupes importants, si vous voulez. C'est la gamme des produits généraux et la gamme des produits techniques. Je vais vous donner ici un catalogue, si vous voulez donc, qui va vous décrire les produits que nous avons. Donc, vous avez ici, par exemple, dans la gamme générale, le balai essuie-glace; nous faisons un balai de très haute qualité; le balai Unipart était spécialement développé pour satisfaire les besoins de la clientèle moderne.

Int: D'accord. Donc tous les produits Unipart sont préparés comme ça, emballés et prêts à la vente?

Rep: C'est ça. Tous les produits Unipart donc sont emballés d'une façon très agréable. Vous avez donc tout le texte en français, aussi dans d'autres langues bien sûr. Et ce sont des produits très attrayants pour la clientèle. Donc surtout en libre-service et bien sûr aussi dans le domaine des professionnels.

Int: Voilà. Parce qu'il faut savoir que, étant donné que la vente se fera en France et plus particulièrement dans la région bordelaise, il faut donc, qu'il y ait, il est certain, un descriptif en français.

E2 Dialogue 2: The satellite dish

A vous

This time it is up to you to make up what you say, according to the cues given in the brackets. Cover up the right-hand column and read down the left-hand column to prepare what you want to say. The dialogue is recorded on the study cassette with blanks when it is your turn to speak.

At a trade fair, you see that Visiosat has a stand next to yours. You go over to introduce yourself and to ask more about the satellite dish of which details are given in the article on the following page.

65

THE LANGUAGE OF BUSINESS

ANTENNE SATELLITE

Entièrement réalisée en matériaux composites, elle résiste à la corrosion, aux variations thermiques, au rayonnement ultraviolet, à l'humidité et à l'atmosphère saline. Sa taille permet de l'installer à l'intérieur. Elle reçoit TDF1, TV-Sat, Astra, Télécom 1, etc. Environ 6,000F.

You: *Bonjour Monsieur.*

Rep: Bonjour, Monsieur.

You: (tell him your name and say you're a sales rep. for company X.) — *Permettez-moi de me présenter. Je suis X, je suis directeur des ventes de la société X.*

Rep: (lui serrant la main) Enchanté, Pierre Leroux. Je suis représentant chez Visiosat.

You: (delighted to meet him, your stand is next door.) — *Enchanté de faire votre connaissance. Notre stand se trouve juste à côté du vôtre.*

Rep: Ah bon, donc nous sommes voisins. Que puis-je faire pour vous?

You: (in fact, you would like to know more about their satellite dish.) — *J'aimerais avoir des renseignements sur l'antenne satéllite.*

Rep: Ce serait pour votre société?

You: (you're interested personally.) — *Non, je m'y intéresse à titre personnel.*

Rep: Et vous ne pouvez pas vous en procurer une en Angleterre?

You: (you have a flat in Nice; in a residential quarter and they — *Si, mais c'est que j'ai un appartement à Nice. Il est dans un*

66

THE TRADE FAIR

	may not allow a dish outside.)	*quartier résidentiel, et je ne sais pas si on peut installer ce genre d'antenne à l'extérieur.*
Rep:	Justement, puisqu'elle est de petite taille, elle peut être installée à l'intérieur.	
You:	(That might be exactly what you need. Ask what it measures.)	*C'est peut-etre exactement ce qu'il me faut. Pouvez-vous me dire combien elle mesure?*
Rep:	Elle a un diamètre de 60 cm.	
You:	(Ask if it has to go outside, near to the sea, is this a problem.)	*Et si je décidais de l'installer dehors, tout près de la mer, est-ce que cela poserait des problèmes?*
Rep:	Pas du tout. Voyez-vous, l'antenne est réalisée en matériaux composites qui résistent même à l'atmosphère saline.	
You:	(You think you're needed on your stand; could you have a flier and prices?)	*Oh, je crois qu'on a besoin de moi au stand. Pouvez-vous me donner un dépliant et les prix?*
Rep:	Bien sûr, voilà. Je me permets de vous faire remarquer que l'installation de l'antenne est comprise dans le prix.	
You:	(Good, you'll think it over.)	*Bien. J'y réfléchirai. Merci beaucoup, et à bientôt.*

Language comment

Formal and informal register

There is much greater difference between a formal and a colloquial style in French than there is in English, and the impression you make will depend

THE LANGUAGE OF BUSINESS

partly on hitting the right note, linguistically speaking. The French use a wealth of colloquial terms knowingly, and sometimes tongue in cheek. While you need to understand these, it is better for you to stick to the more formal end of the scale, especially in business situations. For that reason, we are marking colloquial vocabulary with (fam.) = le français familier. Some common examples would be:

Standard	Colloquial
36 000 francs	36 000 balles
une chose	un truc, un machin
une voiture	une bagnole
travailler	bosser
manger	bouffer
une société, un lieu de travail	une boîte

Examples of differences in grammar are the dropping of ne (fam.), in negative expressions and uninverted question forms. Informally, you can ask a question simply with rising intonation; **est-ce que** is a standard form, and verb-subject inversion is used in a formal situation. Notice that the client seeking information about the heater uses the formal form (**par qui puis-je me procurer ce produit?**), which should have been all the more reason for the rep. to say **36 000 francs** rather than 36 000 balles!

Modes of address

For similar reasons, you should stick to **vous** until you know a French person so well that *they* suggest using **tu**. Always use a title, ie, **Bonjour, Madame/Mademoiselle/Monsieur/docteur**. You do not need to add the surname, except when identifying or calling to someone. While using **Monsieur/Madame**, you always use the **vous** form. The French use Christian names less than we do, though they are starting to do so more now. Even with a Christian name, you will use **vous**, except with personal friends of long standing, or friends with whom you share a close common interest.

Sketch: La France aux Français!

As we will say 'buy British' so the French believe in buying French, particularly when it comes to cars. *La France aux Français*, is the rallying cry of Le Pen's party, The National Front... and after all that, Albert owns a Toyota!

THE TRADE FAIR

Key words and phrases

Ma voiture est en panne — my car has broken down
il me manque une pièce — I'm missing a part
bricoler — tinker with, patch up
une carte d'accès gratuit — a free entry card.

Business notes: Trade fairs and exhibitions

In the past, French manufacturers were not keen to see non-French competitors on stands at trade fairs and exhibitions in France. If trade fairs were promoted abroad, it was mainly to attract buyers of French goods rather than foreign suppliers, such was the fear of competition that many French companies felt.

This has changed rapidly, however, as the French have realised that more foreign exhibitors very often means more visitors overall and hence what was once viewed as a threat is now seen as an opportunity. Although it has taken British companies a long time to increase their presence at French shows, the situation is perceptibly changing. At the SEHM menswear exhibition in Paris (considered by some to be the best in Europe), for example, over one-tenth of the exhibitors are now British. One preconceived notion held by many British companies is that French fairs are not international enough, compared with those in West Germany. Even if this were true, and there are many French fairs which can claim to be truly international – SICOB, data processing and office technology; MIDEST, sub-contracting; CVIR, leather; SIMA, agricultural machinery; *Equip'mag*, shopfitting and display; SIAL, food products – it must always be remembered that, given the regional nature of many French markets and the more fragmented nature of the distribution system, distributors may well be scattered far and wide across the country and it is precisely trade fairs which bring them together in one spot. In the Trade Fair video sequence, Unipart has well understood this point and hence this is one of the many reasons for its presence at the *Equip'auto* show. The French themselves certainly view fairs as very important for this very reason, with well over two-thirds of companies in some sectors being represented. If the main aim is to attack the *French* as well as the international market, then fairs must be seen as a highly effective way of seeing what is on offer, in terms of both products and competitors.

As in many other areas, most roads lead to Paris and, whereas there are many more separate centres in West Germany, Paris is indeed reputed to be the single largest centre in Europe for fairs, shows and conferences. Notable regional exceptions to the monopoly of Paris are *Vinexpo*, for wines and spirits in Bordeaux, SIG for winter sports equipment and fashion in Grenoble, the clothing fair in Lille (home of many of the mail-order firms) and various exhibitions in Lyon. Although a number of these are not promoted as heavily as those in Paris – France's old centralising reflexes again! – it should be borne in mind that these fairs increasingly attract visitors from greater transnational regions which are growing in importance in continental Europe (Lyon, for example, which brings together people from Southern Germany, Switzerland, Italy and Spain). Unlike the regional fairs in West Germany, which are individually promoted by their organisers. One government sponsored organisation in France, Promosalons (British address: The Colonnades, 82 Bishops Bridge Road, Bayswater, London, W2 6BB, tel: 071–221 3660) is an umbrella organisation charged with the overall promotion of both the Paris and regional fairs (but only if 25 per cent of the exhibitors are foreign companies). One sign of the more liberal and competitive attitude towards business in France is the recent mushrooming of exhibitions often competing for the same trade. This can cause problems, however, such as not enough visitors, too many competing stands, unofficial status of the exhibitions themselves, etc., and it is wise to check with Promosalons the precise standing of a fair or show in which your company may be interested.

Services offered by Promosalons include:

- information on precise shows and dates
- help with organisation and travel arrangements
- meetings with trade press, etc.

In the case of many fairs and exhibitions, Promosalons works closely with the Department of Trade and Industry which operates both 'Task Forces' for various sectors (selective marketing initiatives targeted at a specific gap in the market with the aim of increasing British market penetration) and a support scheme for individual companies through their trade associations (sponsors). Qualifying companies may claim up to 50 per cent of all direct costs (travel, purchase of space, design and erection of stand, etc) for which they enter into a direct contract with the DTI. Whereas support was once for an unlimited number of occasions, under existing rules companies may only claim for up to three visits to one particular country. This is a significant change as in many sectors a repeated presence at fairs is essential. The French will often not buy from a company when it first exhibits but merely check whether it might be a viable supply option. It may only be on the second or third occasion that an order is placed and subsequent appearances are vital if a company is to prove it is serious to the French.

Further information on these schemes and other services available under its 'Export Initiative' may be obtained from DTI Regional Offices, the French Desk, Exports to Europe Branch, 1–19 Victoria Street, London, SW1H 0ET (in the case of Task Forces), or in the case of trade fairs, from the DTI Fairs and Promotions Branch, Dean Bradley House, 52 Horseferry Road, London, SW1P 2AG.

But why go to a fair in the first place?

- It is ideal for exposing new customers and potential distributors to a company's product range.
- It is used by both established and new companies and hence allows companies to check on new developments and competitors.
- For companies without established contacts, it may be the only way to reach potential customers and distributors.
- It gives newcomers an idea of the size and extent of potential competition before entry into the market.

- Specialised magazines and the trade press may be too small for advertisers and therefore prospective customers attend fairs. The amount spent on advertising in France is still low by Anglo-Saxon standards and therefore, particularly for industrial goods, distributors, agents and salesmen have a key role to play. Word of mouth is still a very powerful instrument in France for capital goods.
- It allows existing sales and contacts to be maintained.
- The business culture can be very different in France and a fair gives an opportunity to experience this at first hand.

To summarise the above: it is a useful way of gaining market intelligence, selling products and appointing agents or distributors, but it is important to define objectives in order of priorities. Manning levels, products to be displayed, the level of technical competence of those manning the stand, prices and delivery dates to be quoted, and literature may all differ according to the objective set.

Trade fair check-list

- Think about the layout and display aids required. Visit a French trade fair first and see how the most successful stands are organised. Ask the sort of questions you might expect to be asked yourself and check the exact status of those manning the different stands. Ask about prices, payment terms and delivery dates in particular to get a feel for what constitutes standard practice.
- Ensure all literature is in *totally accurate* French. Horrendous gaffes still occur because no use was made of professional translators and consequently misspellings and wrong expressions occur. Nothing can look more slipshod and amateur than incorrect written French.
- All staff representing the company should preferably speak French – if not all, at least one staff member *must* be able to. Remember, too, that technical questions are often asked or demonstrations required – check whether the level of French is adequate in this respect. If necessary, employ someone locally. With regard to technical details, a frequent criticism of literature for British goods is that specifications are not shown. This also implies that a thorough check of standards and regulations which may affect your products is required.
- Staff should be trained to look and be energetic and dynamic. Again, a frequent criticism is that staff are reading newspapers or fail to approach visitors correctly.

THE TRADE FAIR

Trained to look and be energetic and dynamic

- All staff should know something about the geography, institutions, economic situation and industry of France. Complete ignorance is again amateurish and nothing flatters the French more than a foreigner knowing about and *being interested in* their country!
- If possible, arrange for your stand to be near a main entrance, bar or information desk to maximise the number of potential visitors.
- Particularly in Paris, make hotel booking arrangements way ahead of the fair date. Hotel accommodation is exceedingly difficult to find during the biggest shows.
- Envisage advertising in the trade and specialist press or send details, photographs, etc., for any preview they may carry. This can be particularly useful to those *not* able to visit the fair. The largest generalist magazines such as *L'Usine Nouvelle*, *Le Moniteur* and *Industrie et Technologie* also often carry reports on the major exhibitions. Possible contact with them should be considered.
- Alert all existing customers and contacts to your presence at the exhibition. Send invitation cards to potential customers, in collaboration with your agent. According to surveys such cards are the most

THE LANGUAGE OF BUSINESS

remembered source of information about exhibitions. Mail shots to new and existing customers (in French!) can also be effective.

- Calculate how much representation at an exhibition really will cost – travel, material, insurance, staff time (often forgotten).
- Focus on the products and information you wish to show. A cluttered stand confuses and does not attract attention.
- The French like activity, flair and original audio-visual displays. Envisage mounting an activity at certain times of the day, if suitable.
- Be ready to quote prices in francs and CIF!
- Check on electrical power requirements.
- After the exhibition, follow up enquiries either with a letter, a visit or an invitation to visit your own company.

Business magazine 1. Trade fairs

Trade fairs can be one of the most effective forms of promotion, but also one of the most expensive. In this Business Magazine you can hear how different UK companies have learnt to use trade fairs to their advantage, either as a part of a DTI sponsored group or as independent exhibitors.

Chapter 2

Direct selling
'C'est un produit qui est unique, qui est spécial'

Introduction

Direct selling is still one of the most popular ways for both small and large companies to enter a new market.

In this video sequence you will see Denis Pike of Merricks Sico give a product presentation to the general manager of a top hotel. He will be trying not only to sell him some folding tables but also to get him to take on board the whole Merricks Sico concept of adaptability.

Being able to give an effective sales presentation, and persuading someone to buy your product, really means being able to speak French.

In this chapter you will:
- learn how to use **on** and **se** (very common in business language);
- find out how to talk about the future;
- emphasise what you are saying;
- learn how to persuade people;
- describe how things work.

Now watch the Direct Selling video sequence (10 19 05).

THE LANGUAGE OF BUSINESS

Key words and phrases

The following keywords and phrases should help you understand the dialogues.

La démonstration du lit

il suffit de retirer le dessus-de-lit	it's enough just to .../ all you have to do is take off the bedspread
la tablette qui sert à cacher les pistons	the flap for hiding the pistons (which serves to hide)
ce lit escamotable	this foldaway bed
la sangle qui va retenir le matelas	the strap which will hold the mattress in place
on bascule le lit	you swivel/tip the bed

Rendez-vous avec Monsieur Duvauchelle

la prestation	service, performance
haut de gamme (f.)	up-market
le matériel (pl. les matériaux)	equipment, materials
il y a une réunion en cours	there is a meeting taking place
on déplie la table et on la dresse	you unfold the table and put it in an upright position
c'est assez élevé	it is rather high (expensive)
un concurrent	a competitor
Si c'est abîmé	if it is damaged
les dégâts (m.)	damage
une usine	factory
les roulettes (f.) font 5 pouces	the castors are 5″
le règlement d'une facture	settling a bill

Faux amis (pitfalls)

important	(1) sizeable, (2) important, significant
une réunion	a meeting
éventuellement	possibly, if necessary
dresser (une table, une liste)	to put up, draw up, raise
avoir de la place	to have space

DIRECT SELLING

A Listen and understand

After watching the video sequence, cover up the right-hand column and try to answer the questions in A1 and A2. Then compare your answers with those on the right to see whether you have understood the video sequence properly.

A1 Getting the gist

1. M. Duvauchelle est à la recherche de quel produit?

Il est à la recherche d'une table roulante pour servir le café pendant les conférences.

2. Qu'est-ce que M. Duvauchelle cherche surtout quand il achète un produit?

Il cherche la qualité.

A2 Getting the details

1. De quel genre d'établissement M. Duvauchelle est-il directeur?

Il est directeur d'un hôtel haut de gamme.

THE LANGUAGE OF BUSINESS

2. En ce qui concerne le service après-vente, qu'est-ce qui est crucial selon M. Duvauchelle?	*C'est la rapidité. S'il y a des pièces défectueuses, il faut que les pièces de rechange arrivent dans un délai très rapide.*
3. Quel est le produit que M. Pike lui propose?	*Il lui propose une petite table qui s'ouvre pour devenir table de réunion ou bar mobile.*
4. Cette table est-elle facile à déplacer?	*Oui, elle se déplace facilement sur ses quatre roues.*
5. Est-ce qu'elle prend beaucoup de place?	*Non, puisqu'elle se plie, on peut la mettre dans un coin.*
6. Que dit M. Duvauchelle à propos du prix?	*Il trouve que c'est un peu élevé.*
7. Quelle est la réponse de M. Pike?	*Il maintient que c'est un produit unique.*

A3 Summing up the scene

A vous

When giving instructions, explanations or commands you can use either **on** or **vous**, as well as the imperative, as you will have seen when M. Duvauchelle was demonstrating the bed. Try now to summarise the instructions for operating the foldaway bed, transforming **on** to **vous** all through. Just the basics are given below, so you can pad these out.

- d'abord on retire le dessus-de-lit
- en deuxième lieu on range les oreillers dans les placards
- puis on retire la tablette qui sert à cacher les pistons
- ensuite on met la sangle qui retient le matelas et la couverture
- finalement, pour basculer le lit, on le prend à l'extrémité, et voilà!

DIRECT SELLING

A4 Equivalents

A vous

Watch the video sequence again (10 19 05) and try to find French equivalents for phrases 1–5, and English equivalents for phrases 6–10.

1. in the context of (within the framework of) conferences
2. for/with regard to our customers
3. compared to your competitors
4. as far as settling the bill goes
5. in as short a time as possible

6. un établissement d'une certaine renommée
7. on est amené à utiliser une table avec des tasses
8. on est obligé de la déplacer
9. on peut la remplir de dessus
10. une table à un seul étage

Answers: *1. dans le cadre des conférences; 2. auprès de notre clientèle; 3. par rapport à vos concurrents; 4. au niveau du règlement des factures; 5. dans le plus bref délai possible; 6. a business/hotel with a good reputation; 7. you have occasion to (are led to) use a table for the cups; 8. you have to move it around; 9. you can fill it from above; 10. a trolley (table) with only one shelf (storey)*

B Develop your skills

B1 The present revisited

A vous

Here you have another chance to practise present tense forms. Look at the exercise below and change each of the sentences to a third person plural, as indicated. Then listen to the answers on the study cassette and repeat them using the pause button.

Example: Il vend des meubles de haute gamme. (Ces magasins)
Ces magasins vendent des meubles de haute gamme.

1. Je sors de la réunion pour prendre un café. (Les délégués)
2. Je comprends très bien votre problème. (Elles)

79

THE LANGUAGE OF BUSINESS

3. On met tout sur la table en même temps. (Les serveurs)
4. La table fait un mètre de longueur. (Elles)
5. La couverture en plastique permet d'éviter les dégâts. (Les couvertures)
6. Vous dites que c'est un produit unique. (Ils)
7. Tu ne prends pas de risques. (Les banques)
8. Ce piston sert à rabattre le lit. (Ces pistons)
9. Je vis en France maintenant. (Ils)
10. La représentante descend souvent à cet hôtel. (Les représentants)
11. Cette sangle retient la couverture. (Ces sangles)
12. Il bat tous les records. (Ils)

B2 Reflexive verbs (Asseyez-vous confortablement!)

A vous

Use this exercise to practise the present indicative of reflexive verbs.

Example: Elle – des clients   Elle s'occupe des clients

Complete the following sentences, choosing one of the verbs below:

s'occuper (à), s'intéresser (à), s'arrêter, se boucher, s'asseoir, se composer (de).
1. Je _____ à votre appareil.
2. Nous _____ de la publicité.
3. C'est un tuyau d'échappement qui ne _____ jamais.
4. La machine _____ toute seule.
5. Le directeur ne va pas tarder; en attendant, _____ confortablement.
6. La foire _____ d'une centaine de stands.

Answers: *1) m'intéresse; 2) nous occupons; 3) se bouche; 4) s'arrête; 5) asseyez-vous; 6) se compose.*

B3 Expressions with on and se

Expressions with **on** and **se** are very common in business language, for instance, when you are describing the advantages of the workings of something, as you will have when M. Duvauchelle gave instructions on how to use the table.

For example, you may say:

On peut ranger cette table dans un petit coin, et on peut la transformer en table de réunion.

or:

Cette table se range dans un petit coin, et elle se transforme (ou: ça se transforme) en table de réunion.

Now use these structures to do the exercise below. You will again find a possible solution on your study cassette.

A vous

Vous avez inventé ou vous essayez de vendre
- un nouveau gadget électro-ménager pour les hôtels et restaurants
- un lave-voitures domestique.

Cela sert à | battre 15 oeufs d'un seul coup
           | éplucher 5 kilos de pommes de terre
           | découper . . .
           | laver et à cirer votre voiture chez vous

Cela peut s'employer même pour | la haute cuisine
                                | les camions

Cela | s'installe/se plie/se range/s'utilise
     | ne s'use jamais

Les piles se rechargent automatiquement

Les repas se préparent tous seuls
Les voitures se nettoient toutes seules

It is up to you to add more characteristics of your gadget.

B4 The present subjunctive (Il faut que vous le sachiez!)

In the previous chapter we saw that the present tense in French has two moods: the indicative and the subjunctive. While relatively rare in English (e.g. 'I wish it *were* . . .'), the subjunctive is still very much alive and kicking in French. Since there are certain expressions which are always followed by the subjunctive, it is a matter of learning a) the forms and b) when to use it.

THE LANGUAGE OF BUSINESS

The form

To form the subjunctive, you take the **ils/elles** form of the present indicative, remove the **-ent** ending, and add **-e, -es, -e, -ions, -iez, -ent**, as in the following examples:

il faut que je vende tout
il faut que tu descendes tout de suite
il faut qu'elle mette tout cela par écrit
il faut que nous comprenions son point de vue
il faut que vous battiez tous les records
il faut qu'elles finissent le rapport

A vous

Now you fill in the correct form of the verb **fournir** in the sentences below. (**Fournir** is conjugated like **finir**.)

1. il faut que je _____ la marchandise pour demain.
2. il faut que tu _____ les articles.
3. il faut qu'il _____ la commande dans le courant de la semaine prochaine.
4. il faut que nous _____ un bon service.
5. il faut que vous _____ à notre atelier de Paris.
6. il faut qu'ils _____ par chemin de fer.

Answers: *fournisse; 2. fournisses; 3. fournisse; 4. fournissions; 6. fournissiez; 7. fournissent.*

When to use it

Apart from the very common use of the subjunctive after 'il faut que', here are some other expressions with which it occurs. First, conjunctions which indicate an *aim or intention*, those which express *some sort of reservation*, and some of those expressing *time*.

de sorte que ⎱	in order that, so that
pour que ⎰	
bien que	although
sans que (+ ne)	without
pourvu que	provided that

à moins que (+ ne)	unless
jusqu'à ce que	until
avant que (+ ne)	before

Secondly, it is used after verbs expressing *emotion* (surprise, pleasure, fear etc), *preference, commanding* (ordering, allowing, forbidding), and *doubt*.

regretter
s'étonner
avoir peur/craindre   } que
être étonné/content/fâché

vouloir, préférer, souhaiter   que

permettre
demander
exiger   } que
douter
ne pas penser/croire

Before you do an exercise on this, a few things to note:

- The 3rd person plural generally sounds the same in the indicative and the subjunctive.
- There are a few "irregular" stems, such as
- pouvoir → puisse
  faire → fasse
  savoir → sache
- The subjunctive of **être** and of **avoir** are

  sois sois soit soyons soyez soient
  aie aies ait ayons ayez aient

- Other uses will be mentioned in chapter 3. More expressions which are followed by the subjunctive are given in the Grammar Kit.
- Many verbs which change stem in the present indicative also do so in the subjunctive, for example:

  il faut qu'il vienne/que nous venions
  il faut qu'il protège ses intérêts/que nous les protégions.

THE LANGUAGE OF BUSINESS

A vous

All the verbs in brackets in the following sentences need to be in the present subjunctive – it is up to you to find the right form!

1. Il est souhaitable qu'il (vivre) à Paris pendant la semaine.

Il est souhaitable qu'il vive à Paris pendant la semaine.

2. Vous pouvez ranger le lit sans que les couvertures se (défaire).

Vous pouvez ranger le lit sans que les couvertures se défassent.

3. On appuie sur le bouton pour que le lit se (remettre) en place.

On appuie sur le bouton pour que le lit se remette en place.

4. Nous exigeons que les matériaux (être) de la plus haute qualité.

Nous exigeons que les matériaux soient de la plus haute qualité.

5. Notre visiteur aimerait mieux que nous (commencer) tôt le matin, pour qu'il (pouvoir) prendre l'avion de cinq heures.

Notre visiteur aimerait mieux que nous commencions tôt le matin, pour qu'il puisse prendre l'avion de cinq heures.

6. Je ne pense pas qu'il y (avoir) de problèmes de ce côté-ci.

Je ne pense pas qu'il y ait de problèmes de ce côté-ci.

7. Nous attendrons jusqu'à ce que la situation économique (devenir) plus claire.

Nous attendrons jusqu'à ce que la situation économique devienne plus claire.

8. Nous pouvons retirer cette modèle, sans que cela ne (faire) aucun mal à notre image de marque.

Nous pouvons retirer cette modèle, sans que cela ne fasse aucun mal à notre image de marque.

9. Les délégués s'étonnent que le café ne (être) pas prêt.

Les délégués s'étonnent que le café ne soit pas prêt.

10. Le directeur de marketing souhaite que vous (dresser) une liste des compagnies susceptibles d'être intéressées.

Le directeur de marketing souhaite que vous dressiez une liste des compagnies susceptibles d'être intéressées.

11. Le ministère regrette que le ministre ne (venir) pas en personne.

Le ministère regrette que le ministre ne vienne pas en personne.

12. Je doute qu'il (savoir) ce qui s'est passé.

Je doute qu'il sache ce qui s'est passé.

13. L'hôtel permet que nous (utiliser) leur piscine.

L'hôtel permet que nous utilisions leur piscine.

14. Nous allons demander que vous (tenir) votre promesse.

Nous allons demander que vous teniez votre promesse.

B5 Negative expressions in comparisons (Ce ne sont pas des produits, c'est un système.)

> We saw in the previous chapter that **un, une, du, de la**, and **des**, become **de** after a negative expression.
>
> Nous n'avons **pas de** catalogues en ce moment.
>
> However, when comparing things we are not dealing with absolute negatives. This means that **un, une, du, de la** and **des** remain as they are.
>
> Ce ne sont pas **des** catalogues, ce sont des manuels d'emploi.
> Ce n'est pas du plastique, c'est du cuir.

A vous

1. Ce n'est pas (petrol) dans le cylindre, c'est (diesel).

Ce n'est pas de l'essence dans le cylindre, c'est du gas-oil.

2. Ce n'est pas (copper); c'est (pewter).

Ce n'est pas du cuivre, c'est de l'étain.

3. Ce n'est pas (beer), c'est (apple juice).

Ce n'est pas de la bière, c'est du jus de pomme.

4. Ce ne sont pas (faulty parts), ce sont (new parts).

Ce ne sont pas des pièces défectueuses, ce sont des pièces nouvelles.

B6 Emphasising what you're saying with ce qui/que ... c'est/ce sont

Ce qui and **ce que** are relative pronouns, used to express 'what' as subject or object of the main verb, in sentences such as:

I know **what** is happening – je sais **ce qui** se passe
I understand **what** you mean – je comprends **ce que** vous voulez dire

Ce qui and **ce que** can be used at the beginning of the sentence for emphasis, and are then picked up again by **c'est/ce sont**.

e.g. **Ce qui** se passe, **c'est** que l'usine est fermée.
Ce que nous voulons, **ce sont** des pièces de rechange.

When a relative pronoun is used in combination with the preposition **de**, the French use **ce dont**.

Ce dont nous avons besoin, c'est d'un excellent service après-vente.

A vous

Transform the following sentences as in the example and compare them to the answers in the right-hand column.

Example: Nous voulons des meubles de haut de gamme
Ce que nous voulons, ce sont des meubles de haut de gamme.

1. L'entreprise cherche un représentant qui parle français.	Ce que l'entreprise cherche c'est un représentant qui parle français.
2. Nous avons besoin d'une livraison rapide. (Attention!)	Ce dont nous avons besoin, c'est d'une livraison rapide.
3. Il nous faut quelque chose de solide.	Ce qu'il nous faut c'est quelque chose de solide.

B7 Talking about the future

The future in French can be expressed by either the present, or **aller + infinitive**, or the future form of the verb (**infinitive + -ai, -as, -a, -ons, -ez, -ont** – except for irregular futures. If you are uncertain of any future forms, check the grammar section). Although these three are often interchangeable, a general rule of thumb is that the present, and **aller + infinitive** (called 'futur proche') are used for the immediate future. They may also be considered more colloquial than the future proper.

DIRECT SELLING

> NB. **quand, lorsque** (= when), + **dès que, aussitôt que** (= as soon as) are not usually followed by the present in French but by the future or the future perfect, when they refer to something which will happen, or will have happened.

A vous

Read out the sentences below and fill in the missing parts.

Situation	Présent	Futur proche	Futur
Example: Le secrétaire répond au VRP (voyageur-représentant-placier (sales-rep))	Monsieur Duvauchelle arrive à l'instant.	Il va arriver dans quelques minutes.	Il arrivera sous peu.
1. A la gare	Le train part.	Le train ____ partir à l'heure.	Le train ____ dans 20 minutes.
2. Il y a une commission (= errand) à faire à l'épicerie.	Je vais à l'épicerie.	Je ____ à l'épicerie tout à l'heure.	J' ____ à l'épicerie quand le programme sera terminé.
3. On ne veut pas répondre tout de suite.	Je passe à cela dans une seconde.	Je ____ à cela dans une seconde.	Je ____ à cela plus tard.
4. Au stand.	Je vous dis d'abord le prix de revient.	Je ____ vous ____ le prix tout de suite après la démonstration.	Je vous ____ le prix à la fin de la matinée.
5. Au téléphone	Je vous envoie notre catalogue, Madame; comme ça, vous voyez de quoi il s'agit.	Je ____ vous ____ notre catalogue, Madame; comme ça, vous ____ de quoi il s'agit.	Je vous ____ notre nouveau catalogue, Madame, dès qu'il sera publié; comme ça, vous ____ de quoi il s'agit.

Answers: *1. va partir; partira; 2. vais aller; irai; 3. vais passer; passerai; 4. vais vous dire; dirai; 5. vais vous envoyer, allez voir; enverrai, verrez.*

C Extend your vocabulary

C1 Some expressions of time

À vous

Fit expressions from the following list into the sentences below.

(a) dans huit jours; (b) tous les quinze jours; (c) de temps en temps; (d) une vingtaine d'années; (e) à peu près 30 jours; (f) des périodes; (g) au moment où; (h) depuis très longtemps; (i) à partir de l'année prochaine; (j) cela fait un an.

1. Il y aura un délai d' ____ .
2. Je lui rends régulièrement visite, car je passe par Paris ____ .
3. Je peux vous apporter le dossier moi-même, puisque je viens à Marseille ____ .
4. Il y a ____ où l'hôtel est complet, d'autres où il ne l'est qu'à moitié.
5. Les nouvelles lois entreront en vigueur ____ .
6. C'est une société d'origine américaine, mais qui est implantée en France ____ .
7. Nous connaissons bien le marché, car cela fait ____ que nous exportons vers l'Europe.
8. Un manque de pièces? Ça arrive ____ , mais c'est quand même rare.
9. Il parle bien français, parce que ____ qu'il habite à Lille.
10. ____ vous mettez la machine en marche, la lumière s'éteint.

Answers: *1. (e); 2. (b); 3. (a); 4. (f); 5. (i); 6. (h); 7. (d); 8. (c); 9. (j); 10. (g).*

C2 A few prefixes (Up front)

In the previous chapter we showed you could extend your vocabulary by adding certain suffixes. In this chapter you may have noticed words with certain prefixes, most notably **re-** (back, again), but also some with **dé-** (which often means un-).

faire (to do)   refaire (to do again)   défaire (to undo)
monter (to put up, to remonter (to set up,   démonter (to take
go up)   put/go up again)   apart, down)
plier (to fold)   replier (to fold up/   déplier (to unfold)
                      again)

DIRECT SELLING

We will concentrate for the moment on **re-** or **ré-**. You will have noticed the following words being used in the video:
- retirer (to withdraw, take off again);
- retenir (to hold back, retain);
- redescendre (to bring down/go down again);
- remettre en place (to put back in its place).

A vous

In the paragraph below fill in the blanks with the correct form of the appropriate verb from the following list:

réapprovisionner; relever; renouveller; reprendre; retenir

Malgré le fait que vous soyez obligés de (1) vos prix par 6,5 pour cent, nous voulons (2) notre commande tout de suite. Nous voulons cependant savoir si vous êtes prêts à (3) les marchandises qui ne sont pas conformes aux normes françaises. Certaines caisses ont été (4) à la douane. Nous avons besoin que vous nous (5) le plus rapidement possible.

Answers: *1. relever; 2. renouveler; 3. reprendre; 4. retenues; 5. réapprovisionniez.*

D Make your language work

D1 How to win orders and influence people

Watch the video again (10 24 40), and notice how persuasive Mr Pike is in French. You will notice that he uses two tactics in particular. Firstly, he makes his commentary interesting by asking the questions he wants to hear, and answering them himself. Secondly, he uses a lot of reassuring phrases, expressing understanding and agreement.

Here are some of the questions and phrases:

Vous êtes en réunion, et qu'est-ce qui se passe?
Et qu'est-ce qui se passe quand . . .
C'est une table, mais autrement, qu'est-ce que c'est?
Et comment fait-on pour . . . ?
Qu'est-ce que cela veut dire?

Je suis sûr qu'il vous arrive de . . .
C'est comme vous voulez . . . D'accord . . .

THE LANGUAGE OF BUSINESS

Ce qu'on peut faire pour vous
Cela est très important.
Je comprends très bien votre problème.
Si vous avez besoin de n'importe quoi, vous m'appelez.
Nous avons exactement ce qu'il vous faut.
L'idéal, c'est que . . .
On est déjà d'accord que c'est un aspect important.

A vous

Read the instructions below and record your description on a blank cassette. Compare your version with the sample version on the study cassette.

Vous êtes représentant pour une société qui vend une nouvelle marque de fours micro-ondes (micro-wave). En utilisant certaines des expressions données ci-dessus, décrivez les avantages de votre produit.

D2 Describe your product

Look through this check-list of phrases for ways of describing a product. Then, drawing on this list and the expressions you have learned in Chapters

90

DIRECT SELLING

1 and 2, try to describe the qualities of Hoppecke's Duplex battery as persuasively as possible. Compare your description with the article on p. 92.

- **Matière**

  Ce produit / Cet appareil | est | fabriqué / réalisé | en | acier inoxydable / tôle d'acier / matière plastique

- **Dimensions**

  Cet article / Cette machine | fait / mesure | _____ mètres carrés (m²)

  Cela/Ils/Elles | font / mesurent | _____ mètres de large sur _____ de haut

  Sa hauteur / Son épaisseur / Son volume / Son poids | est de _____

- **Description**

  Cet appareil | se compose de / comprend / comporte / possède | _____ éléments.

- **Fonctionnement**

  Cette machine / Cet appareil | fonctionne | très bien / de manière parfaite

  est réglable | par, au moyen de / grâce à / à l'aide de

  est d'une grande | simplicité / souplesse / sûreté | de | fonctionnement / mise en marche

  Sa mise en route / Son arrêt | est | instantané(e) / sans problèmes

THE LANGUAGE OF BUSINESS

| Il / Elle | est | facile / rapide / simple | à | employer / régler / entretenir / nettoyer |

| Il / Elle | est | doté(e) / pourvu(e) | des | tout derniers perfectionnements techniques les plus modernes |

La batterie DUPLEX

L'énergie sûre, c'est quand la voiture démarre au quart de tour, tout le temps, même à −30°C, pendant des années.

La batterie DUPLEX offre, par sa conception, toutes les garanties.

La technique du double couvercle oblige les gaz et brouillards acides à se recombiner sous forme de condensation liquide qui reflue dans la batterie. Deux pastilles poreuses latérales servent à réguler la pression. Antidéflagrantes, elles protègent la batterie contre d'éventuels retours de flammes.

La DUPLEX H est de conception hybride : plaques positives au plomb antimonié, plaques négatives en pochettes au plomb calcium.

Cela leur confère puissance au démarrage, faible autodécharge et une résistance cyclique élevée.

Elles sont 100% sans entretien.

AUJOURD'HUI, L'ÉNERGIE DE DEMAIN

LA DUPLEX PLEBISCITEE

Hoppecke a élargi son offre de batteries de démarrage avec l'introduction, en 1985, de la gamme Duplex.

A l'issue d'un sévère test comparatif effectué pour le compte de la revue automobile allemande Autozeitung, la Duplex a obtenu le plus grand nombre de points, ce qui lui a valu la mention "**fortement recommandée**". De même, au cours du test effectué par le centre de contrôle technique TÜV Rheinland, la batterie Hoppecke Duplex s'est particulièrement distinguée dans les essais de démarrage à froid. D'où cette conclusion officielle:

"**excellente aptitude au démarrage en cas de sollicitations extrêmes**".

L'ALLIANCE D'UNE DOUBLE FORMULE

Cette batterie haut de gamme réunit les avantages de deux types d'alliage: plomb-antimoine et plomb-calcium. Le matériau le plus important dans une batterie, c'est le plomb. Relativement mou, sa stabilité mécanique est obtenue grâce à des alliages spéciaux avec l'antimoine ou le calcium. Ces deux types d'alliage sont utilisés pour la fabrication de batteries de démarrage. En effet, il existe des batteries au plumb-antimoine ou au plomb-calcium.

Ces deux solutions procurent des avantages déterminants sur le plan technique. L'alliage plomb-antimoine a une influence favorable sur la stabilité au cyclage. De ce fait, la batterie survit sans problème au processus de charge et de décharge.

L'alliage plomb-calcium réduit non seulement la consommation d'eau mais aussi le taux d'autodécharge, ce qui en améliore la tenue au stockage en chargé liquide.

Les ingénieurs d'Hoppecke ont donc mis au point une combinaison des deux types d'alliage, réunissant ainsi les avantages des deux formules. Le résultat? C'est la batterie Duplex Hybride. Elle se caractérise par son étonnante performance au démarrage à froid (−40°) par une faible autodécharge, une grande aptitude au cyclage. Elle est de plus 100% sans entretien.

DIRECT SELLING

E Dialogues

E1 Greeting people

There are various ways of greeting people. Listen to some examples on the study cassette, and make up and record on the blank cassette your part in the two short conversations below. It is up to you to initiate the dialogue by making the appropriate comments (for example, you may start: 'Bonjour Mademoiselle, j'ai rendez-vous avec M. Benjamin'). You will find a possible answer on the study cassette.

A vous

1. In the first exchange you arrive at the offices of your French counterpart, and ask to see him.

VOUS:

LA SECRÉTAIRE Bonjour, Monsieur, Monsieur B est en réunion. Il va sortir d'un moment à l'autre.

VOUS

LA SECRÉTAIRE Installez-vous là, vous serez plus à l'aise. Vous avez fait bonne route?

VOUS

2. In the second exchange, you meet a new representative from the French company at the airport in Britain.

VOUS

LUI Oui. c'est moi-même. (Vous vous serrez la main). C'est gentil d'être venu à l'aérogare.

VOUS

LUI Oui, merci, sauf qu'il y a eu un retard d'une demi-heure à Roissy.

VOUS

LUI Non, merci, on a mangé à bord de l'avion. Nous pouvons commencer tout de suite à travailler.

VOUS:

THE LANGUAGE OF BUSINESS

E2 Interview with M. Duvauchelle:

Listen to what M. Duvauchelle says on the study cassette, and then read his part copying his style of presentation and intonation.

DUVAUCHELLE: Ce qu'on recherche, en fait, c'est l'approche d'une qualité. Nous sommes un établissement d'une certaine renommée. Nous avons toujours essayé d'avoir du matériel et une prestation de haut de gamme. Donc, ce que nous recherchons essentiellement, c'est la qualité, aussi bien dans la présentation que dans la solidité et l'utilisation quotidienne.

INT: Et le prix?

DUVAUCHELLE: Le prix rentre bien sûr en ligne de compte. Disons que c'est toujours pareil. Si on essaie d'avoir un produit d'une certaine qualité, il faut aussi y mettre le prix. On ne peut pas acheter à bon marché quelque chose qui est de qualité, d'une finesse dans la finition, par rapport à un produit, disons, qui sera bien sûr meilleur marché mais moins solide et qui n'aura pas, au bout d'un certain temps, la même présentation que le jour de l'achat.

INT: Et vous avez parlé de qualité en parlant de la présentation elle-même. Qu'est-ce que vous entendez par qualité dans ce contexte-là? Qualité de la présentation?

DUVAUCHELLE: La qualité de la présentation, c'est le produit qui, par rapport à notre établissement, répond le mieux à ce que nous recherchons. Donc il faut que l'aspect esthétique rentre en ligne de compte et puisse s'adapter à tous nos salons, dans le cadre de la personne que je vais rencontrer, et donc c'est surtout le mobilier destiné aux conférences ou aux chambres. Il faut que ce soit un produit qui puisse rentrer tout à fait dans le style de la maison.

Language comment

Two brief points:

- Again you will notice that the French speaker uses fairly formal language, while Mr Pike uses colloquial forms, for example, leaving out **ne**.
- Notice that the correct word for a quotation is a **devis** (not **quotation**!) You can say **indiquer un prix** or **établir un devis**.

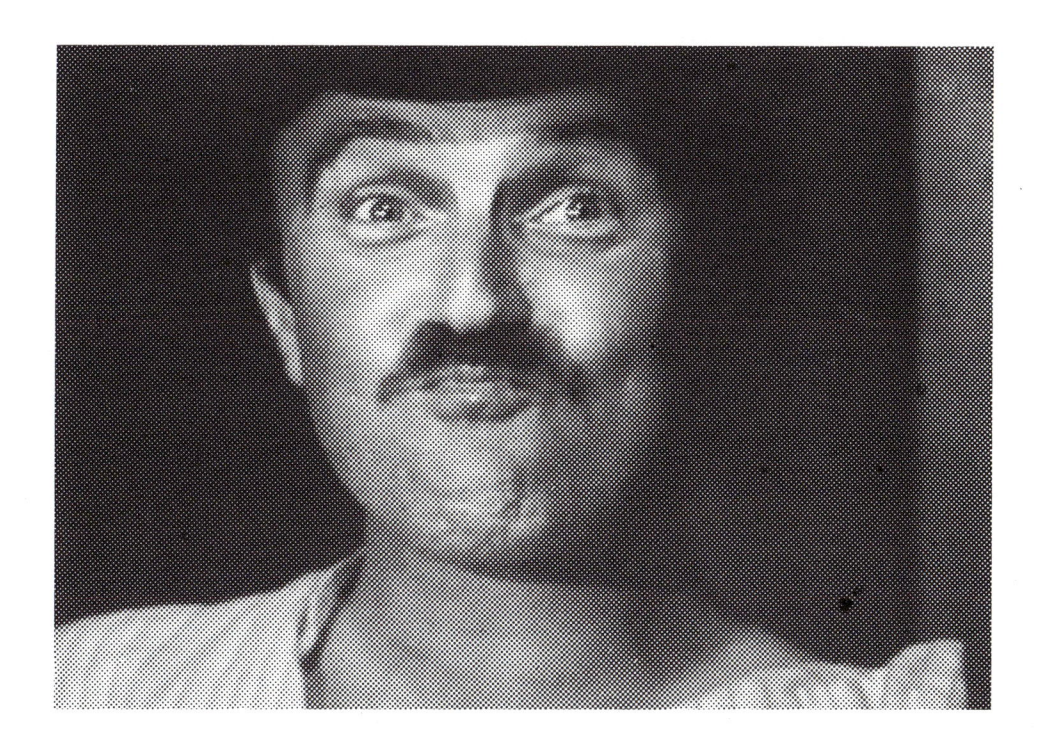

Sketch: De la confiture avec tout

> Well, the French have never really liked English cuisine – they seem to think we eat nothing but boiled meat and that we even serve it with jam. If only they would look at some of their dishes, they would realise that turkey with cranberry sauce isn't that different to some of their traditional dishes . . . like wild boar and blueberry jelly.

Key words and phrases

dégueulasse (vulg.)	– disgusting
un gars (fam.)	– a bloke
un stage	– a training period

Business notes: Direct selling

Home based sales staff

> Selling direct into the French market has already been discussed in Chapter 3 but a number of further comments are worth making.

THE LANGUAGE OF BUSINESS

- It is highly sales-oriented and often needs the support of centralised promotion to supply leads through direct advertising, trade fairs, etc.
- It may be vulnerable to local competitors having greater depth in marketing and service support.
- It requires in-depth local customer and market knowledge. In this respect, language skills are vital. Speaking good French could even be turned into a competitive advantage over French sales staff, since the French do respond well to foreigners speaking French. It is important, too, to train other sales staff to replace those who are ill or leave the company. A one-man band will not suffice to build up a long term relationship.
- Prices quoted can be more competitive where an intermediary's commission is not to be added to production costs.
- When turnover has been increased sufficiently, direct sales should be seen as a stepping-stone to setting up a subsidiary or other longer term establishment, particularly in markets (local authorities, etc.) which, in spite of the Single European Act's aim of opening up public procurement, still remain highly nationalistic and prefer local suppliers.
- Payment methods may cause problems, particularly in France where settlement periods can be long (see the following).

- Regular and prompt deliveries must be ensured, particularly if made to the retail sector. The whole supply chain, from production through distribution to sales needs very careful examination together with the paperwork and communications involved.
- This type of method can also be used by suppliers of own-brand products, with customers usually holding stock directly imported through the exporter. However, transport strikes and storms in the Channel (the biggest apparent worry of Marks & Spencer at their Paris shops!) need to be taken into account.
- This method becomes unsuitable when a high level of market penetration is the objective or when the market has been built up to such an extent that sales staff are overstretched and support services cannot cope with the demand. Failure to come up to expectations can be very costly in France where there are competitors only too ready to jump into the breach left by defective customer service.
- As in the case of SICO in the video sequence, turnover may be greatly increased by switching from using agents, who may represent other products and whose sales effort is thereby fragmented, to direct selling. SICO dealt with intermediaries in the past on a non-exclusivity basis in order to be able to terminate contracts more easily – and more cheaply!

Terms of payment

Payment terms (*le délai de paiement* – not a delay in English, which would be *un retard de paiement*) are traditionally long and even the French themselves consider them to be quite scandalous! Basically, credit squeezed out of suppliers constitutes the main form of short term credit in France (non-discounted bills of exchange may represent up to 40 per cent of a small companies assets!) Overall, intercompany credit is four times higher than short term credit obtained from banks.

Nearly all business payments **within** France are made by bill of exchange (*une lettre de change* or *une traite*, in more common business language). These are usually payable at the end of the month of delivery plus 60, 90, even 120 days (the latter is not at all uncommon). Variations on this would be, for example, 90 days 5th of the next month (e.g. Nouvelles Galeries) or 90 days 10th of the next month (Auchan). Some hypermarkets will pay cash (*au comptant*), i.e., about 14 days for a settlement discount (*remise*) of 3.5–4 per cent, depending both on the company and the sector.

Une traite operates in the following manner:

- The bill of exchange is sent by the supplier to the customer for acceptance.
- On acceptance, i.e., on signing the bill, the customer (*le tiré*) is committed to paying the sum due to the supplier (*le tireur*) on the fall-due date (*l'échéance*).
- On this date, the supplier presents the bill to the customer's bank (*banque de domiciliation*) for payment.
- If the supplier wishes to receive (*toucher*) his money before the redemption date, he can negotiate with the bank, which will advance him the sum due less an amount charged at a determined rate of interest (*le taux d'intérêt*) and bank charges (*l'agio*). This is called discounting (*l'escompte*).

Since most companies still prefer this method of payment, British companies would be well advised to open an account with the branch of a French bank in London which will undertake all the necessary formalities and transactions. This could well avoid those problems with payment which British companies so often find in France. A company's usual invoice, in pounds sterling, payable within 30 days, will just not cut any ice unless it is clearly understood beforehand by customers that payment is to be made by cheque or bank transfer (*le virement bancaire*). Whatever the system used, customers must be contacted firmly and regularly if they are late in signing a bill or final settlement, to show that the company is serious and strict about its business. To compensate for the longer settlement terms, many firms in this country add a certain agreed percentage per month to their prices.

Discounts

It is not unusual for hypermarkets and supermarket chains to want a 12 week stock of many items ('pile 'em high, sell 'em cheap'), mainly to gain the best discount possible. Much ingenuity is shown in inventing new discounts and great care must be taken to understand precisely what they are for. Common examples of those used in the retail sector (both the *grandes surfaces* and specialised shops) are:

- *remise sur tarif* – trade discount
- *remise de fin d'année* – end of year rebate (often up to 23 per cent of list price and claimed when sales forecasts are exceeded)
- *remise transport* – for delivery to central depots

- *remise dépôt* – for warehousing costs
- *remise quantitative* – for quantity
- *remise de diffusion* – calculated according to how many shops the products will be sold in
- *remise d'assortiment* – calculated according to the range of goods ordered
- *remise de progression* – for agreed increase in turnover from one year to the next
- *remise promotionnelle* – buyers will ask for as many as possible; allow only 2–3
- *commande* (order) *conditionnelle* – retailers will ask for unsold articles to be taken back
- *emplacement sur le rayon* (shelf/department) – best shelf positions are 'negotiable'
- *participation (aux frais de publicité* – advertising costs) – shops themselves will ask for this and it can lead to tricky negotiations.

Dealing with buyers

Be Firm. Many of the *grandes surfaces* chains have central purchasing organisations (*centrale d'achats*) and products are chosen to be a listed item (*être référencié*). In some cases (Casino, Docks de France, Ruche Méridionale), the central buyers choose the suppliers, products, prices, promotion, etc. In others (Leclerc, Intermarché, Codec, Unico) regional and shop managers (and family!) also have a big say in the selection of products, etc. It is therefore essential to check individual organisations' buying habits since the very strong central decision-making, ordering, delivering and invoicing which characterise the UK market is absent in varying degrees throughout French retailing. Relationships between manufacturers and the retail distribution tend also to be much more antagonistic with price being a key factor.

In the case of highly centralised buying patterns, it is best to negotiate on a strict contractual basis. Quantities, agreed increases in turnover, range of products can be agreed centrally, but promotion may be better left to separate dealings with shop managers.

Be Consistent. Do not allow concessions to shops which have not been agreed with the central buying organisation. Write everything down to avoid attempts being made to drive a wedge between you and the *centrale d'achat*.

THE LANGUAGE OF BUSINESS

Trained Staff. This type of negotiation needs highly skilled staff who can be firm and say no.

Shelf Stocking. Ensure that all goods delivered eventually end up on the shelves.

Pricing Policy. Buyers (with good memories!) often change buying organisations. Be careful to offer the same discounts to all customers.

Invoices. If you deliver on the 20th of the month, do not wait until the 10th of the next to send your invoice.

Reminders. If you do not send reminders, 60 days will quickly become 120 days.

Much is often expected of suppliers, even down to constant visits to shops almost to sell their own goods. Retailers in particular appreciate:

- prices marked already on products
- bar codes (*code barres*) – many insist on bencod put on by the supplier
- anti-theft cards – small items need to be on big cards or in plastic blister packs to guard against shoplifting
- consumer information – products are expected to sell themselves, so clear, simple instructions for use are expected
- mechandising (*le merchandising*) – many sales staff pay constant attention to rack-end (*tête de gondole*) displays for which a premium is paid
- backhanders (*les dessous de table*) may occur in fast moving consumer goods in France!

To summarise, then, toughness (the French do expect this) and professionalism are essential qualities in home based sales staff, particularly when dealing directly with the retail sector. Clarity and precision are also needed when discussing details such as prices, discounts, etc. And it should always be remembered that there are plenty of other suppliers willing to offer what buyers want, so be prepared to be more flexible than on your home market. It could pay dividends in the long run.

Business magazine 2: 'Face to Face'

Direct selling to a customer or end user is being used more frequently by British companies selling into the French market. It permits a company to retain control of its marketing which may be important in the case of products sold as part of a 'concept'. In this magazine programme, you can hear how some UK companies have set about direct selling and what results have been achieved.

Chapter 3

Working with an agent
'Ce n'est pas du tout le même système qu'en France'

Introduction

When entering the French market, many companies decide to work with a French agent. Finding the right one is important – someone who does not represent other products that are in competition with your own and someone with whom you can develop a good working relationship.

In this sequence we meet Peter Osbourne who owns a quality giftware company, Troika. Peter is visiting his agent in France, Jean-Daniel Gaillard, to discuss last year's trading. In fact, Peter has now developed his business one step further, with the help of M. Gaillard, and has set up his own *Société à responsabilité limitée* or SARL. This helps make administration in France easier, and many French people still feel more comfortable doing business with a French company. You will also be hearing Troika's accountant in France, Douglas Connell, talking about dealing with the French accounting system.

On the language side you will be learning

- how to discuss future strategies
- to use the conversational past tense
- how to express approximate quantities
- to use the subjunctive
- how to discuss the success of a product
- how to discuss price.

WORKING WITH AN AGENT

Now watch the video sequence 'Working with an agent' (10 34 05). Try to follow the dialogues with the help of the keywords and phrases below.

Key words and phrases

Dans la salle d'exposition

la salle d'exposition (f.)	the exhibition room
j'ai agrandi pas mal (fam.)	I've enlarged (it) quite a lot
ces boîtes (f.)	these tins
entrer en concurrence (f.)	to compete
essayer d'éclairer	to try to shed light on
la flasque 'Ergo'	the Ergo flask
cela marche toujours (fam.)	that's still popular, successful
la vedette	the star
en étain (m.)	in pewter
notre propre fabrication (f.)	our own manufacture, production

La réunion avec le comptable

sa comptabilité	its accounts, its books
des redressements (m.) d'impôts (m.)	back tax adjustments
sur le plan commercial	from the commercial point of view
une marge (bénéficiaire)	a (profit) margin
les frais (m.) de commercialisation	the marketing costs
mon conseil	my advice
un résultat à perte (f.)	a loss result, a loss income statement
le fisc	Inland Revenue, the tax department

Jean-Daniel Gaillard discute de sa stratégie de ventes avec Peter Osbourne

consacrer plus de temps (m.) au suivi	to spend more time on the follow-up
de manière à pouvoir suivre	in such a way as to be able to follow
ces demandes (f.)	these enquiries
exigeant	demanding
des remises (f.)	discounts
des renseignements (m.)	details, information
engager quelqu'un	to hire someone
arriver à s'implanter	to succeed in establishing oneself
dès le départ	right from the start
d'une part ... d'autre part	on the one hand ... on the other hand

103

THE LANGUAGE OF BUSINESS

pas mal de (fam.)	quite a few
des échantillons (m.) de réalisations (f.)	product samples
quelques cadeaux (m.)	a few presents
se barbouiller le visage	to plaster, to daub one's face

Listen and understand

Cover up the right-hand column and try answering the following questions on your own. Then compare them with the suggested answers on the right.

A1 Getting the gist

1. Qui sont Peter Osbourne et Jean-Daniel Gaillard?	*Peter Osbourne est à la fois le propriétaire et le P-DG de la société Troïka. Jean-Daniel Gaillard est l'agent commercial de Troïka, mais il possède également sa propre société.*
2. Où est-ce que Jean-Daniel Gaillard emmène Peter Osbourne? Pourquoi?	*Il l'emmène voir deux salles d'exposition pour lui montrer les modifications qu'il a apportées à ces salles.*
3. Qui est Douglas Connell et de quoi parle-t-il?	*Il est comptable et il parle de la législation fiscale en France.*
4. De quoi discutent Jean-Daniel Gaillard et Peter Osbourne?	*Ils discutent de la stratégie commerciale pour l'année prochaine.*

A2 Getting the details

Dans la salle d'exposition

1. Est-ce que Jean-Daniel Gaillard vend uniquement les produits de Troïka?	*Non, on peut voir dans la première salle d'exposition une sélection de boîtes métalliques qui ne sont pas des produits de Troïka.*

2. Est-ce que ces boîtes entrent en concurrence avec les produits de Troïka?

Non, elles n'entrent pas en concurrence avec les produits de Troïka; elles sont un bon complément.

3. Est-ce que ces boîtes sont chères?

Non, elles ne sont pas chères.

4. Que dit Jean-Daniel Gaillard pour rassurer Peter Osbourne?

Il lui dit que ces boîtes sont une bonne carte d'entrée dans certaines boutiques pour les produits de Troïka.

5. Pourquoi la flasque 'Ergo' est-elle considérée comme la vedette parmi les produits de Troïka?

Parce qu' elle se vend bien partout dans le monde.

La réunion avec le comptable

6. Que risque-t-on si on ne présente pas sa comptabilité selon les règles établies?

On risque d'avoir des redressements d'impôts très importants.

THE LANGUAGE OF BUSINESS

7. En quoi consiste le plan d'action actuel?

Il consiste simplement à couvrir les frais de commercialisation.

8. Pendant combien d'années le fisc pourrait-il accepter un résultat à perte?

Pendant les deux premières années.

9. Quelle est la marge bénéficiaire fixée par Peter?

Elle a été fixée à trente pour cent.

10. Que couvrira cette marge de trente pour cent?

Elle couvrira les frais de distribution et de publicité, ainsi que les frais occasionnés par l'organisation de salons et la participation aux foires.

11. En quoi consiste la rémunération de Jean-Daniel Gaillard?

Il reçoit des commissions sur les ventes.

WORKING WITH AN AGENT

Jean-Daniel Gaillard discute de sa stratégie de ventes avec Peter Osbourne

12. Qu'aimerait faire Jean-Daniel Gaillard l'année prochaine?

Il aimerait consacrer plus de temps au suivi de la clientèle potentielle pour laquelle il n'a pas assez de temps actuellement.

13. Est-ce que Jean-Daniel Gaillard s'occupera personnellement de la clientèle potentielle?

Non, il espère pouvoir employer quelqu'un qui suivra toutes les demandes et qui fera même de la prospection.

14. Pourquoi Jean-Daniel Gaillard considère-t-il la clientèle potentielle exigeante?

Parce qu'elle demande des remises importantes et des délais de livraison impossibles.

15. De son côté, comment Peter Osbourne pourrait-il aider Jean-Daniel Gaillard à réaliser son objectif?

Il faudrait qu'il puisse fournir à son agent des tarifs et des échantillons de réalisations.

A3 Summing up the scene

Watch again that part of the video where Jean-Daniel tells the story about the Nina Ricci presentation to Concorde passengers (10 41 50), and retell it in your own words, using the clues given below. You will find the solution on the travel cassette.

Donc, en France, jusqu'à maintenant nous avons eu .... avec ce produit, ... avec Nina Ricci .... Air France qui a offert .... qui .... en Concorde .... et je crois d'ailleurs que Nina Ricci .... qui voyagent en Concorde, ... une petite notice spéciale car .... d'eau de cologne, ... avec ce produit.

B Develop your skills

B1 The present subjunctive (encore)

To see if you remember the forms of the subjunctive from last time, let us look at it again. The subjunctive is used with a large number of impersonal impressions, such as:

107

THE LANGUAGE OF BUSINESS

il se peut que	it is possible/may be that
il vaut mieux que	it's better for us/him to . . .
il est important que	it's important to . . .
il est impossible que	it's impossible to . . .

A vous

In the following sentences, change the **de + infinitive** to **que + subjunctive**, as in the example. Do not look at the answers until you have completed the exercise on your own. (Remember the Grammar Kit is there to help you.)

Example: Il est préférable de contacter d'abord l'agent. (vous)
Il est préférable que vous contactiez d'abord l'agent.

1. Il est très important d'avoir des renseignements complémentaires. (je)

   Il est très important que j'aie des renseignements complémentaires.

2. Il est temps d'engager quelqu'un pour assurer le suivi de la clientèle. (nous)

   Il est temps que nous engagions quelqu'un pour assurer le suivi de la clientèle.

3. Il est essentiel de nous envoyer beaucoup d'échantillons de manière à ce que nous puissions montrer au client ce qui a été fait sur le marché anglais. (vous)

   Il est essentiel que vous nous envoyiez beaucoup d'échantillons de manière à ce que nous puissions montrer au client ce qui a été fait sur le marché anglais.

4. Il est nécessaire de pouvoir lui accorder une remise de 10 pour cent. (elle)

   Il est nécessaire qu'elle puisse lui accorder une remise de 10 pour cent.

5. Il est impossible de leur remettre des tarifs aujourd'hui. (ils)

   Il est impossible qu'ils leur remettent des tarifs aujourd'hui.

6. Il est préférable d'écrire tout de suite. (on)

   Il est préférable qu'on écrive tout de suite.

In the following set of sentences, replace the constructions in bold with a construction of **que + subjunctive**. Using **que + subjunctive** and changing **ce** to **il** where it occurs, will change the sentence from a colloquial to a more formal one. Try this according to the example.

108

Example: **C'est mieux de savoir** ce qu'il pense. (on)
Il vaut mieux qu'on sache ce qu'il pense.

1. **C'est important d'avoir** un catalogue à jour. (nous)

   Il est important que nous ayons un catalogue à jour.

2. A mon avis, **il faut s'éloigner** de ce qui peut ressembler à la concurrence. (nous)

   A mon avis, il faut que nous nous éloignions de ce qui peut ressembler à la concurrence.

3. **Il est temps de faire** quelque chose. (vous)

   Il est temps que vous fassiez quelque chose.

4. **Ce n'est pas impossible** de finir à temps. (il)

   Il n'est pas impossible qu'il finisse à temps.

5. **C'est indispensable de** se mettre en rapport avec nous d'abord. (elle)

   Il est indispensable qu'elle se mette en rapport avec nous d'abord.

6. **C'est vraiment dommage de** devoir refuser des commandes avant les fêtes. (on)

   Il est vraiment dommage qu'on doive refuser des commandes avant les fêtes.

B2 Direct and indirect object pronouns

me				
te	le	lui		
se	la	leur	y	en
nous	les			
vous				

If you learn the positions of the pronouns as you would the positions of a football team, it will help you to remember the order in which they appear in a sentence when there is more than one. For the moment, we will look only at the pronouns **me, te, nous, vous**, which can be used as both direct objects (me, us, you) and indirect objects of the verb (to me, to us, to you). Note that the pronouns immediately precede the conjugated form of the verb.

THE LANGUAGE OF BUSINESS

Direct

Elle **me** voit = She sees **me**
Il **nous** salue = He greets **us**
Je **t'**aime bien = I like **you**

Elle ne **vous** comprend pas = She doesn't understand **you**

Indirect

Elle **me** parle = she speaks **to me**
Il **nous** répond = He replies **to us**
Je **te** raconte des bêtises = I'm telling **you** nonsense

Elle ne **vous** donne pas le livre = She's not giving the book **to you**/ She's not giving you the book

Notice that in the last two examples, the indirect object in English can be expressed as **you**, but still means to you. So, **je te raconte des bêtises** literally means 'I am talking nonsense *to you*'. Similarly, in **elle ne vous donne pas le livre**, the direct object is **le livre** and the indirect object is **vous**. Remember this because it will be important later on!

A vous

Now watch the video again, where Jean-Daniel Gaillard is discussing his sales strategy with Peter Osbourne (10 39 13), and correct in the following sentences what is different from the recorded version. Pay particular attention to the pronouns. Use the transcript to check your answers.

1. . . . cette clientèle potentielle qui vient te voir et pour laquelle tu n'as pas assez de temps, donc . . .

2. Cette clientèle nous propose ou nous fait espérer des commandes énormes en quantités, me demande des remises importantes, me demande des délais de livraison quelquefois impossibles . . .

3. Donc si j'engage quelqu'un qui travaille uniquement dans ce domaine, je crois que j'arriverai à m'implanter là encore sur le marché.

4. . . . qui me permettent dès le départ, lorsque j'ai une question, donc qui m'est posée, ou de pouvoir déjà donner une idée sur les prix, . . .

5. . . . , donc il faudrait que d'une part, nous puissions vous donner des tarifs, même s'ils sont approximatifs, avec des . . .

6. ... des remises quantitatives par produit et que vous m'envoyiez pas mal d'échantillons de réalisations que vous avez faites sur le marché anglais, ...

7. ... cela va donner une certaine confiance au client, certaines ideés, cela me donnera même certaines ideés de prospection.

B3 How to talk about the past

The perfect tense (**passé composé**) is used in French to express a *completed* action, and corresponds to both English forms: has (have) done and did.

| Le prix de l'acier **a augmenté** | The price of steel **has gone up** |
| Le prix de l'acier **a augmenté** hier | The price of steel **went up** yesterday |

The pefect tense of most verbs is formed by using the present tense of the auxiliary verb **avoir** plus the past participle. All transitive verbs (i.e. verbs taking a direct object) and a large number of intransitive verbs take **avoir**. A small number of verbs takes **être** as auxiliary. These are discussed later in this chapter.

Examples: J'ai acheté un livre   I have bought/I bought a book
          Les prix ont augmenté   Prices went/have gone up

The past participle of the **-er** verbs is formed by adding **-é** to the infinitive stem.

A vous

Complete the following sentences with the correct form of the **passé composé** of the indicated verb.

Example: Ils .... de fournisseur. (changer)
         Ils ont changé de fournisseur.

1. Nous .... cette salle d'exposition. (modifier)
2. On .... d'éclairer le mieux possible. (essayer)
3. Vous .... beaucoup de temps au suivi. (ne pas consacrer)
4. J' .... un représentant supplémentaire. (employer)
5. Ils .... un petit problème. (rencontrer)
6. On nous .... des délais de livraison impossibles. (demander)

THE LANGUAGE OF BUSINESS

Answers: *1. avons modifié; 2. a essayé; 3. n'avez pas consacré; 4. ai employé; 5. ont rencontré; 6. a demandé.*

> The past participle of **-ir** verbs is formed by adding **-i** to the infinitive stem.

A vous

Rewrite the following sentences using the perfect.

Example: La secrétaire accueille les visiteurs.
La secrétaire a accueilli les visiteurs.

1. Nous choisissons les meilleurs représentants.
2. D'abord vous remplissez un bon de commande.
3. C'est le service comptabilité qui établit les factures.
4. On fournira les marchandises aussitôt que possible.
5. Ils n'élargissent pas leur gamme.
6. Il finit son travail à cinq heures et demie.

Answers: *1. avons choisi; 2. avez rempli; 3. a établi; 4. a fourni; 5. n'ont pas élargi; 6. a fini.*

> The past participle of many **-re** verbs is formed by adding **-u** to the infinitive stem.

A vous

Complete the following sentences with the correct form of the perfect of the indicated verb.

Example: Elle .... une demi-heure. (attendre)
Elle a attendu une demi-heure.

1. Nous .... un certain nombre de droits. (perdre)
2. Ils .... des produits à nos concurrents. (vendre)
3. J' .... des rumeurs au sujet du taux de TVA. (entendre)
4. Je vois qu'il .... son chef. (convaincre)

5. Il .... les échantillons. (rendre)
6. Elle .... à mon coup de fil. (ne pas répondre)

Answers: *1. avons perdu; 2. ont vendu; 3. ai entendu; 4. a convaincu; 5. a rendu; 6. n'a pas répondu.*

The past participle of irregular verbs is formed in a variety of ways so each one must be learned separately, e.g.:

être	été
avoir	eu
faire	fait

However, some irregular groups tend to have characteristic past participles, and some general guidance can be given, e.g.:

- The verbs **mettre** and **prendre** and its derivatives form their past participles in **-is**:

mettre	mis
prendre	pris
comprendre	compris

- Verbs with infinitives in **-uire** form their past participle in **-uit**:

produire	produit
reconstruire	reconstruit
conduire	conduit

- Verbs with infinitives in **-aître, tenir** and its derivatives and **venir** and its derivatives form their past participle in **-u**:

connaître	connu
tenir	tenu
convenir	convenu

THE LANGUAGE OF BUSINESS

- Verbs with infinitives in **-aire, -oir**, and some other verbs form their past participle in **- u:**

plaire	plu
devoir	dû
concevoir	conçu
croire	cru
pouvoir	pu
falloir	fallu

- Some verbs whose infinitives end in **- ir** form their past participle in **- ert:**

ouvrir	ouvert
découvrir	découvert
offrir	offert

- Verbs with infinitives in **- eindre/aindre** form their past participle in **- eint/- aint:**

éteindre	éteint
atteindre	atteint
craindre	craint

A vous

Rewrite the following sentences in the **passé composé**.

Example: Nous suivons les consignes.
Nous avons suivi les consignes.

1. On a des problèmes.   *On a eu des problèmes.*
2. Je vois l'usine de Peter.   *J'ai vu l'usine de Peter.*
3. Vous ne faites pas d'erreurs majeures.   *Vous n'avez pas fait d'erreurs majeures.*
4. Elle promet une grosse commande.   *Elle a promis une grosse commande.*
5. Elles ne veulent pas acheter notre produit.   *Elle n'ont pas voulu acheter notre produit.*

6. On me permet de vous accorder un rabais.   On m'a permis de vous accorder un rabais.

A vous

Complete the following sentences with the correct form of the past participle of the indicated verb.

Example: Ils .... ce qu'ils voulaient. (dire)
Ils ont dit ce qu'ils voulaient.

1. J' .... un rabais de tant de francs. (obtenir)
2. Nous .... simplement .... les frais. (couvrir)
3. Nina Ricci .... un cadeau à ses clients. (offrir)
4. Certains .... qu'il s'agissait d'un produit cosmétique. (croire)
5. Nous .... la conviction qu'il avait raison. (acquérir)
6. Il .... lui expliquer plusieurs fois la même chose. (falloir)

Answers: *1. ai obtenu; 2. avons couvert; 3. a offert; 4. ont cru; 5. avons acquis; 6. a fallu.*

B4 Verbs taking the auxiliary **être**

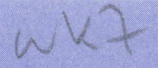

A number of intransitive verbs (ie verbs without object or complement) take **être** as auxiliary. One example of an intransitive verb is **mourir** – to die. **Mourir** cannot have an object; it is impossible to die someone!

Below you will find a list of the main verbs which take **être** as an auxiliary. They will be easier to remember if you see them as pairs of opposites.

aller	venir
entrer	sortir
arriver	partir
monter	descendre
mourir	naître
tomber	rester

(and their compounds, e.g.: **devenir, rentrer,** or words used with the same meaning, eg, **retourner**).

THE LANGUAGE OF BUSINESS

> In the case of those verbs being conjugated with **être**, the past participle ending agrees with the subject.
> La dernière livraison est arriv**ée**
> Les paquets sont tomb**és** par terre
> Les deux secrétaires sont all**ées** à la poste

A vous

Now look at the example and fill in the **passé composé** in the following sentences:

Example: Tous les délégués .... (arriver)
Tous les délégués sont arrivés.

1. Ils .... au premier étage pour assister à la conférence. (monter)
2. Malheureusement les conférenciers .... (ne pas arriver)
3. La présidente de la séance .... pour téléphoner. (descendre)
4. On lui a dit que les conférenciers .... ce matin de bonne heure. (partir)
5. Il semble qu'ils .... dans un embouteillage. (tomber)
6. Et ils y .... bloqués pendant une bonne heure. (rester)
7. Les voilà qui arrivent! La présidente .... pour annoncer la nouvelle aux délégués. (remonter)

Answers: *1. sont montés; 2. ne sont pas arrivés; 3. est descendue; 4. sont partis; 5. sont tombés; 6. sont restés; 7. est remontée.*

B5 Further into the past

The main point you need to remember about the perfect tense is how it is formed: **avoir** or **être** + past participle.

If you have mastered that, here are a few further points which help you understand some of the forms you will see and hear in future chapters. The points are brief because they will be dealt with later.

- If verbs like **descendre, monter** are used transitively (ie: with a direct object) they are conjugated with **avoir**.

Compare: Elle **est** descendu**e**   She came down
          Elle **a** descend**u** les   She brought/took the luggage
          bagages   down

and

> Ils **sont** rentrés They came in
> Ils **ont** rentré les voitures They brought the cars in

- 'Reflexive' verbs, eg **s'asseoir, se taire** are conjugated with **être**, and the past participle agrees with the pronoun if the latter is the direct object.
- The past participle of verbs conjugated with **avoir** agrees with a direct object coming before the verb.

e.g.: Où sont les valises? Where are the suitcases?
Je les ai mont**ées** dans la chambre I've taken them up to the room

Compare: Je l'ai **vu** I've seen him
Je l'ai **vue** I've seen her

and

Je l'ai comp**ris** I understood him/it (le détail, l'ordre)

Je l'ai comp**rise** I understood her/it (l'explication, la lettre)

A vous

Now, here is a final exercise on the perfect tense. Watch the first few seconds of the video (10 34 05) carefully, so that you can describe Peter's gestures and actions, using the perfect. Try and fill in the following exercise and check it against the answers below.

Hier, Peter ....(1) chez son agent en voiture. Il ....(2) sa voiture en face du bâtiment, et on suppose, puisqu'on ne peut pas voir ce qu'il fait à l'intérieur de la voiture, qu'il .... (3) le moteur, qu'il .... (4) la clé de contact du tableau de bord et qu'il .... (5) la clé dans sa poche. Il .... (6) de la voiture en claquant la portière derrière lui. Il .... ensuite ....(7) la portière arrière pour prendre sa malette, qui se trouvait sur le siège arrière. Il ....(8) la portière et il ....(9) vers la porte d'entrée du bâtiment. A mi-chemin entre la voiture et la porte, il .... (10) la malette de main, il .... (11) sa montre pour vérifier s'il était à l'heure pour son rendez-vous et il .... (12) dans le bâtiment.

Comme les bureaux de son agent se trouvent au premier étage, Peter .... (13) les escaliers d'un pas alerte. Jean-Daniel, qui .... sûrement .... (14) arriver Peter, ... (15) à sa rencontre. Il .... (16) quelques marches et il .... (17) la main de Peter pour lui dire bonjour et lui souhaiter la bienvenue. Les deux partenaires .... alors .... (18) quelques mots de politesse dans les escaliers et .... (19) vraisemblablement au bureau de Jean-Daniel pour y déposer les affaires de Peter avant d'aller visiter les salles d'exposition.

Answers: 1. est arrivé; 2. a garé; 3. a éteint; 4. a retiré; 5. a mis; 6. est descendu; 7. a ouvert; 8. a refermé 9. s'est dirigé; 10. a changé; 11. a regardé; 12. est entré; 13. a monté; 14. a entendu; 15. s'est précipité; 16. a descendu; 17. a serré; 18. ont échangé; 19. sont allés.

C Extend your vocabulary

C1 More ways of expressing time

A vous

These half-sentences are jumbled up. Pair them together correctly, so that they make sense.

Example: 1. + a. gives : Notre chef reviendra dans 4 ou 5 jours.

1. Notre chef reviendra
2. Nous avons jusqu'au 15 juin
3. Elle a travaillé chez Brimax
4. Ils ont fait des pertes
5. Les nouveaux tarifs sont applicables
6. Votre facture est prête
7. A ce moment-là je ne comprenais pas la comptabilité;

a. dans 4 ou 5 jours.
b. depuis jeudi dernier.
c. à partir du 4 juillet.
d. pour livrer la marchandise.
e. maintenant je commence à comprendre.
f. dès le début.
g. pendant 10 ans.

Answers: 2. + d; 3. + g; 4. + f; 5. + c; 6. + b; 7. + e.

C2 From verb to noun

WK 7

Many verbs can be transformed into nouns by using the suffix **-tion**, or one of its variations. Some endings are:

-tion	construire	→	construction
-action	réagir	→	réaction
-ication	modifier	→	modification
-ation	utiliser	→	utilisation
-ssion	progresser	→	progression
-sion	exploser	→	explosion

A vous

In the following sentences change the verb in bold to a noun ending in **-tion**, and make any necessary changes.

Example: On **utilise** le tunnelier étanche. Cela permet de travailler dans des terrains très humides.
*L'**utilisation du** tunnelier étanche permet de travailler dans des terrains très humides.*

Watch what happens to **de** in the answer phrase. For more information on this subject see the Grammar Kit.

1. On **automatise** la production. Cela améliore fortement la compétitivité.	*L'automatisation de la production améliore fortement la compétitivité.*
2. On **fabrique** des produits de haute qualité. Cela répond aux besoins de nos clients.	*La fabrication de produits de haute qualité répond aux besoins de nos clients.*
3. On **délègue** des responsabilités. Cela stimule la participation.	*La délégation de responsabilités stimule la participation.*
4. On **réalise** un premier prototype. Cela permet de faire des essais et des modifications.	*La réalisation d'un premier prototype permet de faire des essais et des modifications.*
5. On **forme** le personnel. Cela intéresse beaucoup les syndicats.	*La formation du personnel intéresse beaucoup les syndicats.*
6. On **conçoit** la pièce à l'aide d'un ordinateur. Cela permet de mieux étudier ses caractéristiques.	*La conception de la pièce à l'aide d'un ordinateur permet de mieux étudier ses caractéristiques.*

THE LANGUAGE OF BUSINESS

C3 Nouns expressing qualities

These nouns are more often derived from adjectives than from verbs. More specifically, the ending **-ité** is used to indicate the qualities of materials used in manufacturing a product.

acide	→	acidité
élastique	→	élasticité
étanche	→	étanchéité
flexible	→	flexibilité
instable	→	instabilité
malléable	→	malléabilité
ductile	→	ductilité

Nouns such as **malleabilité** and **ductibilité** are used to describe specific qualities of metals.

A vous

In the following exercise you are asked to replace the adjective in brackets with the corresponding noun.

Example: Le tunnelier est équipé de joints spéciaux, qui lui assurent une (étanche) totale.
Le tunnelier est équipé de joints spéciaux, qui lui assurent une étanchéité totale.

1. Lors de la conception de nos machines, la (fiable) était notre principale préoccupation.
2. Nous n'avons aucun doute en ce qui concerne l'(efficace) de notre nouvelle méthode de travail.
3. Le taux de (rentable) de votre investissement n'est pas très élevé.
4. Ce matériel est d'une (solide) à toute épreuve.
5. Le revêtement employé conserve une bonne (stable) dimensionnelle à haute température.
6. Nous avons accru la (mobile) de cet appareil en réduisant son encombrement.

Answers: *1. fiabilité; 2. efficacité; 3. rentabilité; 4. solidité; 5. stabilité; 6. mobilité.*

WORKING WITH AN AGENT

D Make your language work

D1 Publicising your product

Any salesman needs to know how to highlight the qualities and advantages of his product. You may need to use a dictionary to check the meaning of some words. The checklist of phrases below are designed to help you to do so, they aim to attract the customer's attention and to persuade him or her to buy.

Phrases d'introduction

| Nous nous permettons
Permettez-nous | d'attirer (tout) particulièrement votre attention sur |

Vous remarquerez, en premier lieu que . . .

Les caractéristiques qualitatives

| Ce meuble
Cette machine
Cet article | est de conception | moderne
très classique
nouvelle |

| Cet article est d'une qualité | courante
excellente
inégalable
irréprochable
sans concurrence |

| Ce produit | possède
offre | des qualités de (robustesse, solidarité, résistance, etc.) |

| Ce produit | est recommandé
est apprécié | pour | ses qualités de . . .
ses qualités mécaniques |

| Cet article | est d'une
de | fabrication
exécution
réalisation
construction | impeccable
irréprochable
supérieure
soignée
robuste
standard
hors série |

121

THE LANGUAGE OF BUSINESS

Cet article est d' | un fini / une finition | parfaite / soigné(e) / impeccable

Cet article est fabriqué
- en | pure laine / bois / matière plastique
- matière | inoxydable / inaltérable / intachable
- avec des matériaux de premier choix
- dans une matière plastique solide

Cet appareil
- est doté des | (tout) derniers | perfectionnements techniques
- offre / comporte / a été amélioré par | les | perfectionnements les plus modernes

Caractéristiques d'utilisation

Cet appareil / Cet article
- répond aux désirs essentiels de la clientèle
- assure (un parfait nettoyage)
- convient à …
- est couramment employé | pour … / dans … / comme …
- est particulièrement recommandé pour …
- permet de résoudre vos problèmes
- a été spécialement | conçu / étudié / fabriqué | pour …

Caractéristiques esthétiques

Il / Elle | possède / présente / offre | une ligne | élégante / jeune / moderne / sobre

WORKING WITH AN AGENT

Il est / Elle est — d'une présentation
- agréable
- élégante
- attrayante
- soignée
- luxueuse

Ce produit/cette machine est — présenté(e) / livré(e)

dans un(e)
- beau coffret
- boîte de 5 kilos
- paquet de 1 kilo
- coffret
- étui en plastic

- sans housse
- avec accessoires nécessaires de pose
- avec notice explicative de montage
- avec mode d'emploi
- prêt à peindre

Caractéristiques promotionnelles

I Le succès d'un article, d'un produit

C'est un article qui est

- actuellement / très / hautement
  - demandé (par)
  - connu (des)
  - apprécié (par)
  - recherché (par)

- particulièrement / fort / très
  - bien accueilli par le public

C'est un article qui

- jouit de / a / connaît
  - une grande renommée auprès de ...
  - la faveur
    - du public
    - des connaisseurs

- connaît / rencontre / remporte
  - le plus vif
  - un gros
  - un grand
  - succès auprès de ...

123

THE LANGUAGE OF BUSINESS

	qui plaît	infiniment énormément beaucoup	à nos clients à la à notre aux femmes au public	clientèle
C'est un article	qui fait	sensation fureur	parmi les jeunes	
	dont	les qualités la solidité	lui ont a	valu le plus vif succès
que	l'on s'arrache			

II Le prix

	Adverbes	Qualificatifs
Vous bénéficierez d'un prix Vous profiterez d'un prix	particulièrement extrêmement réellement vraiment	bas honnête modéré attractif réduit raisonnable exceptionnel

Un prix calculé au plus juste, spécialement étudié

• Par rapport au prix de la concurrence

Un prix est reconnu comme étant	concurrentiel compétitif imbattable inégalable	eu égard à la qualité

Un prix	sans pareil sans égal sans concurrence défiant toute concurrence

WORKING WITH AN AGENT

- En considération des possibilités de la clientéle

Un prix
- abordable – inabordable
- accessible – inaccessible
- avantageux
- intéressant
- excessif
- exorbitant

Un prix
- de lancement
- d'occasion
- d'ami
- à la portée de tous (de toutes les bourses)
- accessible à tous les budgets
- dans vos / mes moyens

A vous

Read carefully through the example below. Then read through the promotional description and decide for each of the paragraphs which categories of characteristics they belong to (**qualitatives, d'utilisation, esthétiques, promotionnelles**).

Example: Nous vous présentons un ensemble de 49 pièces double face, parfaitement réalisées, à la fois très en relief et très fin.

qualitatives et esthétiques

Une ménagère de couverts et couteaux

Nous vous présentons un ensemble de 49 pièces. Dans un style d'actualité, le riche décor double face, parfaitement réalisé est à la fois très en relief et très fin. Ces superbes couverts et couteaux rehaussent l'éclat des tables de fête. Les couteaux en particulier sont entièrement en acier inoxydable massif.

Cette ménagère est luxueusement présentée dans un bel écrin dont l'intérieur rouge est du plus bel effet, avec un coussin en satin dans le couvercle.

Vous disposerez d'un ensemble homogène et vous aurez dans vos tiroirs une ménagère élégante et solide, toujours à votre disposition en toutes occasions, tant pour vos repas quotidiens que pour vos réceptions. Vous apprécierez les qualités de cet ensemble très complet.

Elégance et raffinement : lignes modernes, enrichies d'un décor romantique de roses dessinées en relief.

Robustesse : sa matière, l'acier inoxydable, normalement ne se ternit pas, ne rouille pas, ne se tache pas, n'a besoin d'être polie.

A vous

Read the exercise below in its entirety and then try to complete the text below using the following words:

attrayant, réalisé, résistant, agréable, muni, glissière, latérales, léger, sécurité, joindre, possède, intérieure, mode, atout, dimensions, agréable, possède.

Consult pp 121–5 if you need any help.

Un sac de voyage

Il est ....(1) et très ....(2), il est jeune et très à la ....(3). Il est ....(4) en polyamide enduit. Il ....(5) deux poignées gainées et pour ....(6) l'utile à l' ....(7) une poignée sur le côté. Ce sac est ....(8) de deux poches ....(9) à ....(10) et d'une poche ....(11). Il ....(12) une longue fermeture avec une serrure de ....(13). Ses ....(14) sont 50 × 40 × 23 cm. Leur prix ....(15) est un ....(16) supplémentaire.

Answers: *(1) léger; (2) résistant; (3) mode; (4) réalisé; (5) possède; (6) joindre; (7) agréable; (8) muni; (9) latérales; (10) glissière; (11) intérieure; (12) possède; (13) sécurité; (14) dimensions; (15) attrayant; (16) atout.*

For the second passage, choose from the expressions given on pp 121–5. In addition, you will need the following words:

décors, intachable, proposée, pièces.

WORKING WITH AN AGENT

Des meubles de salon

Tous ces meubles ont mérité notre certificat 'Valeur Sûre' pour leur .... soignée et la ....de leurs finitions. Entièrement réalisés en ....et de style ...., ils plairont par leurs lignes .... et .... Ce sont de jolies .... d'ébénisterie mises en valeur par une couche de vernis ....et très facile à entretenir. La ....de nos modèles s'intègre à tous les .... Nos prix pour la qualité ....sont sans égal.

D2 Getting people to meet their obligations

You learned from the accountant in this sequence that you will need to know how to prompt your customers in France to pay! First of all, read through this slightly modified version of what the accountant said, and see how many different expressions you can jot down for expressing necessity or obligation.

Conseils du comptable

En ce qui concerne les paiements en France, je suis obligé de vous prévenir que c'est un point assez délicat. Dans la mesure où les paiements sont réclamés, ils doivent être suivis directement par votre service comptabilité. Il est essentiel que vous établissiez une certaine routine et il faut absolument que vous respectiez cette routine. Lorsque vous livrez de la marchandise en France, il faut que vous assuriez un suivi, que vous ayez un échancier, que vous établissiez un système pour que, 10 jours après la réception de la commande si votre client ne vous a pas retourné sa traite, il reçoive immédiatement une première lettre de rappel lui signifiant votre étonnement de ne pas avoir reçu ce règlement. Par la suite, si votre client ne répond pas à votre première lettre, il est indispensable que vous réécriviez très rapidement pour que votre client comprenne que vous allez suivre le règlement dès le départ. Car malheureusement, beaucoup de boutiques, enfin beaucoup de nos clients sont des personnes qui sont honnêtes, mais quelquefois un peu fantaisistes dans la manière de tenir leur comptabilité ou n'en ont pratiquement pas. Donc si vous ne réclamez pas le paiement des factures, vous serez rarement payé.

A vous

In a moment, we shall be asking you to look at three follow-up letters of varying degrees of urgency. First of all, look at the table below which will help you to fill in the blanks in the second half of each letter.

THE LANGUAGE OF BUSINESS

You try the rest:

| Délai de règlement | Dès que possible

a | Par retour de courrier

b | Sous 48 heures

c |
|---|---|---|---|
| Menaces | A défaut, nous remettrons votre dossier à l'agence de recouvrement qui entamera une procédure de recouvrement

a | Nous insistons sur un règlement rapide afin d'éviter les frais d'une procédure de recouvrement contentieux

b | (Aucune menace)

c |
| Formule de politesse | Nous vous prions d'agréer, M..., nos salutations distinguées

a | Veuillez agréer, M..., nos salutations

b | Avec nos remerciements, veuillez agréer, M..., nos salutations empressées

c |

Opposite you see some examples of follow-up letters. The phrases in the first half of each letter have been mixed up. Try to put them in the right order so that the letter makes sense. The second half of each letter contains some blanks. See if you can fill these in. Refer to the table above if you need any help.

128

WORKING WITH AN AGENT

La première lettre de rappel:

Adresse du fournisseur	Adresse du client
Objet : N/facture n°	Lyon, le ....

Monsieur,

(1) En procédant à; (2) nos comptes, ; (3) de notre part; (4) vous avez omis; (5) la vérification de; (6) la facture; (7) sauf erreur; (8) citée en référence; (9) que; (10) nous constatons; (11) de nous régler.

Nous vous serions très obligés de bien vouloir réparer cet oubli en nous adressant (quand?) ...., par tout moyen à votre convenance, la somme de ....F.

(Menace)

(Formule de politesse)

Answers: *First paragraph: (1); (5); (2); (10); (7); (3); (9); (4); (11); (6); (8).*
Délai de règlement: a
Menace: c
Formule de politesse: c

La 2ᵉ lettre de rappel:

Objet: N/facture n°   Lyon, le ....

Monsieur,

(1) Malgré notre rappel du ....; (2) notre facture; (3) que; (4) nous constatons; (5) est toujours impayée; (6) citée ci-dessus.

Comme nous devons nous-mêmes faire face à nos engagements, nous vous prions de nous faire parvenir un chèque de ....F (quand?) ....

(Menace)

(Formule de politesse)

THE LANGUAGE OF BUSINESS

Answers: *First paragraph: (1); (4); (3); (2); (6); (5).*
Délai de règlement: b
Menace: b
Formule de politesse: a

La 3ᵉ lettre de rappel:

Objet: N/facture n°   Lyon, le ....
        Mise en demeure

Monsieur,

(1) Nous avons le regret de constater que,; (2) le.........; (3) qui aurait dû être réglée; (4) malgré; (5) est toujours impayée; (6) nos deux précédents rappels,; (7) notre facture n° ....

Il ne nous est pas possible de patienter plus longtemps: aussi, nous vous demandons d'effectuer (quand?) .... le paiement de la somme de ....F.

(Menace)

Nous espérons néanmoins ne pas être obligés de prendre de telles dispositions.

(Formule de politesse)

Answers: *First paragraph: (1); (4); (6); (7); (3); (2); (5).*
Délai de règlement: c
Menace: a
Formule de politesse: b

    And finally, you may find yourself obliged to send a letter like the one below. Read it carefully, and answer the questions on it.

Objet: N/facture n° 245   Le 8 février 19..

Monsieur,

Notre banque nous retourne impayée, et sans indication du motif de refus, la lettre de change de 1700,00F à échéance du 31 janvier que nous avions tirée sur vous le 4 décembre en règlement de notre facture du 30 novembre dernier.

Nous sommes d'autant plus surpris de cet impayé que vous aviez accepté la traite.

Nous vous demandons de nous faire parvenir, par tout moyen à votre convenance, la somme de 1800,00F correspondant à votre dette augmentée des frais de retour, avant le 15 février. Sinon, nous nous trouverons obligés, à notre grand regret, de remettre votre dossier à notre agence de contentieux, afin qu'elle puisse recouvrer notre créance.

Dans l'espoir d'un règlement rapide, veuillez agréer, Monsieur, l'expression de nos salutations distinguées.

1. Pourquoi le fournisseur s'empresse-t-il à écrire au client? — *Parce que le client n'a pas payé la traite à la date d'échéance.*

2. Qui a retourné la lettre de change impayée? — *C'est la banque du fournisseur.*

3. Quelle est la date d'échéance indiquée sur la traite? — *Le 31 janvier.*

4. Quand le fournisseur a-t-il tiré la traite sur le client? — *Il l'a tirée le 4 décembre.*

5. En règlement de quelle facture? — *De la facture du 30 novembre dernier.*

6. Pourquoi le fournisseur est-il surpris de cet impayé? — *Parce que le client a accepté la traite.*

7. Est-ce que la somme de 1800,00F correspond à la somme indiquée sur la traite? — *Non, elle a été augmentée des frais de retour.*

8. Trouvez un exemple de participe passé qui s'accorde avec l'objet direct qui le précède. — *. . . la lettre de change . . . que nous avions tirée.*

9. Donnez les expressions qui visent à minimiser l'impact psychologique négatif de la lettre de rappel. — *Par tout moyen à votre convenance; à notre grand regret; dans l'espoir . . .*

10. Donnez un exemple d'expression suivie du subjonctif. — *. . . afin qu'elle puisse recouvrer notre créance.*

THE LANGUAGE OF BUSINESS

E Dialogue

Before attempting the dialogue, you'll need to read through this letter, paying particular attention to points 1–5.

Adresse du fournisseur   Adresse du client

JCV/MAD   Le 9 mars 1990

A l'attention de Madame Christiane PRADERE

Madame,

Nous vous remercions pour le très aimable accueil que vous avez bien voulu réserver à Monsieur Jean-Claude Forni, lors de sa récente visite pour la présentation de notre collection couvertures.

Suite à notre entretien, nous vous faisons parvenir, sous pli séparé, des échantillons d'articles qui ont le plus spécialement retenu votre intérêt.

Chaque échantillon est muni d'une fiche technique vous rappelant les caractéristiques de l'article concerné.

Sur le tarif spécial que nous vous remettons, ci-joint, vous trouverez, récapitulés, nos prix les plus étudiés à votre intention.

Nous vous précisons que ces prix s'entendent:

1) Remise de 5% sur facture pour les commandes prises au Salon

2) Franco de port à 3000 F.H.T.

3) RFA: 2%

4) Prix valables jusqu'au 31 mars 1990

5) Règlement comptant 3% sous 10 jours ou traite à 60 jours fin de mois

Nous restons à votre entière disposition pour toute information complémentaire qui pourrait vous être utile.

Nous vous prions d'agréer, Madame, nos salutations distinguées.

                                                    Le Directeur Commercial,

                                                    Jean-Claude Forni

WORKING WITH AN AGENT

Listen to the conversation between a British Managing Director (MD) and his French agent (A) on the study cassette. Below you will find a transcription of the agent's part of the conversation. You are asked to take the part of the MD, using the instructions in English as a guide to what to say in French and using the pause button when it is your turn to speak.

The right-hand column again contains sample answers. Do not look at these until you have completed the exercise on your own.

MD Au cours de notre discussion vous avez mentionné à plusieurs reprises la remise. Vous ne pouvez pas préciser un peu.

A Bien sûr. La remise, cela marche bien parce que sur le plan psychologique, il faut absolument, lorsque quelqu'un veut vous acheter une grosse quantité d'un article, il faut absolument pouvoir faire une remise.

MD (Clients presumably have to tell their superiors that they've managed to get a discount.)

Je suppose que les acheteurs qui viennent vous voir ont à rendre compte à leurs supérieurs de leurs opérations et il faut qu'ils puissent dire voilà, j'ai obtenu un rabais de tant de francs sur le prix.

A C'est ça. Mais il y a également le fait que si vous partez avec un prix plancher qui ne vous permet pas de faire une remise, vous perdez certaines affaires que vous auriez enlevées si vous aviez vendu 10 pour cent, 20 pour cent plus cher au départ.

MD (You'll have to review next year's pricing policy. You also noticed he used several different words for 'discount'.)

Nous allons donc revoir notre politique des prix pour l'année prochaine. A propos, j'ai remarqué que pendant la discussion vous avez utilisé des termes différents pour désigner 'discount'.

THE LANGUAGE OF BUSINESS

A C'est vrai. Tout à l'heure vous avez dit rabais et je ne vous ai pas corrigé. J'aurais dû le faire. Pour mieux comprendre prenons par exemple cette lettre que ma secrétaire vient de taper. On peut lire: 'remise de 5% sur facture pour les commandes prises au Salon'. Dans ce cas précis, c'est une réduction à titre promotionnel.

MD (So one uses 'remise' for a special offer, eg: during a trade fair, and for a large order.)

On peut donc utiliser remise lorsqu'on parle de réductions promotionnelles, généralement accordées pendant les salons et foires, et de réductions sur des quantités.

A Exactement! Par contre, les réductions pratiquées exceptionnellement sur le prix de vente convenu pour tenir compte, par exemple, d'un défaut de qualité ou de conformité sont appelées 'rabais'.

MD (You'll have to be careful as you generally use 'rabais'. Now what about 'franco de port à 3000 FHT' no delivery charge on an order over 3000F? 'Prix valables jusqu'au 31 mars 1990': no comment. What about RFA 2 per cent?)

Je vois. Je dois faire attention car j'ai toujours tendance à utiliser le mot rabais. Continuons! 'Franco de port à 3000 FHT': je suppose que cela signifie qu'il n'y a pas de frais de transport si la commande est égale ou supérieure à 3000 F. 'Prix valables jusqu'au 31 mars 1990': pas de commentaire. RFA, 2 pour cent: je ne connais pas ce sigle.

A RFA, c'est la ristourne de fin d'année qui est calculée sur la totalité du chiffre d'affaires réalisé par le client et réglée à la fin de l'année.

MD (There's more: 'règlement comptant 3 pour cent sous 10 jours ou traite à 60 jours fin de mois')

Et ce n'est pas tout! Le dernier point: 'règlement comptant 3% sous 10 jours ou traite à 60 jours fin de mois'.

A C'est ce qu'on appelle l'escompte. En fait, la différence qui existe entre toutes les autres réductions et celle-ci, c'est que l'escompte est une réduction financière qui est accordée pour paiement comptant ou avant la date d'échéance.

MD (That's my French lesson for today!)

Je crois que j'ai eu ma leçon de français pour aujourd'hui!

Language comment

- **Pas mal de . . .** is a colloquial expression, meaning 'quite a few, a lot of . . .'. In any formal situation, or when in doubt, use the more standard expression.

    Colloquial
    Nous recevons pas mal de commandes de l'Allemagne

    Standard
    Nous recevons un grand nombre de commandes de l'Allemagne.

    J'ai pas mal de problèmes.

    J'ai beaucoup de problèmes.

- **Une boîte** occurs in this sequence with its standard meaning of 'box, tin, carton'. You'll also hear it widely used in colloquial speech for 'company', or 'place of work' or in another context a 'disco'.

    ITM est une boîte internationale.
    Il a changé de boîte.

- Note that some adjectives have two meanings depending on whether they come before or after the noun.

    notre propre fabrication = our own manufacture
    une fabrication propre = a non-polluting system of manu-facturing

ma propre voiture =	my own car
une voiture propre =	a clean car
mon ancienne maison =	my old (former) house
une maison ancienne =	an old house

- Watch your pronunciation! Peter would communicate even better in French if he remembered that:
  - you must pronounce the last **é** of the past participle, to distinguish **calculé** from **calcule**
  - many final consonants are not pronounced, eg: prix précis
  - consonants are usually pronounced when followed by a vowel, e.g.: there is liaison in 'les deux premières années'

Sketch: Un produit européen

With most of Europe moving towards a common market, the term 'made in Europe' may well become the norm. For Josianne and Albert, however, to be truly European a product must also be French, hence their interest in where the stylish flask comes from. Every nation seems to have its own view as to its importance to 'Europe'.

WORKING WITH AN AGENT

Key words and phrases

un machin	– a thing
un remontant	– a pick me up
avoir de la gueule	– to look good
dans le coup	– in on it
traîner	– to hang about

Business notes: Establishing a company

In this sequence, the giftware company Troïka has decided to adopt a hybrid scheme for its exports to France. Mainly to appear to be established in France and allay French customers' fears of trouble with customs procedures, it has set up a company Troïka France, a *Société à Responsabilité Limitée* (SARL). It has, however, appointed an agent (who has his own company – Franco-Britannique de Diffusion – and represents two other British firms) as its manager. The company does not hold stocks in France – deliveries are made from the UK within 3 weeks. It is domiciled in France, is subject to French commercial law and has a British firm of accountants in Paris looking after its accounting. Invoicing, etc., is carried out back in England, however, and it is precisely this arrangement which has caused most problems to Peter Osbourne's company.

Firstly, it took a matter of months before the company fully understood that the main form of payment in France is the *traite* (remember this is not a *guarantee* of payment but an *acknowledgement of debt* which can be recovered in French courts; payment by cheque essentially waives the right to insist on the payment of a debt). Having discovered its proper use, the company then used the wrong size of form (not all *traites* have the same format) and consequently its French bank's computer was unable to process them! Most important of all, the company failed to contact those customers who did not return the accepted *traite* within the customary ten days. It cannot be stressed enough that any action on the part of a British company in this respect will be quickly taken advantage of (small boutiques 'lose' the *traite*, etc.) and the consequence could well be thousands of pounds worth of stock lying around in France unpaid for. In Troïka's case, some *traites* which had been accepted by customers were rejected by their own banks, since they had insufficient funds to cover them. This is where the principle of a *traite* being an acknowledgement of debt (and therefore legally recoverable) is important.

VAT returns must be made monthly in France (payment is by the 20th of the following month). Failure to do so can incur immediate penalties (ten per cent of total payable) as the tax authorities (*le fisc*) apply the rules rigidly. (This system of *majoration* (increase) is widespread in France and is often applied not only by the tax authorities but also by all public utilities – telephone, water, electricity, etc. for all cases of late payment. There are no reminder letters!) This caused the second major problem for Troïka since communication between the UK headquarters and its accountant in France was slow, causing repeated delays in its VAT returns and thus incurring the consequent penalties (it is worth pointing out, too, that there is *no* exoneration from VAT for any company in France, whatever its size). Present VAT rates (1990) are 5.5 per cent, 18.6 per cent and 23 per cent (the latter being for luxury items and notably cars).

Whilst on the subject of taxation in France, the following major points should be borne in mind:

1. There is a greater multiplicity of taxes in France than in the UK, the most important being:

   - Corporation tax (*impôt sur les sociétés – IS*), currently (1990) standing at 37 per cent for companies reinvesting their profits and 42 per cent if dividends are distributed.
   - Local business tax (*taxe professionnelle*) which is calculated partly on rentable value of tangible fixed assets (buildings, plant, etc) and partly on the payroll – in this sense it can be seen as a tax on jobs and has consequently often been a bone of contention in France. The *taxe professionnelle* is payable to the local *communes* (of which France has more than all of the other EC countries put together, a fact which can lead to local in-fighting and conflict of responsibilities). In addition, also at the local level, there are *droit de mutation*, a transfer tax for land and buildings and the *taxe locale d'équipement*, a proportional tax on an investment project.
   - Apprenticeship tax (*taxe d'apprentissage*), levied on all companies employing more than 10 people, at the rate of 0.5 per cent of the gross wage bill. Twenty per cent of the tax must be spent on internal or external apprenticeship schemes and seven per cent is paid to Chambers of Commerce, which provide many different forms of vocational training in France. Companies can choose how to spend the remaining 73 per cent and many business schools rely on companies paying it to them to cover the bulk of their financial needs.
   - Training tax (*participation au financement de la formation professionnelle continue*). Again all companies employing more than ten staff are

obliged to pay 1.3 per cent of their gross wage bill towards the financing of training, whether internal or external. All of which entails detailed paperwork and a higher degree of bureaucracy than found in the UK. And, of course, to these taxes must be added social charges (*les charges sociales*) which are high in France (some 60 per cent of the direct salary). Taking all taxes together, they represent 44.3 per cent of GDP – the highest of the EEC countries (37.4 per cent in West Germany, 37.7 per cent in the UK). As can be seen, many legal considerations such as tax, consultation bodies, trade union rights, etc, are determined by the number of people employed, with the effective threshold levels being 10, 50, 100, 200, 500, 1,000 and 1,500 although there are many intermediate stages, all of which illustrates the legislative nature of the French business environment.

2. Accounts in France are essentially for tax purposes and hence there is a general tendency for profits to be understated. This is particularly important when acquiring a French company – assets (warehouses full of goods) might well be 'hidden' for tax reasons!

3. Whereas the British come to an agreement with the tax authorities on how much tax is to be paid, in France companies make their computation, file their returns and nothing happens... until the tax authorities suddenly decide to carry out a tax audit (*contrôle fiscal*). This is the medium used by the French administration to verify all forms of tax declaration made by individuals or companies relating to revenue taxes, wealth tax, VAT, stamp duty, etc. The process is usually triggered by an event which has brought the company or individual to the attention, not just of the tax authorities (*le fisc*) but of the French administration. Very often this is the French equivalent of Chapter 11 in the UK, the *Dépôt de Bilan* (filing for bankruptcy) which results in either a period of administration (*redressement judiciaire*) or liquidation (*liquidation judiciaire*). A *contrôle fiscal* may be caused by other events, however, such as constant lateness in filing VAT returns, etc. Penalties for tax infringements can range from fines to interest on late payment and tax increases.

When acquiring a French company, great care must be taken to ensure that there are no liabilities outstanding as a result of a *contrôle fiscal* and a suitable detailed warranty agreement (*contrat de garantie*) must be sought through lawyers working on behalf of the acquiring company. Without it no redress is possible against the vendors. It is also worth paying for reputable accountants but even these may miss certain points since in the case of many small and medium-size companies, the books

THE LANGUAGE OF BUSINESS

might not have been audited. In view of the problems which may occur, it is advisable to consider paying part of the purchase price into a blocked account until any risk has disappeared.

4. Returns must be made within three months of the end of the financial year, otherwise, as with VAT, penalties will be incurred.

To return to Troïka, its experience has taught it how complex administrative procedures in France are and that they need constant and careful attention. If a SARL is to be managed from the UK, then staff (with a knowledge of French!) must be appointed to deal with these procedures on a permanent, serious basis. Troïka has now employed someone with sole responsibility for the administration of its French operations, an absolutely essential measure if a company is to be responsible for the administration of its French company from the UK.

Agents

Much has already been said about the advantages and disadvantages of agents (and good ones are difficult to find!). In the case of Troïka's agent, a two-year contract has been signed. Many British companies believe that gentlemen's agreements are possible with French companies and no doubt many exist. Remembering the legalistic approach of the French, however, such an agreement may be highly dangerous, particularly when the British company believes it can part company with its French agent on good terms. There are many examples of such agents successfully suing their principals for loss of business, even when there has been no legal contract signed, and therefore terms and conditions have not been made clear. Legal advice **must** be taken, therefore.

Useful terms to remember in an agency contract are:

- *Le texte authentique* (authentic text). It is essential to know which text is legally binding if the contract is drawn up in both French and English.
- *Les obligations et les pouvoirs de commettant* (the duties and powers of the principal). A number of potential Troïka customers were approaching the company direct in the UK rather than going through the agent, Jean-Daniel Gaillard. A contract would normally cover this point. Such a clause will obviously affect the level of commission paid, however, in view of the higher degree of security bestowed.
- *Une clause 'ducroire'*. A 'del credere' clause whereby an agent is responsible for bad debts through insolvency.

- *La concurrence déloyale.* Unfair competition which will cover the use of trade marks (*marques de fabrique*), patents (*brevets*), etc.
- *Établissement d'une filiale.* Setting up a subsidiary deals with the rights of the principal to set up a subsidiary or other form of company or not. In many cases, an agent might usefully be employed or offered other sales possibilities within the new company, thus avoiding painful (to the principal!) termination of his contract.
- *Des rapports périodiques.* Periodical reports. These are important to show seriousness and to obtain on-going information about the market.
- *Un stock minimum.* Minimum stock. In the case of Troïka, no stock is held in France, as deliveries are made directly from the UK, thus avoiding capital being tied up in France.
- *Le chiffre d'affaires.* Minimum turnover with a stated rate of commission (*un taux de commission*).
- *Le service après-vente.* After-sales service and the provision of spare-parts (*les pièces de rechange*).

Distributors

The main differences between agents and distributors have been outlined in Chapter 3, but it is perhaps well worth making several final comments:

1. In the case of a consumer good (*un bien de consommation*) where a large number of sales outlets (*des points de vente*) are involved, a distributor may be a better bet than an agent, since by holding his own stock he is able to supply the market more easily.
2. With a distributor and therefore essentially one single client to pay for his goods, the danger of having many credit risks is avoided. Control may thereby be effected, however, since the distributor will then be responsible (and not the manufacturer or supplier) for determining the level of stocks to be held and therefore business to be generated.
3. A distributor may often expect a contribution towards the cost of advertising and promotion and this may present a difficulty to small companies.
4. The problem in France is often not one of finding distributors but keeping them! In many sectors (particularly, for example, in car parts and accessories) it is a very aggressive market and every effort has to be made to serve the distributor well (regular visits, after-sales service, help and advice with promotion, training, etc.).

THE LANGUAGE OF BUSINESS

Business Magazine 3: 'The Right Choice'

Whether to work with an agent, operate through a distributor, or set up your own company in France involves a complex set of decisions. In this Business Magazine you can hear how different companies, including Troïka, have made their choices.

Chapter 4

Business at a local level
'Mais on va travailler ensemble, de toute façon'

Introduction

Once you have set up a business in France, the problems are not over. Local customs, bureaucracy and habits all have to be taken into account. The problems are the same, regardless of the size of the company. However, do not think matters are difficult just because you are British – French companies trying to work in a different region can find local bureaucracy just as 'foreign' and usually employ a local fixer, who knows both the administration and the necessary people.

In this chapter you will:

- watch a major UK company, Norwich Union, as it negotiates the final terms of a contract for a new shopping mall in Grenoble;
- meet their letting agents Healey and Baker and see how they are forced to take local feelings and habits into account.

On the language side you will:

- revise the imperfect and perfect tenses;
- learn how to use the imperfect in clauses with 'if';
- discover how to refer to the immediate past;
- familiarise yourself with a number of different pronouns;
- extend your vocabulary using phrases with avoir;
- learn how to express disagreement.

THE LANGUAGE OF BUSINESS

Now watch the Working Together video sequence (10 47 02) using the key words and phrases below to help you understand the dialogues.

Key words and phrases

Dans la cour

le jeu de lumière	the lighting effects
effectivement	indeed
la verrière	the atrium
le soleil a du mal à raser l'immeuble	the sun hardly reaches the building
comment ça se raccroche sur le quartier	how it fits in with the area
une honte nationale	a national disgrace
je tiens à le dire	I insist on saying so

Pendant la réunion

nous avons ressenti le besoin	we felt the need
quelques risques (m) de dépassement	some risk of over spending
le pilotage	the supervision
un portage financier	a financing cost
le preneur	the tenant, candidate
l'entreprise générale	the main contractor
le gars (fam.)	the chap
aménager	to fit out
réceptionner	to take delivery of
voire même	even going as far as
le maître d'oeuvre	the project supervisor
sa coque	its shell
le mail	the mall
le chantier (m)	the building-site

Entrevue avec M. Bouvelot

la place se prête à	the square lends itself to
figé	fixed
des gens terre à terre	down to earth people
on se croirait revenu à la province profonde	one might think oneself back in the country

BUSINESS AT LOCAL LEVEL

Faux amis (pitfalls)

un engagement	a commitment, undertaking

Watch out for the following:

J'ai un rendez-vous à 8 heures	I have an engagement at 8 o'clock
Nous avons le plaisir de vous annoncer les fiançailles de notre fille	We have pleasure in announcing the engagement of our daughter
Le téléphone sonne occupé	The phone is engaged
sentir	to feel (as in 'to feel ill')
ressentir	to feel (the need for)

Listen and understand

After having watched the video sequence, try answering the questions in A1 and A2. Cover the answers in the right-hand column until you have answered all questions on your own and then compare the two.

A1 Getting the gist

1. Pourquoi le groupe se retrouve-t-il dans la cour?

Parce qu'il veut voir comment la verrière et la galerie commerciale s'harmonisent avec le site existant.

2. Pourquoi M. Andrew Percival a-t-il décidé de convoquer une réunion?

Parce que Andrew Percival et Norwich Union, la société qu'il représente, ont ressenti d'une part, le besoin d'avoir plus de précision sur les finitions de la galerie et d'autre part, ils veulent évaluer la situation au niveau du budget.

3. Pourquoi le problème de pilotage des travaux des preneurs suscite-t-il autant d'émotion?

Parce que normalement l'entreprise générale assure la responsabilité des opérations jusqu'au bout, mais dans ce cas précis, il a été décidé que le pilotage serait assuré par le maître d'oeuvre.

4. Quelle a été la réaction de M. Bouvelot lorsqu'on lui a demandé son avis sur l'emplacement d'une brasserie place Clavaison?

Sa réaction a été catégorique; M. Bouvelot ne ferait pas la brasserie à cet endroit-là.

A2 Getting the details

Dans la cour

1. En parlant de la construction de la verrière, quel est, d'après M. Andrew Percival, l'élément qui jouera un rôle essentiel?

D'après lui c'est la lumière, le jeu de lumière.

2. Est-ce que la cour est actuellement très ensoleillée?

Non, car le soleil a actuellement du mal à raser l'immeuble, c'est-à-dire qu'il a du mal à passer.

3. Comment réagit le représentant de Norwich Union lorsqu'on aborde la question des escaliers et en particulier un des escaliers?

Il admet qu'il n'a jamais compris pourquoi les autorités municipales pouvaient insister de garder un tel escalier. Pour lui, c'est une honte nationale.

Pendant la réunion

4. Pourquoi M. Cantais trouve-t-il impossible de faire les finitions?

Parce qu'on doit les faire en même temps que les preneurs font leur commerce.

5. L'engagement de livrer la galerie commerciale pourra-t-il être tenu?

Il semble que oui, puisque l'engagement était de livrer la galerie 17 mois après le début des travaux.

6. Quand les problèmes de finition dans les galeries commerciales surgissent-ils?

Ils surgissent quand on mêle le preneur et l'entreprise générale qui doit livrer le mail.

7. A quel problème est-on réellement confronté?

On est confronté à un problème de responsabilité.

8. De quoi faut-il convaincre M. Percival?

Il faut le convaincre que la solution proposée par M. Cantais est la seule pratique et efficace.

9. Pourquoi, selon M. Cantais, le problème se pose lorsque les preneurs viennent équiper leur coque?

Parce qu'il est difficile de les faire sortir lorsqu'ils sont là.

10. A quel moment est-ce que la situation devient ingérable?

Elle devient ingérable si on ne finit pas le mail à temps.

Entrevue avec M. Bouvelot

11. Pourquoi a-t-on prévu une brasserie dans le secteur indiqué par Mme Celia Berry?

Parce que la place Clavaison se prête très facilement à une installation sur la terrasse.

12. Quelle est selon M. Bouvelot l'erreur qui a été commise en voulant établir la brasserie place Clavaison?

L'erreur c'est qu'on veut essayer de changer la façon de vivre des Grenoblois.

13. Pourquoi n'y aura-t-il jamais aucun passage place Clavaison?

Parce que pour les Grenoblois, qui sont des gens un peu terre à terre, le centre-ville c'est place Grenette. Terminé!

BUSINESS AT LOCAL LEVEL

A3 Summing up the scene

Rewind the video and watch again the section where M. Patrice Cantais explains the problems involved in setting a completion date (10 51 50). Summarise this section using the phrases below.

Il faut savoir alors, ………., de dire aux gens qui ………. les boutiques, de ………. dire: "vous avez donc jusqu'à ………. et on ………. la boutique et ………. on vous la ………. le 1er septembre." Ça c'est ………. Mais c'est la seule ………. pour faire ………. Je ne peux pas faire ………. des ……….., des ……….., de l' ………. et de la ………. en même ………. que les gars qui ………. Parce qu'ils n'ont ………. pour ………. Et puis, ce n'est pas ……….

B Develop your skills

B1 The **imparfait** (imperfect tense) (Quand j'étais jeune . . .)

Formation

The imperfect tense is formed by dropping the **-ons** ending from the first person plural of the present tense and adding the endings **-ais, -ais, -ait, -ions, -iez, -aient**. The singular and the third person plural forms all sound alike although they are spelt differently.

    avons   avais, avais, avait, avions, aviez, avaient
    faisons   faisais, faisais, faisait, faisions, faisiez, faisaient
    finissons   finissais, finissais, finissait, finissions, finissiez, finissaient

The imperfect tense of the verb **être** has an irregular stem to which the regular endings are added.

étais, étais, était, étions, étiez, étaient

Use

The imperfect always translates 'was (were) doing' and 'used to do', 'would do':

J'achet**ais** des pièces chez ITM.	I used to/would buy parts from ITM.

149

THE LANGUAGE OF BUSINESS

>   Elle attend**ait** notre colis. She was waiting for our parcel.
>   Quand j'ét**ais** jeune, j'all**ais** souvent en France. When I was young I often went (ie: used to/would go) to France.
>
> The imperfect tense is used to describe activities in the past. The word perfect means completed. Imperfect means not completed. Thus, the imperfect tense is used to indicate actions which started in the past but are not necessarily completed.

A vous

Now watch the video (10 53 30), and compare the following sentences with the video dialogue. Correct what is different from the recorded version. Pay particular attention to the verb endings. You can check your answers against the video transcript.

1. C'était pour ça que nous réglions le problème en disant ce que vous aviez l'air, disons, d'être d'accord là-dessus, ...
2. ... nous finissions la galerie en dehors de certains équipements qui ...
3. ... vous protégiez cette galerie efficacement, ...
4. ... ils la réceptionnaient, ...
5. ... nous savions comment ils étaient, ...
6. ... nous la protégions complètement au niveau tant des murs que des sols, ...
7. ... et nous donnions donc l'autorisation aux preneurs de venir, ...

B2 Habitual/repeated actions in the past

> Some common adverbial expressions which indicate continuance and are thus frequently used with the **imparfait** are:
>
> | | |
> |---|---|
> | toujours | always |
> | fréquemment | frequently |
> | d'habitude | usually |
> | quelquefois | sometimes |
> | de temps en temps | sometimes, from time to time |
> | tous les jours (lundis) | every day (Monday) |
> | en ce temps là | at that time |
> | chaque année (jour, mois) | every year (day, month) |
> | souvent | often |
> | régulièrement | regularly |

BUSINESS AT LOCAL LEVEL

> Ils **utilisaient toujours** le même transporteur.
> They always used to use the same transporter.
>
> J'**allais fréquemment** à l'étranger.
> I went abroad frequently.
>
> C'est vrai que **de temps en temps** nous **avions** des ennuis.
> It is true that from time to time we had difficulties.
>
> The imperfect tense is used to describe what people are doing rather than report what people did.
>
> Ils **parlaient** aux ouvriers pendant que je **discutais** avec l'ingénieur.
> They were talking to the workers while I was having a word with the engineer.

A vous

Put the verb below into the **imparfait**.

Example: Tous les mois, il .... son loyer en liquide. (payer)
Tous les mois, il payait son loyer en liquide.

1. Chaque mois, les ouvriers .... une grosse prime. (toucher)
2. D'habitude, le cloisonnement .... selon la demande du preneur. (se faire)
3. Nous .... souvent négocier les contrats nous-mêmes. (devoir)
4. Je .... régulièrement les travaux. (contrôler)
5. En ce temps là, les niveaux inférieurs .... déjà .... par des centres commerciaux. (être occupé)
6. Avouez que quelquefois vous ne me .... pas .... de tous vos projets. (tenir au courant)

Answers: *1. touchaient; 2. se faisait; 3. devions; 4. contrôlais; 5. étaient déjà occupés; 6. teniez pas au courant.*

B3 Description in the past (when time of starting is not indicated)

> The **imparfait** is also used to describe something in the past or to designate a condition in the past that no longer exists.

151

THE LANGUAGE OF BUSINESS

A vous

Find the French equivalents for the following expressions.

1. The weather was nice. *Il faisait beau.*

2. The prices were not shown. *Les prix n'étaient pas indiqués.*

3. She was interested in business. *Elle s'intéressait aux affaires.*

4. Miss Leclerc was ill *Mlle Leclerc était malade.*

5. There was a lot of traffic. *Il y avait beaucoup de circulation.*

6. The factories were well lit. *Les usines étaient bien éclairées.*

B4 Imparfait in 'if' clauses

Si + **on** or **nous** + imperfect tense can be used as a kind of imperative.

Si on discutait du projet? How about discussing the project?
Si nous discutions du projet? How about discussing the project?

A vous

Rephrase the following imperative sentences following the example.

Example: Discutons de cela la semaine prochaine. (nous)
Si nous discutions de cela la semaine prochaine?

1. Allons d'abord voir les escaliers! (nous) *Si nous allions d'abord voir les escaliers?*

2. Démolissons ce vieux mur! (on) *Si on démolissait ce vieux mur?*

3. Finissons les plafonds! (nous) *Si nous finissions les plafonds?*

4. Prévoyons des cloisonnements! (nous) *Si nous prévoyions des cloisonnements?*

5. Evacuons les gravats! (on)   *Si on évacuait les gravats?*

6. Commençons à en parler maintenant! (on)   *Si on commençait à en parler maintenant?*

Another example of the use of **si** with the **imparfait** is the following exclamation expressing regret:

Si seulement il avait le temps!   If only he had time!

Follow the model.

Example: Est-ce qu'elle parle français?
Ah, si seulement elle parlait français!

1. Est-ce que vous êtes en forme? (je)   *Ah, si seulement j'étais en forme!*

2. Est-ce qu'il sait ce qui se passe?   *Ah, si seulement il savait ce qui se passe!*

3. Est-ce que vous comprenez le plan? (nous)   *Ah, si seulement nous comprenions le plan!*

4. Est-ce qu'il veut apprendre une langue étrangère?   *Ah, si seulement il voulait apprendre une langue étrangère!*

5. Est-ce que nous pouvons commencer le 15 août?   *Ah, si seulement vous pouviez commencer le 15 août!*

6. Est-ce qu'elles font ce qu'on leur dit?   *Ah, si seulement elles faisaient ce qu'on leur disait!*

In the following sentences use **si** + **imparfait** followed by a conditional in the main clause. The various parts of these sentences are jumbled up: assemble them in a logical order, following the example below.

Example: je n'hésiterais pas/une assurance tous risques/à prendre/Si j'étais vous/
Si j'étais vous, je n'hésiterais pas à prendre une assurance tous risques.

153

THE LANGUAGE OF BUSINESS

1. modifier quelque chose/ce serait le local/Si je pouvais.

Si je pouvais modifier quelque chose, ce serait le local.

2. de démolir/il faudrait/de la municipalité/l'autorisation/Si on décidait/cet escalier.

Si on décidait de démolir cet escalier, il faudrait l'autorisation de la municipalité.

3. les faire sortir/Si/nous permettions/d'équiper/aux preneurs/leur coque/nous ne pourrions plus.

Si nous permettions aux preneurs d'équiper leur coque, nous ne pourrions plus les faire sortir.

4. à ma place/qu'est-ce que/vous étiez/Si/vous feriez?

Si vous étiez à ma place, qu'est-ce-que vous feriez?

5. la façade/serait/la cour était dégagée/beaucoup plus ensoleillée/Si/de la brasserie.

Si la cour était dégagée, la façade de la brasserie serait beaucoup plus ensoleillée.

6. changer/les commerçants vous seraient/la façon de vivre/reconnaissants/Si/elles parvenaient à/des Grenoblois.

Si elles parvenaient à changer la façon de vivre des Grenoblois, les commerçants leur seraient reconnaissants.

B5 Imparfait and passé composé

The **passé composé** and **imparfait** can occur alongside each other in an account of events. The **imparfait** is used to indicate that an action was in progress when another isolated action occurred, the **passé composé** is used to indicate the occurrence of this isolated finite action, without emphasising its duration.

A vous

In the following sentences, put the first verb into the imperfect to indicate the background action and the second verb into the perfect to indicate the action that interrupted it.

Example: Il ferme le magasin; j'arrive.
         Il fermait le magasin quand je suis arrivé.

1. Ils lisent le bilan; on entre dans le bureau. — *Ils lisaient le bilan quand on est entré dans le bureau.*

2. Je soumets un projet au chef; vous entrez. — *Je soumettais un projet au chef quand vous êtes entré.*

3. On range les dossiers; le téléphone sonne. — *On rangeait les dossiers quand le téléphone a sonné.*

4. Nous ne connaissons pas la nouvelle; elle nous en parle. — *Nous ne connaissions pas la nouvelle quand elle nous en a parlé.*

5. Vous discutez avec les ouvriers; l'accident arrive. — *Vous discutiez avec les ouvriers quand l'accident est arrivé.*

6. Il n'y a qu'une place de libre; je réserve ma place. — *Il n'y avait qu'une place de libre quand j'ai réservé ma place.*

B6 Immediate past

To indicate that an action has just taken place, you use the present tense of **venir** + **de** + **infinitive**.

So: Il est malade? Is he ill?
Mais **je viens de** le **voir** au café! But **I've just seen** him in the café!

A vous

Reply in the affirmative using the present tense of **venir de**.

Example: Avez-vous exécuté le sol? (on)
Oui, on vient d'exécuter le sol.

1. A-t-elle aménagé sa boutique? — *Oui, elle vient d'aménager sa boutique.*

2. Est-ce que vous lui avez donné votre avis? (nous) — *Oui, nous venons de lui donner notre avis.*

155

3. Est-ce qu'ils se sont installés dans la galerie commerciale?

Oui, ils viennent de s'installer dans la galerie commerciale.

4. Est-ce que vous vous êtes rendu compte que la galerie n'est pas au centre-ville? (je)

Oui, je viens de me rendre compte que la galerie n'est pas au centre-ville.

5. Vous avez réglé le problème d'étanchéité de la verrière? (on)

Oui, on vient de régler le problème d'étanchéité de la verrière.

6. Est-ce que vous leur avez expliqué le cahier des charges? (nous)

Oui, nous venons de leur expliquer le cahier des charges.

Similarly, **je venais de le voir** means I had just seen him. In this exercise use the imperfect of **venir de** to provide complementary information using the clues given in brackets.

Example: Le propriétaire a augmenté mon loyer. (je, aménager)
Et cela au moment où je venais d'aménager.

1. L'EDF a coupé l'électricité. (nous, commencer les travaux)

Et cela au moment où nous venions de commencer les travaux.

2. La banque a augmenté le taux d'intérêt. (je, emprunter une grosse somme)

Et cela au moment où je venais d'emprunter une grosse somme.

3. Il a décidé de se retirer du projet. (il, recevoir l'autorisation de construire)

Et cela au moment où il venait de recevoir l'autorisation de construire.

4. Vous avez fermé l'usine. (vous, faire des bénéfices)

Et cela au moment où vous veniez de faire des bénéfices.

5. Les commandes ont baissé. (l'on, engager 3 nouveaux ouvriers)

Et cela au moment où l'on venait d'engager 3 nouveaux ouvriers.

6. Elles ont démissionné. (elles, être promu)

Et cela au moment où elles venaient d'être promues.

B7 Disjunctive pronouns

The conjunctive pronouns (remember the 'football team' approach in Chapter 3) are always located very close to the verb. The disjunctive pronouns, on the other hand, are used apart ('disjoined') from the verb.

Some of the disjunctive pronouns or emphatic pronouns are the same as the subject pronouns.

Subject	Disjunctive	Subject	Disjunctive
je	moi	nous	nous
tu	toi	vous	vous
il	lui	ils	eux
elle	elle	elles	elles
on	soi		

The disjunctive pronouns are used:

- for one word answers:

    Qui veut partir? – Lui!   Who wants to leave? – He (does)!

- for emphasis:

    Moi, je continue, mais vous, vous pouvez arrêter.   I am continuing but you can stop.

- after **c'est** and **ce sont**:

    C'est nous qui travaillons dur et ce sont eux qui sont récompensés.   It is we who are working hard and it is they who are rewarded.
    (Note that the verb in the qui clause must agree with the subject.)

- After the prepositions (**chez, avec, de**, etc.):

    J'ai parlé avec elle.   I spoke to her.

- After a comparison:

    Elle est plus intelligente que lui.   She is more intelligent than he is.

- As a part of a compound subject:

    Vous et moi, nous avons mérité un jour de congé.   You and I have earned a day off.

THE LANGUAGE OF BUSINESS

> • In confirmation with même:
>
> | | | | |
> |---|---|---|---|
> | moi-même | myself | nous-mêmes | ourselves |
> | toi-même | yourself | vous-même(s) | yourself, yourselves |
> | lui-même | himself | eux-mêmes | themselves |
> | elle-même | herself | elles-mêmes | themselves |
>
> J'enverrai la télécopie **moi-même**. – I will sent the fax myself.
> **Soi** is used when the subject is general: **on, chacun, nul, personne**, etc.
> Chacun pour **soi**. – Each one for himself.

A vous

Reply in the affirmative using a pronoun, as in the example.

Example: Vous êtes allé manger chez les Dupont, n'est-ce pas?
Oui, je suis allé manger chez eux.

1. Qui m'a téléphoné? Le réprésentant, n'est-ce pas?

   Oui, c'est lui qui vous a téléphoné.

2. Il veut partir à l'étranger sans sa secrétaire, n'est-ce pas?

   Oui, il veut partir à l'étranger sans elle.

3. Vous restez? Et votre associé il part, n'est-ce pas?

   Oui, moi je reste, et lui il part.

4. Ce cadeau est pour les ingénieurs, n'est-ce pas?

   Oui, ce cadeau est pour eux.

5. Vous l'avez fait vous-même, n'est-ce pas?

   Oui, je l'ai fait moi-même.

6. Il est arrivé avant mon collègue et moi, n'est-ce pas?

   Oui, lui il est arrivé avant nous.

B8 Demonstrative pronouns

The demonstrative pronouns are used to replace a noun and are usually translated by 'this one', 'that one', 'these', 'those' and they are:

	Singular	Plural
Masculine	celui	ceux
Feminine	celle	celles

Demonstrative pronouns can be used in a number of ways.

- When followed by a relative pronoun (**qui, que, dont**) the demonstrative pronouns mean the person who, the one who.

Celle qui vient d'arriver c'est ma secrétaire.	The one who has just arrived is my secretary.

- Demonstrative pronouns followed by **de** can indicate possession.

Le local de M. Dupont et **celui** de M. Leclerc.	M. Dupont's premises and M. Leclerc's.

- The suffixes **-ci** (this) and **-là** (that) are added to distinguish between 'this one' (or 'these') and 'that one' (or 'those'), and to express 'the latter' and 'the former'.

Entre ces deux articles, je préfère **celui-ci**.	Of the two items I prefer **this one**.

Ces appartements sont jolis, mais **ceux-ci** sont plus chers que **ceux-là**.	These flats are nice, but **these** are more expensive than **those**.

When two things are mentioned, **celui-ci** means the latter and **celui-là** means the former.

M. Lejeune avait rendez-vous avec M. Dupont à 10 heures. Celui-ci est arrivé en retard.	M. Lejeune had an appointment with M. Dupont à 10 o'clock. The latter arrived late.

THE LANGUAGE OF BUSINESS

A vous

Answer the following questions using a demonstrative pronoun according to the model.

Example: C'est votre restaurant? (mon ancien collègue)
Non, c'est celui de mon ancien collègue.

1. C'est sa brasserie? (son mari)   *Non, c'est celle de son mari.*

2. Ce sont vos produits? (nos concurrents)   *Non, ce sont ceux de nos concurrents.*

3. Ce sont vos nouvelles gammes? (nos concurrents)   *Non, ce sont celles de nos concurrents.*

4. C'est votre voiture? (ma société)   *Non, c'est celle de ma société.*

5. C'est votre bic? (mon assistant)   *Non, c'est celui de mon assistant.*

6. Ce sont vos livres? (de la bibliothèque)   *Non, ce sont ceux de la bibliothèque.*

B9 Possessive pronouns (mine, yours, his, etc):

Possessive pronouns are used to replace the construction possessive adjective and noun, or, more generally when ownership needs to be indicated. In French, the possessive pronoun agrees with the being or thing owned, not the owner.

Masc.	Fem.	Plural	
le mien	la mienne	les miens/les miennes	mine
le tien	la tienne	les tiens/les tiennes	yours (fam)
le sien	la sienne	les siens/les siennes	his, hers, its
le nôtre	la nôtre	les nôtres	ours
le vôtre	la vôtre	les vôtres	yours
le leur	la leur	les leurs	theirs

eg: Votre ordinateur me plaît, mais je préfère **le mien** – I like your computer but I prefer mine.

BUSINESS AT LOCAL LEVEL

> In combination with prepositions **à** and **de**:
>
> eg: Votre méthode de production est différente de la nôtre.
> Your production method is different from ours.
>
> Comparé à la leur notre machine est démodée.
> Compared to theirs our machine is old-fashioned.

A vous

Answer in the affirmative or the negative, using the appropriate possessive pronoun.

Example: C'est leur sous-traitant? (non)
Non, ce n'est pas le leur.

1. C'est son paiement? (oui)   *Oui, c'est le sien.*

2. C'est notre client? (non)   *Non, ce n'est pas le nôtre.*

3. Ce sont ses dossiers? (non)   *Non, ce ne sont pas les siens.*

4. C'est leur boutique? (oui)   *Oui, c'est la leur.*

5. Ce sont vos factures? (oui)   *Oui, ce sont les miennes.*

6. C'est notre nouvelle installation? (oui)   *Oui, c'est la nôtre.*

This time, reply to the questions with the help of the words in brackets, as shown in the example.

Example: C'est votre appareil? (la secrétaire)
Mon appareil? Non, ce n'est pas le mien, c'est celui de la secrétaire.

1. C'est votre convocation? (mon chef)   *Ma convocation? Non, ce n'est pas la mienne, c'est celle de mon chef.*

2. Ce sont nos produits que vous refusez d'acheter? (votre concurrent)   *Vos produits? Non, ce ne sont pas les vôtres, ce sont ceux de votre concurrent.*

161

3. Ce sont vos collaborateurs? (mon collègue)

Mes collaborateurs? Non, ce ne sont pas le miens, ce sont ceux de mon collègue.

4. C'est sa société qui a déposé le bilan? (son agent)

Sa société? Non, ce n'est pas la sienne, c'est celle de son agent.

5. Ce sont les décisions des délégués syndicaux? (le conseil d'administration)

Leurs décisions? Non, ce ne sont pas les leurs, ce sont celles du conseil d'administration.

6. Ce sont les règles de sécurité de votre usine? (l'inspection du travail)

Nos règles? Non, ce ne sont pas les nôtres, ce sont celles de l'inspection du travail.

B10 Indefinite pronouns and indefinite adjectives

Aucun(e) — anyone, none
Aucun(e) ...... **ne** — no

Look at the following examples of how these are used:

Aucun d'eux **n'**est arrivé.	None of them arrived.
Aucune d'elles **n'**est arrivée.	None of them arrived.
Avez-vous des difficultés?	Do you have any difficulties?
Aucune.	None.
Aucune solution **ne** peut être rejetée.	No solution can be rejected.
Il **n'**y a **aucun** problème.	There is no problem.

A vous

Fill in the blanks with the appropriate form of **aucun**.

Example: Les preneurs n'ont ...... respect pour les travaux des autres.
Les preneurs n'ont aucun respect pour les travaux des autres.

1. En .... cas, nous ne pouvons leur permettre de venir nous interrompre.
2. .... employée n'acceptera un tel travail.

3. Ça fait maintenant 8 mois que je suis vraiment dans le centre-ville et place Clavaison il n'y a ...... passage.
4. .... solution ne peut être envisagée sans l'autorisation de l'entreprise générale.
5. .... d'entre eux n'a pu nous donner satisfaction.
6. Il n'y a .... doute, nous livrerons la galerie commerciale pour la date prévue.

Answers: *1. aucun; 2. aucune; 3. aucun; 4. aucune; 5. aucun; 6. aucun.*

B11 Anything you can do . . . Indefinite pronouns

To say 'anyone can do it', 'put it anywhere', etc, in French, you use the following expressions:

n'importe qui	– anyone	n'importe où	– anywhere
n'importe quoi	– anything	n'importe quand	– anytime
n'importe quel(le)	– any	n'importe comment	– anyhow

Choose an appropriate expression from the above list to fill the blanks below.

A vous

Example: Si on n'a pas le temps de protéger le sol, le preneur qui aménage sa boutique fait ......
Si on n'a pas le temps de protéger le sol, le preneur qui aménage sa boutique fait n'importe quoi.

1. Vous pouvez poser la question à ...... Grenoblois.
2. C'est un excellent vendeur, il vendrait ...... à ......
3. Proposez une date. Nous sommes prêts à vous rencontrer .....
4. ...... ingénieur sait que notre produit est le meilleur.
5. Je leur ai dit que nous étions d'accord d'implanter une usine en France, mais pas ......
6. Vous pouvez constater vous-même que le travail a été fait ......

Answers: *1. n'importe quel; 2. n'importe quoi, n'importe qui; 3. n'importe quand; 4. n'importe quel; 5. n'importe où; 6. n'importe comment.*

C Extend your vocabulary

C1 Expressions with avoir

avoir faim	to be hungry
avoir soif	to be thirsty
avoir chaud	to be hot
avoir froid	to be cold
avoir raison	to be right
avoir tort	to be wrong
avoir . . . ans	to be . . . years old
avoir de la chance	to be lucky
avoir honte	to be ashamed of
avoir besoin de	to need
avoir mal à	to have an 'ache' (e.g. backache)
avoir du mal à faire quelque chose	to have difficulty in doing something
avoir l'air (de)	to look (to seem to)
avoir envie de	to feel like
avoir l'occasion de	to have the chance to
avoir lieu	to take place

Watch your pronunciation: **faim** is pronounced like **la fin** (ending) not like 'la femme' (woman). The 'f' in **soif** is pronounced.

A vous

Using the list given above, fill in the blanks below.

Cela faisait quelques jours que j'........(1) de vous dire que vous..........(2) d'embaucher ce gars. Et puisqu'aujourd'hui j'..........(3) de vous en parler, eh bien, je vais en profiter. Mais surtout ne me dites pas que nous n'avons pas eu..........(4). Je sais que nous..........(5) d'urgence d'une personne supplémentaire, mais quand même! Je dois cependant avouer qu'à première vue le candidat......(6) d'être en bonne santé et en forme. Malheureusement pour nous, une semaine après il a commencé à se plaindre qu'il..........(7) au dos. Ce n'est pas étonnant puisqu'il........(8) 59 ans! Je suppose après tout que vous..........(9) à trouver quelqu'un de convenable.

Answers: *(1). avais envie; (2). avez eu tort; (3). ai l'occasion; (4). de chance; (5). avions besoin; (6). avait l'air; (7). avait mal; (8). a; (9). avez du mal.*

BUSINESS AT LOCAL LEVEL

Idiomatic expressions

en avoir pour son argent	to get your money's worth
en avoir pour un certain temps	to take a certain time, to need a while
en avoir marre (de quelque chose)	to be fed up (with something)
ils n'ont qu'à attendre	they'll just have to wait
il n'y a pas de quoi	it's alright, no problem, don't mention it
se faire avoir	to be had/done/cheated
qu'est-ce qu'il(s) a(ont)?	what's the matter (wrong) with him (them)?
qu'est-ce qu'elle(s) a(ont) cette(ces) radio(s)	what's the matter (wrong) with this (these) radio(s)?

A vous

Choose an appropriate expression from those above and adapt them where necessary to fill in the blanks below.

1. – Je vous remercie de tout ce que vous avez fait pour nous.
   – ....
2. Moi, j'ai très bien mangé. Les portions étaient copieuses et la qualité y était également. Bref! On ....
3. – Alors tu as fini?
   – Presque, j'....... encore .... 10 minutes.
4. Alors là vraiment! Une tournée pour 150F! Je crois qu'on ....
5. – Pourquoi tu ne viens pas avec nous?
   – Parce que j' ....des rapports ......terminer.
6. – ....?
   – Je ne sais pas, il était déjà de mauvaise humeur en arrivant.
7. ....cette machine? Il y a 5 minutes elle marchait très bien.
8. – Comment met-on en marche ce projecteur?
   – Vous n'..........appuyer sur le bouton.
9. J'..........vraiment..........de ce boulot, de cette boîte!

Answers: *1. il n'y a pas de quoi; 2. on en a eu pour notre agent; 3. j'en ai encore pour; 4. on s'est fait avoir. 5. j'ai des rapports à terminer; 6. qu'est-ce qu'il a; 7. qu'est-ce qu'elle a; 8. vous n'avez qu'à; 9. j'en ai vraiment marre.*

THE LANGUAGE OF BUSINESS

C2 Expressing disagreement

Gentle disagreement:

Non . . . pas vraiment	No . . . not really
pas tellement	not a lot, much
pas toujours	not always
Je ne suis pas tout à fait d'accord	I do not totally agree
Je ne suis pas très convaincu(e)	I am not very convinced
Je n'en suis pas sûr(e)	I am not sure (about it)
Ce n'est pas sûr (certain)	It's not sure

Strong disagreement:

Non . . . Je ne suis pas d'accord	No . . . I do not agree
Ce n'est pas vrai	That is not true
Absolument pas!	absolutely not!
Pas du tout!	not at all!
C'est une plaisanterie!	You must be joking!
C'est une blague!	
Vous vous moquez de moi!	You are having me on!
Vous plaisantez!	You are joking!
Je ne suis absolument pas de votre avis	I am of a quite different opinion.

A vous

Now take the part of B and express your disagreement to what A says, as indicated in brackets and using the above expressions.

1. A Pensez-vous que la galerie commerciale soit bien située?
   B ....(I am not sure)

2. A Seriez-vous intéressé à louer une boutique dans la galerie?
   B ....(Not really)

3. A Vous ne trouvez pas que les loyers sont raisonnables?
   B ....(Not at all! You must be joking!)

4. A L'accès à la galerie commerciale en voiture est bon, n'est-ce pas?
   B ....(I do not agree)

5. A On m'a dit qu'il y a un grand parking au centre-ville, c'est vrai?
   B ....(No, it is not true)

BUSINESS AT LOCAL LEVEL

6. A Vous pouvez faire un bon chiffre d'affaires à cet endroit.
   B ....(I am not convinced)

Answers: *1. Je n'en suis pas sûr(e); 2. Pas vraiment; 3. Pas du tout! Vous plaisantez; 4. Je ne suis pas d'accord; 5. Non, ce n'est pas vrai; 6. Je ne suis pas convaincu(e).*

C3 Problems, problems

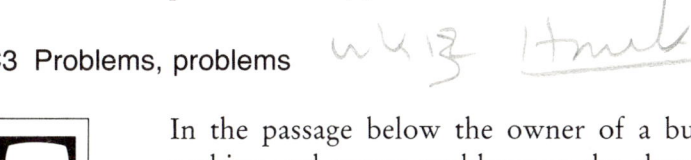

In the passage below the owner of a business is in a meeting describing parking and access problems to the shopping centre where his business is located. Before you read through the passage and try to fill in the blanks, watch the video sequence again (10 57 13), paying particular attention to the way in which people broach and articulate problems in French. Identify as many of the expressions below as possible and use them in the blanks below.

se rendre compte que . . .   régler un problème
résoudre le problème de . . .   le problème qui se pose est . . .
être confronté à un problème   se rendre compte
je propose que . . .   aborder une question (par tous les bouts)

traiter un problème
le problème auquel on vous   rendre le problème plus compliqué
demande de réfléchir . . .

Le problème qui ....(1) est celui du parking d'une part, et de l'accès au centre commercial d'autre part. Je ....(2) qu'on ....(3) les différentes questions séparemment car si on commence à les ....(4), le danger c'est qu'on ne s'y retrouve plus. Donc, je me propose de ....(5) en premier lieu le problème de parking. Parce qu'on est en centre-ville et qu'il n'y a pas de parking pour se garer à proximité, on est ....(6) à un sérieux problème. Ce qui ....(7) le problème encore plus compliqué, c'est le fait que la ville réalise actuellement d'importants travaux dans le secteur de la vieille ville. Alors là c'est simple, depuis que les travaux ont démarré le 27 avril nous avons eu une baisse du chiffre d'affaires de 50%. On ne peut même pas dire que les clients soient gênés par les travaux parce qu'on leur interdit l'accès du centre-ville, puisqu'on a fermé les sens de circulation qui pénétraient dans la ville. La seule solution envisageable pour ....(8) le problème de stationnement c'est la place Notre-Dame qui se trouve à proximité du centre-ville, mais pour que les commerçants ne crient pas trop on leur a

167

permis de garer leur voiture toute la journée. Donc, il me semble que la seule solution pratique à court terme pour ....(9) ce problème est de demander à la municipalité l'autorisation de stationner sur la place Notre-Dame qui se trouve à proximité du centre-ville. Je me ....(10) que ce n'est pas une tâche facile, mais le problème ....(11) pour la prochaine réunion est celui de l'accès de nos clients au centre commercial.

Answers: *1. se pose; 2. propose; 3. aborde; 4. aborder par tous les bouts; 5. traiter; 6. confronté; 7. rend; 8. régler; 9. résoudre; 10. rends compte; 11. auquel on vous demande de réfléchir.*

D Make your language work

D1 Contrat de bail commercial

The following document and checklist give you phrases and expressions used in letting contracts. Read them carefully before doing the exercises that follow.

ENTRE LES SOUSSIGNES

    M et Mme Jean PRALUS, Propriétaires, demeurant à ROANNE: 36, place des promenades

D'UNE PART

ET

    Madame BUISSON Marie-Claude, 55, rue Georges Clémenceau 69470 – COURS LA VILLE

D'AUTRE PART

IL A ÉTÉ FAIT ET CONVENU CE QUI SUIT:

Préalablement, il est expliqué que Mr et Mme PRALUS avaient consenti à Mr et Mme DEPIERRE en date à COURS le 19 MARS 1977 un bail concernant divers locaux situés à COURS : 55, rue Georges Clémenceau.

Ce bail avait pris effet le 1er JANVIER 1976 pour se terminer le 31 DECEMBRE 1984.

Madame BUISSON s'est trouvée aux droits de Madame DEPIERRE.

Les locaux loués se composent de :

– partie d'une maison d'habitation comprenant au rez-de-chaussée 4 pièces dont une servant de magasin.
– cave et grenier.

Ceci étant exposé, les parties conviennent de renouveler ledit bail pour une nouvelle période de NEUF ANNEES entières et consécutives prenant effet au 1er JANVIER 1985 (PREMIER JANVIER MIL NEUF CENT QUATRE VINGT CINQ) pour se terminer au 31 DECEMBRE 1993 (TRENTE ET UN DECEMBRE MIL NEUF CENT QUATRE-VINGT TREIZE).

Ces précisions étant apportées, toutes les autres clauses et conditions du bail sont inchangées à l'exception du prix fixé à la somme de F. 14.100,00 (QUATORZE MILLE CENT FRANCS) payable par SEMESTRE à TERME ECHU.

FRAIS

Le preneur paiera tous les frais, droits, honoraires et émoluments des présentes, et tous ceux qui en seront la suite et la conséquence sans aucune exception ni réserve.

Fait en double exemplaire, à ROANNE, le 25 MARS 1985.

Lu et approuvé pour le prix de quatorze mille cent francs par an.
Jules Vigne

Lu et approuvé

Lu et approuvé
Pierre Delof

Extracts of phrases used in lease contracts.

Durée. – Le preneur qui aura, seul, la faculté de dénoncer la présente location à l'expiration de chaque période triennale, devra signifier son congé au bailleur au moins six mois à l'avance par un acte extra-judiciaire.

...

Activités autorisées. – Le preneur déclare qu'il utilisera les locaux objet du présent bail, savoir:

Fonds de commerce de . . .

La destination ci-dessus est stipulée à l'exclusion de toute autre et sans que le preneur puisse changer cette affectation par substitution ou addition d'activités.

...

Etats des lieux – Entretien – Jouissance. – Le preneur s'engage:

1° A prendre possession des locaux qui lui sont concédés dans l'état où ils se trouvent sans pouvoir exiger du bailleur aucun travail de finition, de remise en état ou de réparations pendant la durée du bail, à l'exclusion des grosses réparations.

2° A entretenir les locaux loués en parfait état de réparation et de les rendre en fin de bail en bon état,...

THE LANGUAGE OF BUSINESS

> 3° A maintenir en bon état d'entretien, de fonctionnement, sécurité et propreté, l'ensemble des locaux loués, et à remplacer, s'il y a lieu, ce qui ne pourrait être réparé.
>
> ...
>
> Révision du loyer. – Le loyer sera révisé à l'initiative du bailleur tous les trois ans à la date anniversaire de la date de prise d'effet du bail d'après l'évolution de l'indice du coût de la construction du 4ème trimestre (l'indice de référence est celui du 4ème trimestre 1984 soit 773).
>
> Cession. – Le preneur a la faculté de céder son droit au présent bail pour la totalité des locaux loués, à l'acquéreur de son fonds de commerce ou de son entreprise, sans que le bailleur puisse s'y opposer ou prétendre à une quelconque indemnité.
>
> Etc.

Mme Buisson, the tenant, received from her landlord, M. Jean Pralus, a letter advising her of an adjustment in her rent. Although he has a right to do this, she is surprised. She leaves a note for her assistant to reply to M. Pralus' letter in light of her present situation.

Taking the part of her assistant, please write Mme Buisson's response taking into account the instructions she has left below. You could then try this as a telephone conversation – recording it onto your blank cassette. You'll hear a possible answer on the study cassette.

> Répondre à la lettre de M. Jean PRALUS du 14 mai 1990.
>
> Le 19 mai 1990
>
> 1. Lui signaler notre surprise de recevoir une demande de révision du loyer.
>
> 2. Lui rappeler qu'il avait promis de faire les réparations sur la façade (attendons toujours!).
>
> 3. Attirer son attention sur l'article 1° de la clause "Etats des lieux" selon lequel les grosses réparations sont à charge du bailleur.
>
> 4. En outre, la majoration du loyer excède le pourcentage de variation de l'indice trimestriel du coût de construction.

> 5. Demander l'autorisation de faire faire les travaux et déduire le montant de ceux-ci du prochain loyer.
>
> 6. Formule de politesse; veuillez croire etc.
>
> Important: lui envoyer lettre recommandée avec avis de réception.

E1 Putting across your point of view

You will have noticed that M. Bouvelot does not beat about the bush! To show his complete disagreement he uses expressions such as 'je ne ferais pas la brasserie..., il n'y aura jamais aucun passage, terminé!'. While it is sometimes useful for you to be able to recognise and express such strong disagreement, as a foreigner you may more frequently wish to express your reservations more discreetly. You should be frank in your exchanges with the French but politely so! To this end you will find a dialogue below which differs slightly from the original version on the video. You are asked to play the part of 'vous', paying particular attention to the ways in which one can put forward an argument in French and to the means of expressing reservations. Before attempting the dialogue, make yourself familiar with the expressions given below.

Je me permets de vous mettre en garde contre . . .
Mais je vous signale que . . .
Mais attention! Faites attention!
Mais je vous préviens que . . .
Je tenais simplement à vous prévenir de . . .
Un homme averti en vaut deux

Now listen to the dialogue on the study tape

Vous	La surface du rez-de-chaussée est de combien?
Lui	200 mètres carrés.
Vous	(And the first floor?) *Et celle du premier étage?*
Lui	Au premier étage, elle doit être à peu près de 330m².

THE LANGUAGE OF BUSINESS

Vous	(That makes 530m².)	Ça fait 530m².
Lui	Oui.	
Vous	(So from 530m² you're supposed to get a 'brasserie' for 250 places. That's a bit hopeful; as it stands, it'd be more like 150 which is ample for a town like Grenoble. The optimum number is 100. Unless you can sit outside…)	Donc, 530m² c'est une brasserie qui devrait faire 250 places. Je me permets de vous mettre en garde contre un optimisme excessif, mais telle qu'elle est conçue on ne dépassera pas 150 places, ce qui est largement suffisant pour la ville de Grenoble. Je dirais que le 'top' niveau d'une brasserie, c'est 100 places. C'est vraiment le 'top' niveau. Pour peu qu'on puisse mettre une terrasse…
Lui	Maître Kanter il a combien de places?	
Vous	(Maître Kanter has 450 places. But he's unique and it'd be a big risk to duplicate what he does. Someone has just started to try in the rue Alsace Lorraine with 450 places and they serve about seven customers a day for a meal!)	Alors Maître Kanter, lui, il a 450 places. Mais je vous signale qu'il n'y a qu'un seul Maître Kanter. Il y en a un et tous ceux qui essaieront de dupliquer Maître Kanter risque gros. Il y en a un qui vient d'ouvrir actuellement rue Alsace Lorraine avec 450 places. Il fait 7 couverts par jour!
Lui	Sept!	
Vous	(That's it: seven. 450 places and seven customers!)	Oui, sept. Il a 450 places et il fait sept couverts!
Lui	Il va donc se casser la figure.	
Vous	(Well, he knew that before he opened. Except in the centre of town, a 'brasserie'	Ah mais, il le savait avant d'ouvrir. Je dirais qu'une brasserie en centre-ville excepté, on pourrait aller un peu

172

BUSINESS AT LOCAL LEVEL

	could do well having more space, but it depends on the location.)	*plus loin en surface. Mais attention! pas n'importe où.*
Lui	D'accord. Donc à première vue selon vous c'est trop grand?	
Vous	(Much too big! 100 places, 250 – 300m² is quite sufficient for Grenoble. That way you can have a nice little business, the right number of customers without the disadvantage of heavy overheads on your premises . . .)	*Beaucoup trop grand! Je dirais que 100 places, 250 à 300m² sont amplement suffisants pour une brasserie à Grenoble. Ça permet d'avoir une exploitation saine, d'avoir de bons ratios et de ne pas être pénalisé par des charges commerciales trop lourdes au niveau de l'immeuble . . . .*
Lui	Puisque plus vous avez de surface, plus les charges pèsent sur l'exploitation. La surface au sous-sol ou au premier étage est quand même pondérée au niveau des charges.	
Vous	(Right, but I have to say that you can't use the whole of the ground floor. You can't put it to commercial use with that monumental stairway, or at least it'll be a real feat to fit it out.)	*C'est exact, mais je vous préviens que la surface du rez-de-chaussée ne sera pas entièrement utilisée. Avec cet escalier monumental qui est au centre, cette surface ne sera presque pas utilisée commercialement ou alors ça va être un casse-tête chinois pour l'aménager.*
Lui	Si je comprends bien, vous pensez que nous avons commis une grosse erreur en acceptant le défi.	

173

THE LANGUAGE OF BUSINESS

Vous (Let's put it this way, anyone taking on the 'brasserie' will have to fit out the first floor to get maximum returns from it. I just wanted to warn you of the risks. There's a French proverb which means 'Better safe than sorry.')

Disons que l'exploitant de cette brasserie va être obligé d'aménager son premier étage de façon à obtenir le maximum de rendement du premier étage. Moi, je tenais simplement à vous prévenir des risques. C'est tout. Ne dit-on pas en français: 'un homme averti en vaut deux'!

Lui Merci de vos conseils.

Language comment

Even the French can be imprecise in their use of language, when they get carried away. For example, **creux** means 'hollow', but in the context in which M. Cantais uses it in the video sequence it means 'empty' or 'cleared'.
  Furthermore, the phrase:

Le soleil a du mal à raser l'immeuble.

should really have been:

Le soleil a du mal à passer.

Gender faults are the most common mistakes foreigners make when speaking French. A few examples from the video sequence are:

un~~e~~ tell~~e~~ escalier	un tel escalier
c~~e~~ réunion	cette réunion
~~du~~ possibilité	de la possibilité

Another common mistake for foreigners is to forget to make the verb agree with its subject:

Not: Les gens qui passent à l'extérieur ~~va~~ effectivement . . .
But: Les gens qui passent à l'extérieur vont effectivement . . .

Sketch: mesures impériales

As far as Josianne and Albert are concerned it is 'typical of the British' to hang on to a different system of weights and measures. People in glass houses shouldn't throw stones, however, and many French still talk in old francs when buying a ten franc steak (un bifteck pour dix mille francs), or a half-pound of butter (une demi-livre de beurre), or in the North even a pint of milk (une pinte de lait):

Key words and phrases

un cadre	an executive manager
un petit truc	a little thing
prendre congé	to take one's leave

Business notes: Professional Services

Grenoble is the second largest town in the Rhône-Alpes region which ranks as the wealthiest and most dynamic area of France after Ile-de-France. Once known for its glove industry, Grenoble is now considered one of the high-tech centres of France and to back this claim, boasts the highest number of engineering students and researchers in the country.

It is a smart, elegant city and benefited greatly from the siting of the Winter Olympics in the area back in the 1970s. In recent times it has been endowed with the last word in tram systems, a fact which underlies the importance of the French transport industry and the seriousness with which the French view their pubic transport system.

It is because of Grenoble's wealth and spending power that Norwich Union has decided to invest in the development of a shopping centre (*centre commercial*) in the town centre. It is just one example of the way in which British financial services are expanding in the French market in niches which the French might not have hitherto spotted. The major French insurance companies, for example, are absent from this type of investment and Norwich Union has hence decided to go for further small shopping centres throughout France. In doing so, in the view of many international property developers, it has introduced new and high benchmark standards into shopping centres. And it is an area where, as Andrew Percival, himself a surveyor with Norwich Union, explains, British professionals may find a market for their activities, i.e. servicing British investments in France. Breaking directly as a consultant into the French construction sector may be difficult, however, since nearly all the specialist activities of surveying and engineering associated with a major construction project are often grouped together in France in a large one-stop *bureau d'études techniques* (BET – literally 'design office') in which generalist engineers (from *grandes écoles*) are employed and the demarcation between these activities is thus blurred. Quantity surveyors, for instance, are virtually non-existent as a separate profession. The *bureaux d'études* are often subsidiaries of large construction companies and there is not the same tradition in France, therefore, of the independent consultant to the client. To be able to offer the multi-purpose service required in France the separate UK professions would have to consider forming a single entity and working together or, preferably, teaming up with a French partner.

Other key niches can be found in the field of financial services (mortgages, consumer credit, insurance, etc.) but a careful examination of products and the distribution system for these services is needed. Such an analysis will reveal whether services can be marketed from a home base using direct or tele-marketing, whether a marketing arrangement should be made with a French company to 'swap' services or products, whether a subsidiary or sales office should be created (and maybe using France's Minitel system with three million subscribers) or a straight acquisition should be made (many French regional banks, for example, have been acquired by overseas investors keen to gain a toe-hold in France for pushing their products and testing the market). Norwich Union has had a base in France for some years but is still innovating, both upstream in its investments and downstream in its products. It is finding that sales by correspondence are particularly effective in a country so large geographically and with a low population density. So remember the key question to ask – where is the distribution coming from?

In other service areas, too, individual practitioners could well find a promising future in France, particularly since the mutual recognition of qualifications provided for in the Single European Act should sweep away any lasting vestiges of protectionism in the French professions. In accountancy, opportunities for English-speaking chartered accountants (*expert comptable*) are likely to be good, since comparatively few French graduates take up the profession due to its dowdy image, and the lengthy qualification period. In spite of French resistance, the large Anglo-Saxon firms are more and more predominant as businesses internationalise and seek accounting firms with the corresponding international expertise and experience. The French accounting profession is very different from that in the UK, however, in that an *expert comptable* (a practising chartered accountant working as a principal member of the pre-eminent body within the accounting profession, *L'Ordre des Experts Comptables*) cannot work in industry but only as an employee of registered companies of *Experts Comptables*. In addition, since 1 January 1978, no person can become a *Commissaire aux Comptes* (auditor) without being an *Expert Comptable.*

In the property development sector, many British companies (e.g. Jones, Lang Wootton) have been present in the French market for some time and now is a particularly good time in business property as companies are returning record profits and hence investing in new premises. One source estimates that as many as three out of four companies are contemplating making a move. Nowhere is this more noticeable than in Paris, particularly in the so-called 'Triangle-d'Or' (l'Etoile, Monceau and l'Opéra) but increasingly in the Austerlitz and Porte Maillot districts which some have dubbed the 'sites of the 1990s'. Some see the east of Paris at last taking off, no doubt due to the expansion of Roissy's activities, the Euro-Disney Park at Marne-la-Vallée and, generally, to the fact that it is closer to the rest of Europe, a factor continuously underlined by the French in the run-up to the Single Market.

Nor are the provinces missing out on the vigorous growth of this sector. Montpellier, Toulouse, Nice and Marseille are proving to be the most dynamic but in less economically advanced areas of France the trend is far less pronounced. The buoyant state of the market is generally considered likely to last until 1993 and is attracting the interest not only of British but American, Japanese, Swedish and Dutch operators. British architects could well find a niche here, too – particularly where British investments in France are involved, but the demand is so great generally that opportunities must occur with French clients.

At present, however, a French architect would still have to be used as a partner even on British projects since it is a profession which is still highly protected by French law in that application for the *permis de construire* (planning permission) can only be made by a French architect (in the UK anyone can apply). This is a good example of those entry barriers to the French profession which will have to be removed in 1993. The role of the architect is also much narrower in that he is limited to purely aesthetic matters and is not involved (apart from in the public sector) in the detailed management of projects as in the UK.

In the sequence showing the meeting between Andrew and the other parties involved, the atmosphere is fairly typical of a French business meeting with participants vigorously putting their point of view in a sometimes anarchic manner! Andrew is used to this, having spent some ten years in France, and knows well that patience is required. On occasions, he confesses, he is unable to chair such meetings when there may be a Frenchman present who considers he can only deal with the head person in Norwich Union, even though Andrew is the most technically competent. This again illustrates the importance of status in France.

In the final sequence, Celia Berry from Healey & Baker finds that good local knowledge of the market is essential, even if it seems to point in a direction opposite to what is planned!

Business Magazine 4: 'Professional Services'

The opportunities in France for individuals and companies offering a professional service, are fast developing. It's an area in which British experience is often highly valued. In this magazine programme you can hear British professionals who work in France talking about their jobs and the differences which result from being in a foreign business culture.

Chapter 5

The Tunnel and beyond
'Une connotation européenne'

Introduction

The opening of the Channel Tunnel will have a profound impact on distribution routes, not just across the Channel, but throughout Europe. The new system of motorways and rail links will allow people and goods to move quickly and efficiently from one side of Europe to another.

The Tunnel will also have an enormous effect on the communities at each end of the link. On the French side there has already been a drop in the number of people out of work in an area of traditionally high unemployment. As planned business parks at either end of the tunnel are built, there will be new opportunities for investment and employment.

In this video sequence you will see a number of French and English people visiting the Eurotunnel Exhibition Centre at Sangatte. They are receiving a presentation from Mr Bill Coleman of Eurotunnel about the likely impact of the tunnel on their business and their environment.

On the language side you will be learning:

- how to talk about industrial materials, machines and their operations;
- to change words using suffixes and prefixes;
- to make adjectives ending in 'able';
- to use the passive voice;
- to use prepositions with geographical names.

Now watch the video sequence on the Channel Tunnel (11 02 05). Use the key words and phrases below to help you understand the French dialogues.

179

THE LANGUAGE OF BUSINESS

Keywords and phrases

Salle de réception

directeur (m) de qualité	quality control manager
implanté à Calais	set up in Calais
l'industrie (f) pétrolière	the oil industry
des tunneliers (m)	tunnel boring machines (TBMs)
ces engins (m)	these machines
étanche	sealed
son homologue britannique	his British counterpart
démonter	to take apart
découper	to cut up
faire marche (f) arrière	to go backwards
basculer dans un trou	to tip up, empty in a hole
sain	healthy
propre	clean
une couche de craie (f) bleue	a layer of chalk marl
le sol	the soil

Salle de la maquette animée

une maquette animée	a working model
emprunter le tunnel	to enter/take the tunnel

Au fond du puits

au fond du puits	at the bottom of the shaft

Maquette du terminal de Sangatte

le terminal poids (m) lourds	the heavy goods terminal
traiter	to process
des navettes (f) à simple pont	single-decker shuttles
un péage	a toll
le poste de frontière française	the French border post
la ZAC (zone d'aménagement concerté)	a development zone

Entretien avec M. Bernard Weil

ce secteur sera réalisé en . . .	this area will be developed as . . .
l'informatique (f)	information technology
on n'aura pas à faire à	we will not have anything to do with

THE TUNNEL AND BEYOND

Sophia Antipolis

un cerveau	a brain
cela tient au fait que	that stems from the fact that
qui est propre à	which is peculiar to
la bande dessinée	cartoon strip

Faux amis (pitfalls)

un directeur	head of a department
un engin	machine, device.

A Listen and understand

Answer the questions on the tunnel sequence on your own – cover up the right-hand column – and then compare your answers to the ones given.

A1 Getting the gist

1. De quoi M. Bill Coleman parle-t-il aux visiteurs?

   Il leur parle de la technologie des tunneliers utilisée en France.

2. Quels types d'activités industrielles va-t-on implanter sur le secteur de Calais?

   On va y implanter des activités davantage destinées à des industries de pointe.

3. Quel est le concept de base d'une technopole?

   C'est le mariage de la technologie, de l'écologie et de la culture.

4. Selon M. Pierre-Henri Castets, quels sont les facteurs que les entreprises britanniques ne peuvent plus se permettre d'ignorer si elles veulent être présentes sur le marché européen?

   Ces facteurs sont la culture et la communication.

A2 Getting the details

Salle de reception

1. Où et par qui sont construits les tunneliers utilisés en France?

   Ils sont construits au Japon par Kawasaki et Mitsubishi.

THE LANGUAGE OF BUSINESS

2. Comment les engins utilisés du côté français diffèrent-ils par rapport à ceux utilisés en Grande-Bretagne?

Ces engins diffèrent en ce sens qu'ils sont entièrement étanches.

3. Comment les engins sont-ils détruits?

Soit on les découpe, soit on les bascule dans un trou.

4. La vitesse de progression des tunneliers est-elle la même des 2 côtés du tunnel?

Non, puisqu'elle varie selon l'état du terrain.

5. Quelle est la différence majeure entre les tunneliers utilisés par les Britanniques et les Français?

Dans les tunneliers utilisés par les Britanniques on est en contact physique avec le terrain alors que du côté français on est toujours à l'intérieur d'un cylindre.

Salle de la maquette animée

6. Que peut-on voir sur la maquette du terminal de Coquelles?

On peut voir circuler des trains.

Maquette du terminal de Sangatte

> 7. Utilise-t-on le même type de navette pour les différents véhicules?

Non, on utilise des navettes différentes selon le type de véhicule.

Entretien avec M. Bernard Weil

> 8. Quels types de commerces souhaite-t-on attirer autour du terminal?

On souhaite attirer des commerces qui soient thématisés sur les régions d'Europe.

> 9. Quant aux industries, se situeront-elles toutes dans le même secteur?

Non, on en trouvera quelques-unes dans le secteur situé derrière M. Weil, mais c'est surtout sur le secteur de Calais, que l'on voit dans le lointain, qu'elles se situeront.

Sophia-Antipolis

> 10. Les sociétés britanniques sont-elles bien représentées à Sophia-Antipolis?

Non, puisque M. Pierre-Henri Castets ne peut en citer qu'une seule, la société Wellcome.

183

THE LANGUAGE OF BUSINESS

11. Qu'est-ce que les sociétés implantées à Sophia-Antipolis ont en commun?

Ce sont des sociétés à culture multinationale.

184

A3 Summing up the scene

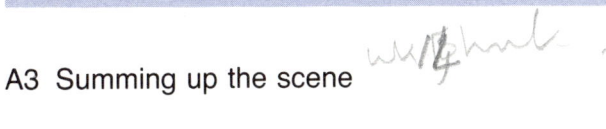

Watch once again the scene on the video (11 14 11) where M. Castets talks about the transformations businesses with a Commonwealth background will have to undergo if they want to play a role at European level. Then try to summarise the scene in your own words or by making use of the phrases below.

Culturellement elle évoluait jusqu'à ...., puisqu'il ...., or aujourd'hui elle ...., de nouvelles .... et pour cela même de .... Il faut que .... Un produit qui serait .... en Grande-Bretagne et qui .... Californien .... du fait de la grande tradition .... De la même manière, un produit qui .... ne passerait pas ...., d'où la nécessité de donner une connotation européenne à ....

B Develop your skills

B1 Direct object pronouns

me				
te	le	lui		
se	la	leur	y	en
nous	les			
vous				

The pronouns **le**, **la**, and **les** can be translated in the following way.

Le = it, him; la = it, her; l' = it, him, her; les = them

The direct pronoun **le** replaces masculine singular nouns; **la** replaces feminine singular nouns; **l'** is used before verbs beginning with a vowel; **les** replaces plural nouns.
  Note that the pronouns can refer to either persons or objects and that they immediately precede the conjugated form of the verb.

Je rends le livre aujourd'hui.   Je le rends aujourd'hui.
Nous regardons la voiture.   Nous la regardons.
Il n'écoute pas la radio.   Il ne l'écoute pas.
Il aide les filles.   Il les aide.
On va laver les mains.   On va les laver.
Pierre ne regarde pas Marie.   Pierre ne la regarde pas.
Marie voit Pierre.   Marie le voit.

THE LANGUAGE OF BUSINESS

A vous

Now answer the following questions using the personal pronouns **le, la, l',
les**.

Example: Où démonte-t-on le tunnelier? (au point de rencontre)
On le démonte au point de rencontre.

1. Où construit-on les tunneliers? (au Japon)

    On les construit au Japon.

2. Vous connaissez la bande dessinée Astérix? (Oui, je)

    Oui, je la connais.

3. Est-ce qu'on embarque les poids lourds sur des navettes à double pont? (Non)

    Non, on ne les embarque pas sur des navettes à double pont.

4. Sortiront-ils l'engin à la fin des travaux? (Non)

    Non, ils ne le sortiront pas.

5. Comment amène-t-on les déblais qui tombent dans la vis d'extraction vers l'arrière du tunnelier? (sur un tapis roulant)

    On les amène sur un tapis roulant.

6. Est-ce que les Calaisiens connaissent bien les Britanniques? (Oui)

    Oui, ils les connaissent bien.

Change the following sentences using the personal pronouns **le, la, l'** and **les**.

Example: On va devoir démonter la machine.
On va devoir la démonter.

1. Nous allons devoir arrêter le tunnelier.

    Nous allons devoir l'arrêter.

2. Le convoi va emprunter le tunnel.

    Le convoi va l'emprunter.

3. Il va falloir remplir ces trous avec du ciment.

    Il va falloir les remplir avec du ciment.

THE TUNNEL AND BEYOND

4. Ils ont pu voir la maquette animée.

Ils ont pu la voir.

5. On n'a pas pu commencer les travaux à la date prévue.

On n'a pas pu les commencer à la date prévue.

6. Soit on devra découper les engins, soit on devra basculer les engins dans un trou.

Soit on devra les découper, soit on devra les basculer dans un trou.

B2 The pronoun 'y' wk16

The pronoun **y** replaces a prepositional phrase introduced by any preposition other than **de** when the noun object is a thing. When **y** replaces the name of a place, it means 'there'.

À vous

Answer the questions below following the example.

Example: Depuis quand la société Brampton Reynolds est-elle implantée à Calais? (depuis bientôt cent ans)
Elle y est implantée depuis bientôt cent ans.

1. Pendant combien de temps avez-vous travaillé en Europe? (pendant 10 ans)

J'y ai travaillé pendant 10 ans.

2. Est-ce que le train entre dans le tunnel? (Non)

Non, il n'y entre pas.

3. Est-ce que ces engins peuvent résister à une pression hydrostatique de 11 bar? (Oui, facilement)

Oui, ils peuvent y résister facilement.

4. Reviendra-t-il à la question que je viens de lui poser? (Oui, un peu plus tard)

Oui, il y reviendra un peu plus tard.

5. Pensent-ils aux difficultés que nous pourrions rencontrer au démontage de la machine? (Non)

Non, ils n'y pensent pas.

THE LANGUAGE OF BUSINESS

6. Souhaite-t-on que les produits qu'on trouvera autour du terminal soient réellement des produits venant de ces régions? (Oui)

Oui, on souhaite que les produits qu'on y trouvera soient réellement des produits venant de ces régions.

B3 The pronoun 'en' wk 16

The pronoun **en** replaces a prepositional phrase introduced by **de**. It means 'of it', 'of them', 'from them', 'from these', 'some' or 'any'. It is used:

- in a prepositional sense;
  Vous venez **de** Lyon? Oui, j'**en** viens.
- in the partitive sense;
  Est-ce que vous buvez **du** vin? Oui, j'**en** bois.
- with expressions followed by **de**;
  Cherchez-vous **du** travail? Non, je n'**en** cherche pas.
- with expressions of quantity.
  Avez-vous **beaucoup de** problèmes? Oui, nous **en** avons beaucoup.
  Elle a **trop de** difficultés? Non, elle n'**en** a pas **trop.**
  Il a **deux** voitures? Oui, il **en** a **deux**.
  Vous avez **plusieurs** fournisseurs? Oui, nous **en** avons **plusieurs**.
  Vous avez **quelques** ennuis avec votre appareil? Oui, j'**en** ai **quelques-uns** en ce moment.
  Vous avez pris **quelques** commandes? Oui, j'**en** ai pris **quelques-unes**.

A vous

Answer the following questions using the pronoun **en**. Do not look at the answers in the right-hand column until you have completed the exercise on your own.

Example: Vous avez entendu parler de l'Université Ouverte? (Oui, je)
Oui, j'en ai entendu parler.

1. Elle fait de la publicité pour sa société? (Non)

Non, elle n'en fait pas.

2. Combien de voussoirs place-t-on par anneau de tunnel côté français? (six)

On en place 6.

3. Avez-vous des questions à poser? (Non)   *Non, je n'en ai pas.*

4. Vous avez un problème en ce moment? (Oui, nous, plusieurs)   *Oui, nous en avons plusieurs.*

5. Le tunnelier fait-il du bruit? (Oui, beaucoup)   *Oui, il en fait beaucoup.*

6. On trouvera des industries dans ce secteur? (quelques-unes)   *On en trouvera quelques-unes.*

B4 Prepositions with geographical names

The preposition **à** is used before names of geographical locations and cities.

Je vais **à** Paris.
Nous étudions **à** Cranfield.

The preposition **en** is used with names of feminine countries or continents. Almost all names of countries ending in an unpronounced **e** are feminine.

Ils iront **en** Afrique.
Nous habitons **en** France.

Exceptions: le Mexique, le Zaïre, ...

The preposition **au** is used with masculine countries, and **aux** with the masculine plural. All names of countries ending in a consonant are masculine.

Elle va **au** Brésil.
Vous allez **au** Canada.

NB: Remember that names of countries or continents are always preceded by a definite article

En superficie, **la** France est plus grande que l'Angleterre.
Le Chili est un producteur de vin.

THE LANGUAGE OF BUSINESS

A vous

Complete the following sentences with the appropriate definite article.

Example: .... Japon domine le marché des composants électroniques.
Le Japon domine le marché des composants électroniques.

1. Dans quelques années, le TGV assurera des liaisons vers.........Belgique.
2. Plus tard sans doute, le TGV assurera des liaisons vers ..... Pays-Bas et ..... Allemagne via Lille, mais aussi en direction de ..... Espagne, de ..... Italie et de ...... Suisse.
3. On voit un convoi qui va emprunter le tunnel sous la Manche vers ...... Angleterre.
4. ..... Grande-Bretagne n'apparaît pas aux yeux des Français comme étant un pays pro-européen.
5. British Rail a révélé le tracé d'une nouvelle ligne directe rapide entre le Tunnel et Londres, d'où les trains pourront poursuivre leur route vers les côtes Ouest et Est en direction des Midlands, du Nord et de .... Ecosse, et assurer la liaison avec ..... Pays de Galles et les lignes de ferries vers ..... Irlande.
6. Les exportations britanniques vers ..... Danemark se sont stabilisées.

Answers: *1. la; 2. les, l', l', l', la; 3. l'; 4. la; 5. l', le, l'; 6. le.*

Complete the following sentences with the correct preposition.

Example: J'ai l'intention de me rendre ..... Belgique le mois prochain.
J'ai l'intention de me rendre en Belgique le mois prochain.

1. Ce sont des tunneliers construits ..... Japon.
2. Ces engins diffèrent des machines que nous utilisons ..... Grande-Bretagne.
3. On a quand même une 'Robbins', une machine américaine qui est fabriquée ...... Etats-Unis.
4. ..... Suède et ..... Norvège on se préoccupe beaucoup de l'environnement.
5. Certaines sociétés anglaises sont déjà bien établies ..... Europe.
6. On implantera sûrement une nouvelle usine ...... Portugal.

Answers: *1. au; 2. en; 3. aux; 4. en, en; 5. en; 6. au.*

THE TUNNEL AND BEYOND

B5 How to express the passive

The passive is often used in technical and administrative language. It is formed by using **être** in the same tense as you would use the verb in the active sentence and adding a past participle, which agrees with the subject.

Le tapis roulant **remplit** les berlines à déblais.	The conveyor belt **feeds** the container trucks.
Les berlines à déblais **sont remplies par** le tapis roulant.	The container trucks **are fed** by the conveyor belt.

A vous

Transform the following sentences in the same way.

1. La machine met en place les voussoirs à l'intérieur même de sa structure.

   Les voussoirs sont mis en place par la machine à l'intérieur même de sa structure.

2. Des pompes de décharge contrôle la vis d'extraction.

   La vis d'extraction est contrôlée par des pompes de décharge.

3. La graisse à haute pression empêche l'eau d'entrer dans les travaux.

   L'eau est empêchée d'entrer dans les travaux par la graisse à haute pression.

4. La machine qui forme un bouchon gaine le tube du tunnel.

   Le tube du tunnel est gainé par la machine qui forme un bouchon.

5. Un petit train achemine les voussoirs vers la tête de forage.

   Les voussoirs sont acheminés vers la tête de forage par un petit train.

6. Un important train technique de 250m de long suit la machine.

   La machine est suivie par un important train technique de 250m de long.

THE LANGUAGE OF BUSINESS

When the initiator of the action is not specified, then there is no **par**... phrase. Turn the sentences below into the passive.

Example: On installe des dépôts de ce côté-ci de la Manche.
          Des dépôts sont installés de ce côté-ci de la Manche.

1. On fabrique presque tous les tunneliers au Japon.

   Presque tous les tunneliers sont fabriqués au Japon.

2. On utilise de nombreuses machines japonnaises dans la construction du tunnel.

   De nombreuses machines japonnaises sont utilisées dans la construction du tunnel.

3. On injecte de la graisse à haute pression à l'intérieur des joints

   La graisse à haute pression est injectée à l'intérieur des joints.

4. On traite les véhicules tourisme séparemment.

   Les véhicules tourisme sont traités séparemment.

5. On appelle la zone située autour du terminal de Sangatte la ZAC.

   La zone située autour du terminal de Sangatte est appelée la ZAC.

6. On entretient les machines régulièrement.

   Les machines sont entretenues régulièrement.

Reflexive verbs are often used in French to avoid overuse of the heavy passive form, and when there is no need to specify a subject. It's up to you to do the same now.

Example: Le terminal de Coquelles est vu de loin.
          Le terminal de Coquelles se voit de loin.

1. Notre nouveau produit est présenté sous forme de granulés.

   Notre nouveau produit se présente sous forme de granulés.

2. Cette plaque est vendue en feuilles de 50 × 50 centimètres.

   Cette plaque se vend en feuilles de 50 × 50 centimètres.

3. Ce nouveau plastique dont le point de fusion est situé entre 280 et 285°C, est employé dans la fabrication de composants électroniques.

Ce nouveau plastique dont le point de fusion se situe entre 280 et 285°C, s'emploie dans la fabrication de composants électroniques.

4. Ce matériau est caractérisé par sa haute résistance à la friction.

Ce matériau se caractérise par sa haute résistance à la friction.

5. Cette matière est obtenu par la calcination à plus de 100°C d'une argile pure.

Cette matière s'obtient par la calcination à plus de 100°C d'une argile pure.

6. Ces matériaux sont utilisés pour dégeler les routes en hiver.

Ces matériaux s'utilisent pour dégeler les routes en hiver.

C Extend your vocabulary

C1 Prefixes **dé**- and **re**-

A vous

Here is some more practice with the prefixes **dé-** and **re-**. Use verbs from the list below to fill in the gaps in the exercise.

charger	→	décharger	→	recharger
embarquer	→	débarquer	→	réembarquer
chauffer			→	réchauffer
enclencher	→	déclencher	→	réenclencher
boucher	→	déboucher	→	reboucher
serrer	→	désserrer	→	resserrer
visser	→	dévisser	→	revisser

1. Les voyageurs .... sur une navette à double pont en France et .... 35 minutes après en Angleterre.
2. Pour .... les plats cuisinés, il suffit simplement de percer le couvercle avant de les passer au micro-ondes.
3. Cela ne m'étonne pas que le mécanicien n'a pas pu .... l'écrou à la main parce qu'il a été .... avec une clé.
4. Après avoir fait le plein d'essence, n'oubliez pas de .... le bouchon.

THE LANGUAGE OF BUSINESS

5. N'oubliez pas de .... les fissures avant de repeindre les murs.
6. C'est parce que le circuit a été surchargé que le disjoncteur a ....

Answers: *1. embarquent, débarquent; 2. rechauffer; 3. desserrer, serré; 4. revisser; 5. reboucher; 6. déclenché.*

C2 The suffix -able

The suffix -able is frequently used in technical or commercial language to describe the qualities of a product.

éjecter	→	éjectable
exploiter	→	exploitable
gonfler	→	gonflable
détecter	→	détectable
encastrer	→	encastrable
emboîter	→	emboîtable

A vous

It is up to you to form a suitable adjective from the list of verbs to complete the sentences below.

jeter, réparer, porter, plier, réutiliser, injecter.

1. Ce photocopieur .... peut être transporté par une seule personne.
2. Pour éviter les gaspillages, il suffit d'employer des matériaux ....
3. La vie du produit a été prolongée par le fait qu'il est ....
4. Les médecins considèrent que les produits .... sont mieux assimilés par l'organisme.
5. Ce briquet est bon marché parce qu'il est ....
6. Puisque cet écran est ...., il n'occupe pas beaucoup de place et peut être facilement rangé.

Answers: *1. portable; 2. réutilisables; 3. réparable; 4. injectables; 5. jetable; 6. pliable.*

C3 Compound expressions

New names have to be found for new tools, components, machines and new technologies. In French these often take the form of compound phrases.

194

THE TUNNEL AND BEYOND

The construction **noun + à + noun** is used to distinguish a tool, a machine, or any other item by its function. The preposition **à** can be paraphrased by **muni de, équipé de, formé de**.

A vous

Transform the following expressions as in the example below.

Example: Les freins équipés de disques.
          Les freins à disques.

1. Un roulement équipé de billes.   *Un roulement à billes.*

2. Un boîtier muni de fusibles.   *Un boîtier à fusibles.*

3. Une soupape munie d'une aiguille.   *Une soupape à aiguille.*

4. Un ressort formé de lamelles.   *Un ressort à lamelles.*

5. Un ascenseur équipé d'un piston.   *Un ascenseur à piston.*

6. Un treuil équipé d'une chaîne.   *Un treuil à chaîne.*

The construction **noun (adjective) + à + noun (adjective)** is often used when the characteristics (shape, nature of the material, particular device, etc.) of a particular product or process need mentioning.

Example: Une machine à commande
          numérique   a NC machine
          un moteur à courant continu a DC motor

The preposition **à** can be paraphrased by **se caractérise par, est caractérisé par, se distingue par**.

A vous

Transform the following phrases as in the example below.

Example: La section de cette lime est triangulaire.
          Une lime à section triangulaire.

195

THE LANGUAGE OF BUSINESS

1. La banquette de cette voiture est rabattable.	*Une voiture à banquette rabattable.*
2. Le micro-processeur de ce composant est intégré.	*Un composant à micro-processeur intégré.*
3. Le verrouillage de ce système est automatique.	*Un système à verrouillage automatique.*
4. Les pales de cette hélice sont métalliques.	*Une hélice à pales métalliques.*
5. Le débit de cette pompe est variable.	*Une pompe à débit variable.*
6. La bande de la carte est magnétique.	*Une carte à bande magnétique.*

C4 More compounds

In order to express the function of a particular machine, tool or instrument, you can use the construction **noun + à + infinitive verb**

Example: un fer à souder – a soldering iron

or **noun + de + noun,**

Example: une barre de guidage – a guiding bar.

The two elements of these constructions can be paraphrased by **sert à, permet de, est utilisé pour, est destiné à, est conçu pour.**

A vous

Find the appropriate preposition to replace the paraphrased expression.

1. Un appareil qui est destiné à protéger.	*Un appareil de protection.*
2. Un tuyau qui est conçu pour évacuer.	*Un tuyau d'évacuation.*

THE TUNNEL AND BEYOND

3. Une machine qui est utilisée pour laver. — *Une machine à laver.*

4. Un écrou qui est utilisé pour bloquer. — *Un écrou de blocage.*

5. Une pince qui sert à dénuder. — *Une pince à dénuder.*

6. Un banc qui permet de faire des essais. — *Un banc d'essai.*

7. Une machine qui sert à écrire. — *Une machine à écrire.*

8. Un fer qui sert à repasser. — *Un fer à repasser.*

9. Un système qui est conçu pour traiter des textes. — *Un système de traitement de textes.*

10. Un outil qui permet de fileter. — *Un outil à fileter.*

11. Un système qui est conçu pour gérer des stocks. — *Un système de gestion des stocks.*

12. Une machine qui sert à coudre. — *Une machine à coudre.*

D Make your language work

D1 How to talk about industrial materials, tools, parts, instruments, machines, etc., with a technical approach

Les matériaux industriels

- **description – aspect général**

  il se présente | sous forme de ...
  on le trouve | à l'état de ...

  Il est ... (adjectif de couleur)
  X est un métal de couleur ...

  Il est vendu (il se vend) | en feuilles
  on peut se le procurer | en tubes

- **propriétés**

    sa densité est de ...
    son point de fusion est de ...
    il fond à ...

    il est caractérisé par ...
    il se caractérise par ...
    ses caractéristiques sont les suivantes: ...

    il se moule (façonne) bien/mal
    il peut être moulé
    on peut le mouler

    ses propriétés | chimiques / thermiques | sont | médiocres / excellentes

- **obtention – méthodes de fabrication**

    il s'obtient par ...
    il est obtenu par ...
    on obtient le ... en calcinant (par calcination)

- **usages**

    ce matériau | sert à ... / sert comme ... / est matière première à ...

    on se sert de ... pour ...
    il est utilisé
    il s'utilise | pour ... / comme ...
    on l'utilise

L'outil, la pièce, l'instrument, la machine

- **origine**

    cette machine a été | conçue par ... / construite par ... / mise au point par ... / lancée sur le marché par ... / développée par ...

cette machine est	commercialisée par ... proposée par ... fabriquée par ...

- **description**

| cette machine | se compose de
est constituée de
comprend
comporte
possède | cinq éléments | qui peuvent
pouvant | recevoir ...
être munis de ...
être équipés de ... |

- **fonction**

| cette machine | a été conçue pour ...
a été construite pour ...
est destinée à ...
permet de ...
sert à ...
est utilisée pour ... |

- **contraintes d'utilisation**

| cette machine | doit toujours tourner
ne doit jamais tourner | à plus de
à moins de | 30 milles tours/minutes |

| on ne doit jamais | faire tourner cette machine
mettre en marche la machine | sans se servir de ...
sans utiliser ... |

on ne peut mettre en marche la machine que lorsque ...

| elle doit être | graissée
révisée
vérifiée | au bout de 10 heures de ...
toutes les 10 heures |

elle doit être soumise à ...

- **consignes de sécurité ou d'entretien**

| en cas de panne
en cas d'arrêt | vérifier le ...
vérifier que ...
bien vérifier que ... |

il est interdit de …
il est conseillé de …
attention, ne jamais …

lors de l'entretien | il faut toujours …

lors du nettoyage
- il ne faut jamais …
- on doit toujours …
- il est obligatoire de …

il convient de …
- car
- sous peine de
- sinon
- pour ne pas
- pour éviter
- pour réduire le risque de

- **utilisation**

introduire le … dans le … en …

après avoir placé le …
- contre
- entre
- sur
- sous

avant de …
- s'assurer que …
- vérifier au préalable que le … est bien …

attendre
- que le … pour …
- quelques secondes avant de …
- jusqu'à ce que …

exercer une pression sur …
appuyer sur …
- de façon à …
- de telle façon que …
- jusqu'à ce que …

pour …
- ne pas prendre appui sur …
- il est nécessaire de …

Les opérations

- **but de l'opération**

cette opération a | pour but de …
                 | pour objet de …

- **description de l'opération**

cette opération consiste à …

cette opération se fait | à froid
                        | à chaud
                        | à très haute température

elle se fait | à l'aide de …
             | en se servant de …
             | en mélangeant …

D2 Comment le dire en quelques phrases

In order to be able to give an adequate description of a product or relevant information on the use of this particular product to a third person, you will need to have some knowledge of the technical language used in these situations.

Depending on your level of French, you will have found the phrases in the checklist on p.197–201 either exhaustive or incomplete. Furthermore, depending on the type of product – which can range from a mass consumer product to a highly technical product – you will have to adapt or complete the checklist to suit your needs.

Because of this (and because we want to introduce you gradually to the use of technical language) we suggest you concentrate on some of the more general examples of the checklist. For the time being, concentrate only on the categories **origine**, **fonction**, **description** and **utilisation**. After all, it is not easy to talk about a product without knowing it in detail!

A vous

In this exercise we ask you to give a summary of the following short articles announcing the launch of a new product, using the above categories as a guideline. We have given you the summary of the first article as an example.

THE LANGUAGE OF BUSINESS

Example

Dégel

Fini, le sel dispersé l'hiver sur les routes gelées, efficace mais pas très écologique. Eco Dégel, développée par Retan, remplit la même fonction sans polluer. C'est une argile pure calcinée à plus de 100°C, et granulée en éléments de 3 millimètres de diamètre. Elaborée selon un procédé breveté, elle possède une multitude de petites cavités remplies d'air. Cette macro-structure confère aux granulés d'épandage une faible densité et des qualités antidérapantes. Le matériau dégèle jusqu'à moins 11°C et s'élimine par les canalisations ou s'intègre à la végétation. Retan, BP 86, Saint-Forgeot, 71400 Autun. Tél.: (16) 85-86-27-26.

Développée par Retan, Eco Dégel permet de dégeler jusqu'à moins 11°C. Il se caractérise par une faible densité et des qualités antidérapantes. Il s'utilise en hiver sur les routes gelées.

A vous

Four

Ce nouveau four construit sur mesure est destiné aux secteurs de la médecine, de l'électronique et de l'aérospatiale. Conçu pour des opérations de traitement thermique, il élimine toute contamination réciproque entre four et bain de trempe par lavage et dégraissage incorporés. La cloche possède plusieurs passages; l'un d'eux est destiné à assurer le cheminement, une sonde servant à soulever et abaisser la charge à traiter durant son transfert au bain de trempe (moins de 30 secondes). L'installation est pilotée par ordinateur et fonctionne de manière automatique.

Plastique

Hoechst lance en Europe un nouveau plastique, le Fortron, déjà commercialisé aux Etats-Unis et au Japon. C'est un sulfure de polyphénylène (PPS), matière thermoplastique partiellement cristalline dont le point de fusion se situe entre 280 et 285°C, ce qui permet de l'utiliser à des températures de 220°C et plus, dans la fabrication de composites de fibres de verre et de fibres minérales, et, à terme, dans la fabrication de composants électroniques.

Mannequin

20% des accidents de voiture se rapportent à des collisions latérales. Pour mieux les connaître et s'en protéger, les Britanniques procèdent à des simulations d'accidents sur le mannequin Eurosid, qui possède vingt et une voies de données transmises aux ordinateurs. Ogle a conçu le thorax et les épaules. Peugeot et Renault le cou et le pelvis, et les Hollandais de TNO l'abdomen. Eurosid est très sensible aux facteurs directement liés à la mécanique des dommages physiques (vitesse de choc, par exemple). C'est sans doute pour cette raison que les constructeurs d'Europe, d'Amérique du Nord, du Japon et du Canada réalisent actuellement des essais poussés avec son aide.

Carburateur

Des cyclomoteurs français seront bientot équipés de carburateurs réalisés en matériau plastique. La société Gurtner a développé un modèle où l'aluminium coulé sous pression est remplacé par un technopolymère, le Poclan, un polybutylènetéréphtalate modifié thermoplaste, renforcé de 30% de fibres de verre. Moulé par injection, il respecte 400 cotes différentes et intègre de nombreux éléments. ce qui réduit les coûts de production. Le matériau employé conserve une bonne stabilité dimensionnelle, tout en résistant aux attaques des carburants, des huiles ou autres produits chimiques.

D3 A presentation

You may, at some time, be called upon to describe a product or discuss a project in more detail. In the following exercise you are asked, therefore, to give a presentation on the Eurotunnel project on the basis of the notes below and the information provided by Mr Bill Coleman in the video sequence.

THE TUNNEL AND BEYOND

Use the details in the tunnel boring machine diagram on p.204 in combination with the checklist of phrases in D1 to explain the technical aspects of this project.

Taking the notes below as a starting point, you could, for instance, elaborate on the terminal site by talking about the activities taking place on either side of the Channel; by describing the equipment used on the French side and giving the reason for the choice of equipment; by explaining how the various vehicles will be transported, etc.

After you have prepared your presentation, record it onto your blank cassette and then compare it to our version on the study cassette.

NOTES: EUROTUNNEL

Longueur du lien fixe transmanche: circa 50 kilomètres (dont circa 38 sous la mer).

Emplacement des terminaux : Calais et Folkestone.

Forage: par onze tunneliers de part et d'autre de la Manche.

Nombre de tunnels: deux tunnels pour la circulation des trains (un dans chaque sens), et un tunnel de service (maintenance, ventilation et sécurité).

Trafic: ferroviaire (marchandises et voyageurs) et routier (passagers et fret; les véhicules sont acheminés à bord de trains faisant la navette).

Vitesse de circulation des navettes: 130 km à l'heure maximum.

Temps pour traverser la Manche: 35 minutes d'un terminal à l'autre.

Fréquence des navettes passagers: toutes les 15 minutes pendant les heures de pointe.

Fréquence des navettes poids lourds: toutes les 20 minutes pendant les heures de pointe.

Ouverture du tunnel: prévue en 1993.

D4 Instructions

Another aspect of technical language we would like to cover is the language of written, as well as oral, instructions. You have no doubt noticed that in written technical French only the 3rd person singular is used.

THE LANGUAGE OF BUSINESS

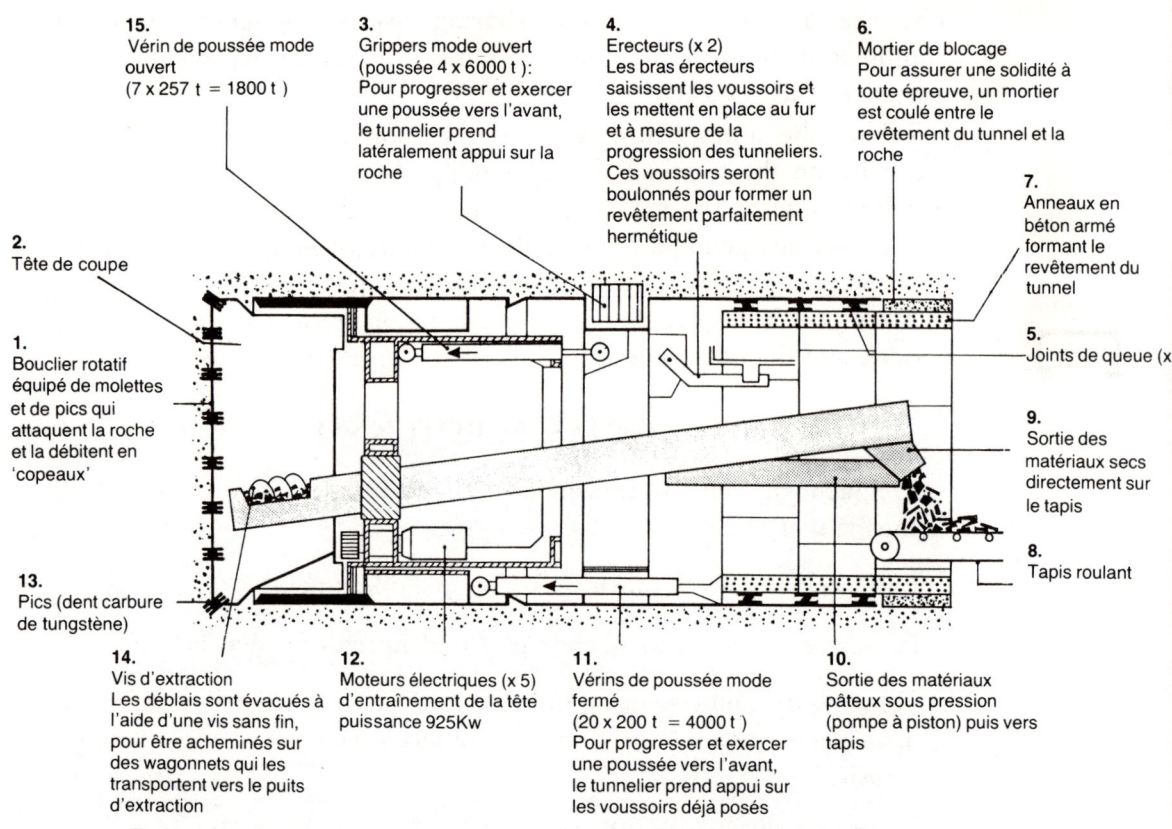

15. Vérin de poussée mode ouvert (7 x 257 t = 1800 t)

3. Grippers mode ouvert (poussée 4 x 6000 t): Pour progresser et exercer une poussée vers l'avant, le tunnelier prend latéralement appui sur la roche

4. Erecteurs (x 2) Les bras érecteurs saisissent les voussoirs et les mettent en place au fur et à mesure de la progression des tunneliers. Ces voussoirs seront boulonnés pour former un revêtement parfaitement hermétique

6. Mortier de blocage Pour assurer une solidité à toute épreuve, un mortier est coulé entre le revêtement du tunnel et la roche

7. Anneaux en béton armé formant le revêtement du tunnel

2. Tête de coupe

1. Bouclier rotatif équipé de molettes et de pics qui attaquent la roche et la débitent en 'copeaux'

5. Joints de queue (x

9. Sortie des matériaux secs directement sur le tapis

8. Tapis roulant

13. Pics (dent carbure de tungstène)

14. Vis d'extraction Les déblais sont évacués à l'aide d'une vis sans fin, pour être acheminés sur des wagonnets qui les transportent vers le puits d'extraction

12. Moteurs électriques (x 5) d'entraînement de la tête puissance 925Kw

11. Vérins de poussée mode fermé (20 x 200 t = 4000 t) Pour progresser et exercer une poussée vers l'avant, le tunnelier prend appui sur les voussoirs déjà posés

10. Sortie des matériaux pâteux sous pression (pompe à piston) puis vers tapis

The machine normally bears on the rock walls (in open mode) or behind, on the segments already in place when it is operating in closed mode in areas of water-bearing ground.

1. Rotating shield fitted with discs and picks which cut the rock and then reduce it to "slivers"
2. Cutting head
3. Grippers open mode (thrust 4 × 6000t):
   In order to advance and begin a thrust forwards, the TBM bears laterally on the rock
4. Erectors (×2)
   The erector arms take the segments and place them in position as the TBMs advance
   These segments will be bolted in order to form a perfectly sealed lining
5. Tail joints (×4)
6. Mortar
   To ensure solidity in any event, mortar is inserted between the tunnel lining and the rock
7. Reinforced concrete rings forming the tunnel lining
8. Conveyor belt
9. Outfall of dry materials directly onto the belt
10. Emergence of materials in pasty form under pressure (piston pump) then towards belt
11. Thrusters (closed mode)
    20 × 200 t × 4000 t
    In order to advance and begin a thrust forwards, the TBM bears on the segments already in place
12. Electric motors (×5) for driving the head power 925 kW
13. Picks (tungsten carbide teeth)
14. Extraction screw
    Spoil is evacuated using an endless screw and is directed towards trucks which transport it to the extraction shaft
15. Thrusters (open mode) 7 × 257 t = 1800 t

On utilise de la graisse spéciale pour ...
Il faut utiliser de la graisse spéciale pour ...

You may have also noticed that, as far as moods are concerned, the imperative only occurs in oral communication. The equivalent in written communication would be the use of an infinitive or the impersonal form.

oral:
Lis/lisez attentivement le mode d'emploi.

written:
Lire attentivement le mode d'emploi.
Il faut lire attentivement le mode d'emploi.

Before you tackle the exercises, look at the written and oral instructions on how to fix a pair of scales to a wall.

Written

Pour fixer la balance contre un mur, percer des trous aux emplacements indiqués et enfoncer les chevilles.

Ensuite, visser dans les chevilles les vis ci-jointes.

S'assurer que les têtes de vis dépassent de 1,5 à 2 mm.

Accrocher la balance.

Oral

Pour fixer la balance contre un mur, percez des trous aux emplacements indiqués et enfoncez les chevilles.

Ensuite, vissez dans les chevilles les vis ci-jointes.

Assurez-vous que les têtes de vis dépassent de 1,5 à 2 mm.

Accrochez la balance.

A vous

Now transform the written operating instructions for the Braun Multipractic Plus food processor into oral instructions using the imperative. Use the written instructions as a basis for your oral instructions.

Record your instructions on the blank cassette and then compare them to the solution we have recorded for you on the study cassette.

Remplissage
Suivant ce que l'on veut en faire, les aliments sont introduits directement dans le bol ④ ou dans le conduit de remplissage ⑤a.

Pour malaxer et pétrir
Pour malaxer et pétrir, utiliser le couteau ⑦. Le Braun Multipractic Plus pétrit toutes sortes de pâtes y compris des pâtes épaisses ou levées. Ne pas préparer plus de quatre pâtes à la suite.

- L'appareil permet de pétrir une quantité maximale de pâte calculée sur la base de 500 g de farine.
- Utiliser une quantité de liquide moins ¼ env. importante que pour une recette normale.
- Pour les ingrédients qui ne doivent pas être trop écrasés, comme les raisins secs, les amandes, les fruits confits, enclencher un court instant à la fin du processus de malaxage la vitesse instantanée.
- En ce qui concerne la pâte levée, par exemple pour le pain brioché, ajouter les ingrédients mentionnés ci-dessus à la main après avoir retiré du bol la pâte pétrie.

Produit et Mode d'utilisation	Durée
Pâte levée régime II	1 minute
Pâte brisée régime II	environ 1 minute
Pâte alimentaire (nouilles fraiches) régime II	1 minute

Pâte
On peut procéder de deux façons différentes:
a) Tout d'abord battre le sucre, les matières grasses et les œufs de façon à obtenir une mousse (env. 1 minute sur vitesse II). Ensuite, ajouter le lait puis faire épaissir avec la farine et les autres ingrédients avec précaution jusqu'à ce que l'ensemble soit parfaitement homogène.
b) Verser tous les ingrédients ensemble dans le bol ④. Ensuite, mettre en marche l'appareil sur vitesse II (au total 1 minute).

Pour broyer, mélanger et battre
Utiliser pour cela le couteau ⑦. Avec le Braun Multipractic Plus, on peut hacher la viande, les légumes, les fruits, les noisettes, les oignons et les fines herbes, broyer les purées ou les bouillies, préparer les cocktails.
Le tableau suivant fournit quelques indications relatives au traitement de différents aliments. Les meilleurs résultats s'obtiennent en respectant les quantités indiquées en exemple dans le tableau. Les durées d'utilisation indiquées sont des valeurs approximatives qui peuvent varier en fonction de la texture des aliments et du degré de finesse désiré.

- Lors du mélange d'aliments liquides, respecter la quantité maximale de remplissage: jusqu'au trait-repère sur le bol (le couteau étant en place).
- Pour la préparation de boissons à base de lait (milk-shakes) par exemple banane et lait, commencer en écrasant les bananes, puis ajouter le lait, le sucre, etc. Ensuite mélanger en ne dépassant pas 15 secondes.
- Les blancs d'œufs et la crème fouettée sont plus consistants que lorsqu'ils sont battus à la main ou avec un batteur mais ils se prêtent très bien à la décoration de gâteaux et de desserts variés. La quantité obtenue est cependant moins importante parce que les blancs ou la crème sont moins aérés.
- Pour battre des œufs en neige, prendre au moins 3 blancs. Pour la crème fouettée, utiliser au moins 0,2 litre.

Pour émincer et râper
Utiliser pour cela le porte-disque ⑧ avec le disque approprié ⑧b, ⑧c ou ⑧d (voir paragraphe «Montage»).
Le Braun Multipractic Plus permet de

émincer:
concombres, choux, betteraves rouges, carottes, oignons, pommes de terre crues, pommes, salades, poireaux;

râper:
fruits et légumes pour salades, bouillies, etc.;

râper
(avec accessoire en option): pommes de terre crues pour boulettes ou pour mousseline, raifort, fromage.

- L'appareil étant arrêté, introduire les aliments dans le conduit de remplissage ⑤a. On peut remplir au fur et à

THE TUNNEL AND BEYOND

mesure, en cours de marche (exception: pommes frites).

- Ne jamais mettre la main dans le conduit de remplissage ⑤a lorsque le moteur tourne. Utiliser toujours le poussoir ⑥ pour pousser les aliments (F).

- Lors de l'utilisation des disques ⑧a – ⑧d, utiliser l'appareil, le commutateur étant sur la position I.

Préparation des pommes frites
Le Braun Multipractic Plus coupe les pommes de terre à la dimension des pommes frites. Utiliser pour cela le porte-disque ⑧ et le disque pour pommes frites ⑧a (voir paragraphe «Montage»).

Important
Pour couper les pommes de terre crues en frites, il convient de respecter **absolument** les instructions suivantes:

- Placer le disque pour pommes frites IV dans la bonne position, c'est-à-dire pointes en bas.

- On obtient les meilleurs résultats en introduisant 3 ou 4 pommes de terre (suivant la taille) dans le conduit de remplissage ⑤a.

- Introduire les pommes de terre uniquement lorsque l'appareil est arrêté (**y compris lors du rechargement**) et placer le poussoir en exerçant une légère pression. Mettre l'appareil en marche et enfoncer légèrement les pommes de terre à l'aide du poussoir ⑥.

- **Travailler uniquement sur la vitesse I.**

- Ne pas trop remplir le bol.

The conversation is recorded on the study cassette at the end of this exercise.

E Dialogues

In the following role play, which you will find on the study cassette, you are asked to play the role of the Eurotunnel representative (ER) talking to a visitor (V). Use the English cues given below, as basis for your replies and press the pause button when it is your turn to speak.

V Alors, le tunnelier, pendant sa progression, met en place des voussoirs à l'intérieur même de sa structure. Où sont construits les voussoirs?

ER (A factory with five production lines is situated at the end of the site, 200m from the shaft. This factory produces lining segments for the six tunnels. These lining segments are stored for about thirty days at the surface and then taken down the shaft. They are transported to the cutting head on narrow gauge trains using special pallettes.)

Une usine avec cinq chaînes de production est au bout du chantier à 200m du puits. Cette usine sort des voussoirs pour les six tunnels. Les voussoirs sont stockés une trentaine de jours en surface et ensuite descendus dans les puits. Ils sont acheminés vers la tête de forage à bord de petits trains sur des pallettes spéciales.

207

THE LANGUAGE OF BUSINESS

V Combien de tunneliers utilisera-t-on pour creuser le tunnel sous la Manche, et l'équipage d'un tunnelier est constitué de combien d'hommes?

ER (A total of 11 TBMs will be used during construction, and each TBM has a team of 30 working in shifts round the clock.)

Au total, il est prévu d'utiliser 11 tunneliers. Chaque tunnelier fonctionne avec un équipage de 30 hommes se relayant de jour comme de nuit.

V Comment les membres de l'équipage se rendent-ils sur le chantier de forage?

ER (They are taken to the tunnel face by train. A special diesel rail car which travels at about 12 km per hour takes up to 22 men at a time.

Le transport du personnel est assuré par des navettes diesel spéciales qui se déplacent à une vitesse d'environ 12 km à l'heure et qui peuvent transporter jusqu'à 22 hommes par voyage.

V Y a-t-il des règles de sécurité particulières pour les hommes travaillant sous terre?

ER (Of course, before descending the shaft each worker takes a safety tag, leaving a duplicate behind at the surface, to show exactly where they will be

Bien sûr, avant de descendre dans le puits chaque homme doit se munir d'un badge de sécurité et laisser le double à la surface afin qu'à tout moment il puisse être localisé.

V Est-ce que tous les tunneliers fonctionnent de la même façon?

ER (No, geological conditions near the French coast mean the TBMs tunnelling from France have to be watertight. They operate in a

Non, les conditions géologiques du côté français sont telles que les tunneliers doivent être hermétiques/ étanches. Ils fonctionnent en mode

'closed' mode, which means the tunnel lining is erected inside the TBM, clear of the wet ground.)

'fermé' ce qui signifie que les voussoirs sont placés sans jamais être en contact avec les terrains aquifères.

V Lorsque vous déclarez qu'à la jonction, le tunnelier devra être démoli, je pense que vous évoquez seulement l'enveloppe extérieure, mais les parties nobles seront récupérées?

ER (The TBM interior is made up of modular components which will be dismantled and brought back to the shaft. Behind the cutting head there is a 250m train pulling fifteen or seventeen trailers which carry pumping equipment, electricity, etc., all of which will be retrieved.)

Tout le matériel à l'intérieur du tunnelier est modulaire et sera démonté et ramené au puits. Derrière la tête de cette machine vous avez un train technique qui fait 250m de longueur et qui comporte quinze ou dix-sept remorques. Chaque remorque ayant des services de pompage et de transformation électrique. Ce train complet bien sûr sera récupéré.

V Vous avez dit, Monsieur, qu'il y a 3500 ouvriers français. Ils habitent où, dans un village spécial à Calais?

ER (The people working on the tunnel here at Sangatte are generally local people. The Regional Council asked TML to employ up to 75 per cent of their workforce locally. TML did better than this and over 90 per cent of the workforce live in the area. There is no special village or large scale movement of the workforce.)

Les Français qui travaillent sur le tunnel ici à Sangatte sont en général des gens de la région. Le Conseil Régional avait demandé à TML d'embaucher des gens de la région, jusqu'à 75 pourcent de leur besoins. TML a dépassé ce chiffre, ils ont embauché plus de 90 pourcent de régionaux, ce qui fait que les gens rentrent chez eux le soir. Il n'y a pas de village ou de déplacement de main-d'oeuvre en masse.

V Faudra-t-il réserver sa place
avant d'emprunter le tunnel?

ER (No, the shuttle system for all road vehicles – both passenger and freight – is designed as a 'turn up any time' system which, under normal circumstances, will operate 24 hours a day.)

Non, le système de navettes pour tous véhicules routiers, aussi bien passagers que fret, a été conçu sur la base du principe 'arrivez n'importe quand'. Dans les conditions normales, ce système de navettes sera opérationnel 24 heures sur 24.

Language comment

Two words to take care with:

1. The word **directeur** has a variety of meanings:
   – it is used for the head of a department, so you have:

   directeur de marketing – marketing manager
   directeur de production – production manager
   directeur commercial – sales manager
   directeur du personnel – personnel manager
   (can also be: chef du personnel)

   – **directeur** on a board of directors = administrateur

   The equivalent of M.D. is **P.-D. G.** (= **Président – Directeur Général**). In the feminine you sometimes hear of Madame la Présidente – Directrice Générale (there are now quite a few of them in France), or else Madame le P-DG!

2. **Le poste/la poste** is an example of a word which changes meaning according to gender.

   le poste has several meanings:

   Passez-moi **le poste** 3432 = telephone extension
   La liste **des postes** vacants = vacancies
   Chercher **un poste** = to look for a job
   Un poste de douane = a customs post
   Un poste de télévision = TV set (also: un téléviseur)
   Un poste de secours = first aid post

Un poste budgétaire = a budget heading
Un poste de 10 heures = a 10 hour shift

la poste = post office
eg. mettre une lettre à **la poste** = posting a letter
la poste principale = the main post office.

Sketch: Routes sans Frontières

There have been so many attempts at building the Channel Tunnel that Albert doubts whether even this attempt will ever actually happen. And as the English worry about the tunnel letting rabies into Britain, so the French worry about all sorts of strange diseases finding their way back across.

Key words and phrases

avoir une peur bleue	be terrified
RATP – Régie autonome des Transports parisiens	Paris bus and underground company

THE LANGUAGE OF BUSINESS

Business notes: The tunnel and beyond

Undoubtedly one of the major events in the coming years, both in terms of engineering and of its significance to travel and trade, will be the opening of the Channel Tunnel in 1993. Its timing is even more appropriate since the Single European Market is officially to take effect at the end of 1992. At the same time, a European network of high speed rail links with the capitals and major towns of Europe has been proposed. This may be seen to bring a whole new dimension to doing business, not just in France but throughout Europe.

The services provided by the tunnel will be as follows:

- Cars, coaches and motor bikes will be carried on passenger shuttles between terminals near Folkestone and Calais. The journey time from one terminal to the other is expected to be 35 minutes, and shuttles will leave every 15 minutes at peak periods, with at least one per hour at night.
- Through passenger rail services between London, Paris and Brussels via Lille. The journey time will be about 3 hours from London and through services are also planned to and from other major cities in the U.K. These trains will travel at up to 300 kph on the new high speed line planned in France.
- Heavy goods vehicles will be carried on freight shuttles, on a concept similar to the passenger shuttles but capable of taking fully laden lorries of up to 44 tonnes in weight. Freight shuttles will leave every 20 minutes during peak periods with at least one per hour at night.
- Through freight trains will operate between major centres in Britain and Continental Europe.

The shuttle services and tunnel system are operated by Eurotunnel. The through passenger and freight services will be operated by the British, French and Belgian Railways but will be subject to Eurotunnel control as they pass through the tunnel.

Frontier controls for road traffic will be undertaken on the 'free exit' principle. This means that all vehicles will pass through both British and French frontier controls before loading onto the shuttles at the terminal of departure. There will be no further controls after they have left the shuttles on completion of their journey.

Immigration checks on nearly all through passengers will be undertaken on the trains in order to avoid departure delays. UK Customs and Excise have not found it possible to process passengers on the trains from London, as happens at virtually every other European frontier.

Infrastructure

The estimated 40 minute saving by using the tunnel may not, in itself, be very significant for a heavy lorry travelling from Manchester to Milan. The no-booking, on-demand service to be offered by the tunnel could, however, provide the incentive for a much greater movement of people and freight between the border regions of the two countries at either end. In particular, the Region Nord Pas-de-Calais is seen by the French authorities and French and British companies to be at a strategic crossroads in the Europe of the 1990s.

The Channel Tunnel is a major link in the European road and rail transport network, and the extent to which the regions of Britain and France benefit from it may depend on the infrastructure investment made to cope with a cross Channel traffic volume which is forecast to double in the next 20 years.

Roads are a crucial part of Britain's infrastructure, but the congestion in the South-East and around London compares unfavourably with the French government's intention to double the number of motorways by 1997.

The imbalance is more marked with the railways. In France, a network of high speed passenger lines is being built or planned. In the UK the through passenger and freight trains will have to use the congested Network SouthEast's lines into and through London before connecting to the faster lines radiating North and West from there.

Rail in continental Europe is seen as a means of reducing the number of heavy lorries on the roads as well as car and air congestion. It is also seen as being environmentally preferable in many instances. A modern rail network, capable of taking bimodal road/rail freight and with depots at strategic locations around the UK, should help the regions of the UK, as far as the North of England and Scotland, compete more effectively with their continental neighbours.

In the shorter term, such imbalances may influence yet more companies to see North-East France as an answer to British bottlenecks, with land prices there one-tenth of prices in Kent.

Calais

In the video sequence, the presentation focuses first on the construction of the tunnel works and, secondly, on the facilities to be provided in and around the terminal near Calais.

THE LANGUAGE OF BUSINESS

For the tunnel construction works in Britain, many specialist workers were recruited from all over the country and housed in a special village near Dover. In France, the rate of unemployment was so high that the Regional Council of the Nord Pas-de-Calais asked the tunnel construction contractors, Transmanche Link, to train and employ as much local labour (la main d'oeuvre) as possible. As a result, 90 per cent of the labour force was recruited from areas around Calais and generally live locally.

The terminal is situated at Coquelles, West of Calais, and will be connected by dual carriageways or 'autoroutes' through Dunkerque to Ostend, to Boulogne and Rouen and to Arras, Lille and Paris. The TGV line from the tunnel to Lille and Paris will have a station at Fréthun near the Coquelles terminal. All of these should be complete by the time the tunnel opens, providing the most modern communications for companies setting up in the area.

The last part in this video sequence features M. Weil, who is in charge of the Eurotunnel subsidiary *Société pour l'Etude et l'Aménagement du Terminal Transmanche (SEATT)*. This organisation is responsible for the development of a 500 acre site, a *Zone d'Aménagement Concerté (ZAC)*, designed to attract companies in the commercial and leisure sectors, as well as the high-tech and research end of industrial activity. Shops, a trade centre, warehousing and even an open university are planned, as well as hotels. Brent Walker is already present. Heavy industry is to be catered for on other sites.

There is some fear in the town of Calais at the prospect of the port losing a large slice of the income generated by ferry traffic. An association has therefore been formed between the authorities of the ports in Boulogne, Calais and Dunkerque to resolve some of the old rivalries that exist and, in particular, to find means of moving away from being highly specialist ports.

The prosperity of Calais has been built on ferry traffic. Deep sea freight traffic is low when compared with Dunkerque which, up to now, has monopolised such traffic, particularly through the growth of its industrial estates offering generous tax and other incentives. Calais has therefore built a new deep sea port area for the shipment of raw materials, and a subsidiary of RTZ has already been attracted to Calais by this. Boulogne intends to diversify from its traditional role as a fishing port, and is investing in some exciting new tourist attractions.

Thus, the building of the Channel Tunnel is perhaps responsible for creating a new dynamic and competitive spirit in the new economic and industrial development of the Region.

Sophia-Antipolis

The final part of the video sequence takes us to quite a different part of France, Sophia-Antipolis, a technology park situated to the West of Nice and close to Cannes, Antibes and Grasse. The park was set up some 20 years ago and is now the largest park of its kind in Europe. Like the Nord Pas-de-Calais region, it stands at a major crossroads, in this case between the East-West links to Italy and Spain with the Rhône valley running North. It is very much on the new TGV and motorway network, making it an attractive area for establishing a company.

The park covers an area of 3,500 hectares and brings together research centres, a business and engineering school and some 700 companies engaged in both research and production, all specialised in high-tech activities such as computers, telecommunications, electronics, chemicals, biotechnology, pharmaceuticals, etc.

Some 13,500 people are directly employed there and this number is forecast to increase to 20,000 by the year 2000. There are plans to expand the park even further to 6,000 hectares.

The park is perhaps typical of the shift in the industrial scene in France from the smoke stack industries of the North to the Sun Belt, or 'Garlic Belt' as it is affectionately known by the Anglo-Saxons. This area, together with the aerospace industry in Toulouse and Bordeaux and the computer and medical activities at Montpellier, attracts both managers and researchers, keen to enjoy the attractions of the south of France.

With the exception of Wellcome, which has a major establishment at Sophia, British companies have hitherto been strangely absent. Yet the attractions of its position cannot be denied, both from the point of view of lifestyle and, equally important, its strategic geographic position. American companies certainly have discovered its advantages as is demonstrated by the presence of Dow Chemicals, Texas Instruments, Digital Equipment, Rockwell and many more. Swiss (Nestlé), German, Japanese (Toyota) and Korean companies are well represented, too – and obviously the French with Thomson-CSF, France Telecom, Air France, soon to be joined by major insurance companies.

Whether leasing or purchasing land and/or property, prices at Sophia-Antipolis are some of the highest in France for such science parks, and are little different from Paris.

THE LANGUAGE OF BUSINESS

Typical 1989 prices per square metre are:

	Lease	Buy
Sophia-Antipolis	FF 650/720	FF 6,000/7,500
Paris	FF 600/750	FF 6,500
Grenoble	FF 370	FF 4,000
Lyon	FF 300	FF 3,000

It should be noted how much lower the prices in Grenoble and Lyon are, in spite of their high-tech and industrial activity.

Offices in the centre of Nice share the same distinction of being the most expensive outside Paris, compared with the more attractive Marseilles:

	Cost per square metre, 1990 prices
Nice	FF 13,000–30,000
Marseilles	FF 7,000–11,000

M. Castets, seen in this sequence, runs a small consultancy firm which helps companies, mainly in the telecommunications field, to find the right method of distribution and to train their staff accordingly. He is particularly interested in British companies since he believes that they need special help in understanding the nature of the French market, especially in the more Latin South where greater emphasis is placed on finding the right middleman, the right prescriber, who will be able to reach the final decision maker. In the UK, more stress is placed on promotion and publicity and in Germany on complying with the right standards.

Business Magazine 5: 'The Way In'

'The Tunnel' focuses with great interest on the Nord Pas-de-Calais region of France – our nearest neighbours. Many British companies are looking at this region to establish both distribution and manufacturing bases. In this magazine programme you can hear more about the opportunities that can benefit British companies with a European focus.

Chapter 6

wk 17 — 19

Establishing a bridgehead
'Les Britanniques débarquent'

Introduction

The Nord Pas-de-Calais region of France has proved an important area for businesses wishing to set up a base on French soil.

If this is the route you are planning to take, it will mean tackling the French legal system and learning to communicate effectively with local dignitaries, officials and even the press!

In this video sequence you will:

- see a UK company, Sandhurst, as it concludes a deal for the purchase of a plot of land
- watch the firm's managing director as he talks to a local mayor about possible future developments
- watch an advertising executive as he investigates the possibilities of finding a French market.

On the language side you will:

- practise the use of the conditional tense
- find out more about **qui, que,** and **lequel**
- learn to make comparisons
- learn how to get things done
- come to grips with some smooth talking.

Watch the video sequence 'Establishing a bridgehead' (11 18 15). Use the following key words and phrases to understand the video sequence.

THE LANGUAGE OF BUSINESS

Key words and phrases

Chez le notaire

un terrain	land, a piece of land
une parcelle	a plot
le cadastre	the land-register
le géomètre	the surveyor
le siège (= siège social)	the headquarters
formant le lot	making up the sub-division
par suite (f) d'une résiliation de vente	as a result of a sale falling through
il n'y a pas d'hypothèque	there is no mortgage
le permis de construire	the building permit
morceler (un terrain)	to divide up
le reçu du chèque	the receipt for the cheque
un lotissement industriel	land for industrial development

Les Attaques

des HLM (= habitations à loyer modéré)	council flats

Radio Métropolys

monter des affaires ensemble	to set up joint businesses
ce qui m'attire	what attracts me
un mouvement de fond	a groundswell
des problèmes avec le chômage	problems with unemployment
(NB trouver un emploi	to find a job)

L'agence Tam-Tam

l'industrie agro-alimentaire	agribusiness
les produits laitiers	dairy products
un éclairage très spécialisé	highly specialised lighting effects
dans/sur un rayon	in a department (of a shop)/on a shelf
ça fait hollandais	it looks Dutch

After you have watched the video sequence answer the questions below on your own. Then compare them with the answers in the right-hand column.

ESTABLISHING A BRIDGEHEAD

A Listen and understand

A1 Getting the gist

1. Pourquoi Messieurs Dean et Jenkinson se réunissent-ils chez le notaire?

Parce que la société Sandhurst veut acheter une parcelle de terrain dans la zone industrielle de Calais.

2. Après leur visite chez le notaire, avec qui vont-ils discuter?

Ils vont discuter avec le maire de la commune.

3. D'où vient M. Kusmirek, et que fait-il?

Il vient du nord de l'Angleterre et il fait partie de la direction d'une agence de publicité, l'agence Two Heads.

4. Dans quel but se rend-il à l'agence Tam-Tam?

Dans l'espoir d'établir des rapports entre les deux agences.

A2 Getting the detail

Chez le notaire

1. A qui appartient le terrain, et pourquoi?

A la ville de Calais, parce que le propriétaire précédant n'avait pas construit sur le terrain.

2. Sous quels délais la société Sandhurst doit-elle terminer de construire?

Dans un délai de 3 ans.

3. Si M. Dean veut céder une parcelle de terrain, que devra-t-il faire?

Il devra obtenir l'accord de la ville de Calais.

Les Attaques

4. Qui décide de ce qui peut se construire sur le terrain?

C'est la municipalité.

5. Quel genre d'habitation le maire est-il prêt à accepter?

Des maisons résidentielles ou semi-résidentielles, mais pas des HLM.

6. Et est-ce qu'on peut y construire des magasins?

Des magasins oui, mais on ne veut pas de supermarchés.

Radio Métropolys

7. Qu'est-ce qui attire M. Kusmirek au nord de la France?

D'un point de vue économique, il trouve que cette région ressemble au nord de l'Angleterre; d'ailleurs il y a habité il y a 27 ans.

8. Selon lui, est-ce qu'il y a une ouverture vers l'extérieur de la part des Britanniques?

Oui, selon lui, il y a un mouvement de fond parmi les hommes d'affaires britanniques.

9. En quoi le nord de l'Angleterre et le nord de la France sont-ils comparables?

Les deux régions souffrent d'un taux de chômage élevé.

L'agence Tam-Tam

10. Quels sont les domaines de spécialisation de l'agence Two Heads?

La publicité dans les domaines de la mode, de l'alimentation (ou du food!) et des produits médicaux.

11. Qu'est-ce que M. Kusmirek montre comme échantillons?

Il montre le packaging de certains produits laitiers.

THE LANGUAGE OF BUSINESS

12. Quelle est la question que son collègue français se pose en regardant la boîte?

Il se demande si elle conviendrait au marché français.

A3 Summing up the scene

In this sequence, you have seen two British businessmen, Tim Dean and Anthony Kusmirek, visiting the Nord Pas-de-Calais region for different reasons. Sum up briefly in French what each is doing. You can either do it entirely in your own words, or by using the outlines given below.

D'une part, il y a Monsieur Dean, directeur de _____ . Cette société, qui a déjà _____ à Lille, veut _____ dans les environs de Calais. Tim Dean est donc venu à Calais dans le but de _____ et de s'informer sur _____ .

Monsieur Kusmirek, d'autre part, est _____ qui souhaite _____ avec une agence française comparable. Monsieur Kusmirek a rendez-vous avec le responsable de l'agence Tam-Tam pour explorer _____ .

A4 English equivalents

You have already met Maître Morillon in his role as notary. He also runs an estate agency in Calais which aims at British people who wish to set up

222

ESTABLISHING A BRIDGEHEAD

a base in the Nord Pas-de-Calais area. Read the brochure below and try to suggest English equivalents for the services mentioned in it.

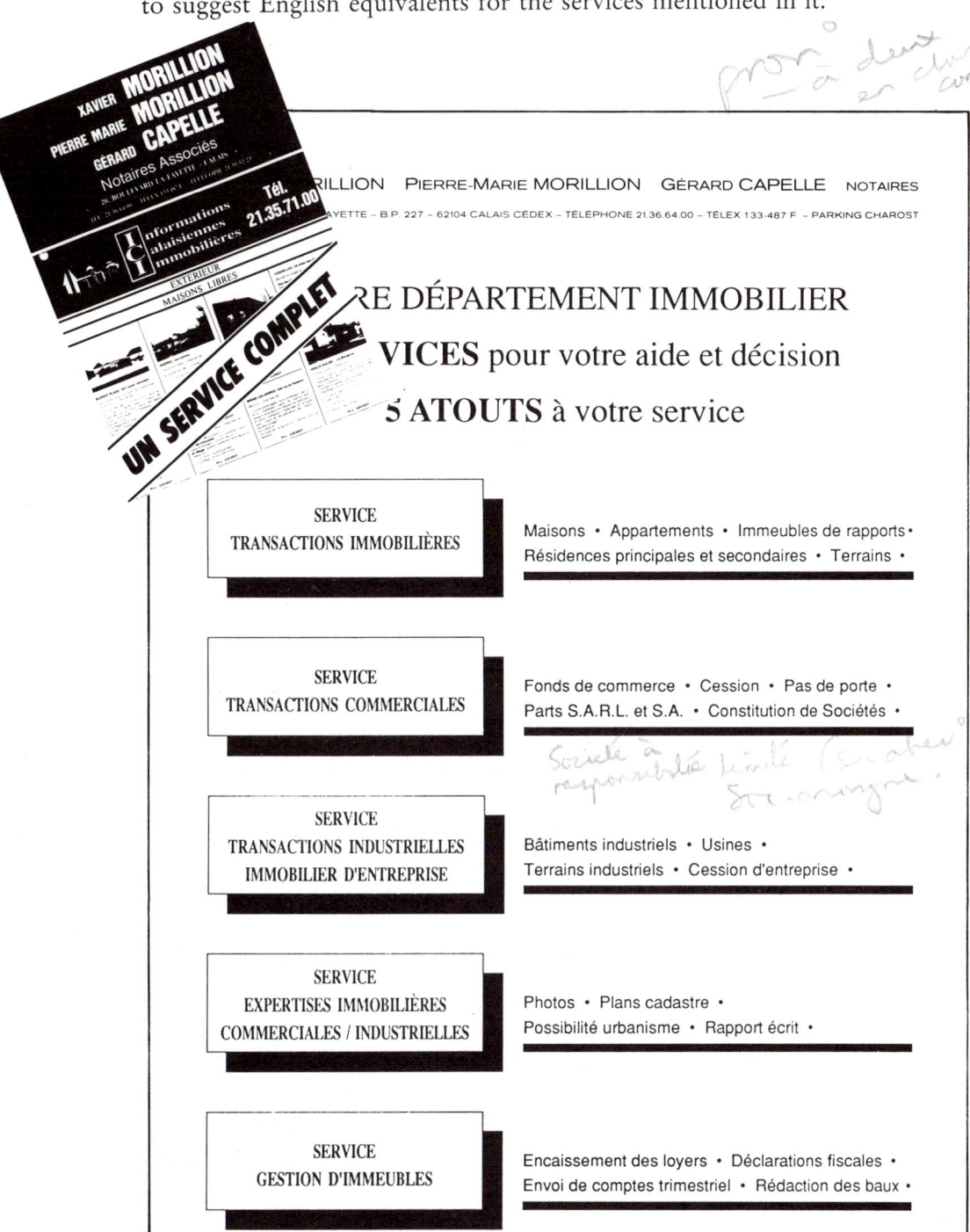

XAVIER **MORILLON** PIERRE-MARIE **MORILLON** GÉRARD **CAPELLE** NOTAIRES

...AYETTE – B.P. 227 – 62104 CALAIS CÉDEX – TÉLÉPHONE 21.36.64.00 – TÉLEX 133-487 F – PARKING CHAROST

...RE DÉPARTEMENT IMMOBILIER

...VICES pour votre aide et décision

5 ATOUTS à votre service

UN SERVICE COMPLET

SERVICE TRANSACTIONS IMMOBILIÈRES	Maisons • Appartements • Immeubles de rapports • Résidences principales et secondaires • Terrains •
SERVICE TRANSACTIONS COMMERCIALES	Fonds de commerce • Cession • Pas de porte • Parts S.A.R.L. et S.A. • Constitution de Sociétés •
SERVICE TRANSACTIONS INDUSTRIELLES IMMOBILIER D'ENTREPRISE	Bâtiments industriels • Usines • Terrains industriels • Cession d'entreprise •
SERVICE EXPERTISES IMMOBILIÈRES COMMERCIALES / INDUSTRIELLES	Photos • Plans cadastre • Possibilité urbanisme • Rapport écrit •
SERVICE GESTION D'IMMEUBLES	Encaissement des loyers • Déclarations fiscales • Envoi de comptes trimestriel • Rédaction des baux •

THE LANGUAGE OF BUSINESS

Answers

PROPERTY SALE AND PURCHASE	Houses · Flats · Investment Properties · Principal Residences and Holiday Homes · Building Plots ·
COMMERCIAL	Businesses · Assignments of Leases · New Leases · Shares in Companies · Company Formation ·
BUSINESS AND INDUSTRIAL	Industrial Buildings · Factories Industrial Plots · Sale of Businesses ·
VALUATION	Photographs · Land Registry Plans · Planning possibilities · Written Reports ·
PROPERTY MANAGEMENT	Rent Collection · Tax Returns · Quarterly Accounts · Drafting of Tenancy Agreements ·

B Develop your skills

B1 The conditional tense

The conditional, which is formed by adding imperfect endings to the future stem, (see Grammar Kit) can be used for a number of reasons. Firstly, to make requests or suggestions sound very polite; M. Coleman, about to explain the Channel tunnelling, asked those present to introduce themselves:

Je vous demanderais de bien vouloir vous présenter.

Secondly, the conditional is used to express something hypothetical, that has not taken place, but *would* do so, if the right conditions were met:

– Dans notre exposition nous souhaitons avoir des produits qui viendraient de toutes les régions d'Europe. (Ideally, they would come from all over Europe.)

> – Nous aimerions nous spécialiser dans le secteur de la mode. (If we manage to set up links here, it is in that area we would like to specialise.)
>
> It is common in French to see the conditional used to report an alleged fact, e.g. in newspaper headlines:
>
> > LE DOLLAR AMERICAIN SERAIT EN BAISSE (It is reported that ...)
> >
> > L'INCULPÉ AURAIT DÉJÀ CAMBRIOLÉ DEUX BANQUES (There is speculation that the police will question the accused about two previous bank robberies).

A vous

In the first group of sentences, put the underlined verb into the conditional, and then say which of the following nuances your sentence has:

a. deference to a superior at work;
b. politely hedging your bets;
c. polite request for information;
d. polite request for a favour;
e. deference to an important person.

1. Pardon, Madame, <u>pouvez</u>-vous m'indiquer le chemin le plus court pour le centre de la ville?
2. Nous <u>voulons</u> vous demander de nous accorder un prêt de 10 000 francs.
3. Ils <u>doivent</u> être en mesure de vous fournir les détails prochainement.
4. Monsieur le maire, mon client <u>souhaite</u> vous poser un certain nombre de questions.
5. Monsieur le Directeur, votre femme <u>veut</u> savoir à quelle heure vous pensez rentrer ce soir.

Answers: *1. pourriez-vous, c; 2. nous voudrions, d; 3. ils devraient, b; 4. il souhaiterait, e; 5. elle voudrait, a.*

THE LANGUAGE OF BUSINESS

> 'If I could, I would!'
>
> You need to be able to express conditions and reservations in French. Naturally, when a sentence has an 'if', there will sometimes be a conditional in the other part of the sentence. Look at these three common patterns:
>
> a. Si vous ne **construisez** pas, la municipalité **reprend** (ou: **reprendra**) le terrain.
>   (statement of fact)
> b. S'il n'y **avait** pas de restrictions sur cette zone, nous **achèterions** une parcelle de terrain.
>   (if there *were* no restrictions, we would buy ... but there are, so we won't!)
> c. Si le propriétaire **avait construit** sur le terrain, la municipalité **ne l'aurait pas** repris.
>   (If he *had built*, they *would not* have reclaimed it, but he hadn't, so they did!)

A vous

Decide whether the following sentences fall into category a, b or c, and conjugate the verbs accordingly.

1. Si son collègue n'avait pas compris 'food', M. Kusmirek (utiliser) le mot 'alimentation'.
2. Si un représentant de l'agence Tam-Tam venait à Hull, M. Kusmirek lui (montrer) la région avec plaisir.
3. Si la société avait eu une filiale en France, ils (pouvoir) éviter certaines difficultés de distribution.
4. Si vous voulez faire des affaires dans la région, il (être) tout à fait possible de vous aider.
5. Il aurait été mieux reçu s'il (traduire) ses brochures en français.

Answers: *1. c, aurait utilisé; 2. b, montrerait; 3. c, auraient pu; 4. a, sera; 5. c, avait traduit*
(Attention! The last verb is in the 'si' clause. Look at the pattern again if you have made a mistake.)

B2 Who's who and who's what

Qui (who), **que** (that) and **lequel** (which) are used to link phrases:

C'est un terrain qui appartient à la ville de Calais.

Le terrain que vous achetez est libre d'occupation.

You will notice that, in these sentences, **qui** links with the subject of the verb, and **que** with its object. In the second sentence, the underlying idea is that *you* (subject) are buying *the land* (object).

Vous achetez un terrain – Le terrain *que* vous achetez ...

After prepositions, you can use **qui** (or **lequel**) for a person and **lequel, laquelle, lesquels, lesquelles** to refer to inanimates.

L'agent comptable *à qui* nous avons parlé
La société française *à laquelle* nous avons écrit.

Remember that in the last sequence, Mr. Coleman started by saying:

Premièrement, je vous demanderais donc de bien vouloir vous présenter, Mesdames et Messieurs, et de nous donner quelques indications sur les sociétés pour lesquelles vous travaillez.

Remember: à + lequel → auquel
              de + lequel → duquel
              de + lesquelles → desquelles, etc.

But: for **de qui** and **duquel**, most French speakers use *dont*.

La banque à laquelle nous empruntons de l'argent ...
L'homme avec qui nous avons discuté
La société Sandhurst dont le siège est à Lille.

In questions you may find **qui, que** or **quel**.

THE LANGUAGE OF BUSINESS

> Qui est le responsable ici?
> (or, more usually: Qui est-ce qui est le responsable ici?)
> Que voulez-vous?
> (or, less abruptly: Qu'est-ce que vous voulez?)
> A qui faut-il s'adresser?
> Quelle est votre banque?
>
> We shall see in Chapter 7 that if you have **que + a passé composé**, you need to look and see if there's something preceding with which the past participle needs to agree:
>
> **Les échantillons que** vous nous avez récemment envoy**és** ...

A vous

Now you try filling in the blanks

1. L'étude de marché _____ nous avons entrepris _ est très encourageante.
2. Les tarifs _____ vous vous référez sont déjà périmés.
3. Le nouveau modèle sur _____ vous vous êtes renseigné vient d'arriver.
4. Les pièces de rechange _____ vous avez besoin sont prêtes.
5. La banque auprès de _____ vous avez déposé une lettre de crédit nous a téléphoné.
6. Nous avons bien reçu votre lettre du 9 mars par _____ vous nous informez de votre situation.
7. Il est parti en voyage d'affaires, au cours _____ il est tombé malade.
8. La première rencontre _____ a eu lieu entre le fournisseur et le client s'est révélé positive.
9. Le nouveau packaging, à propos _____ nous avons discuté à la foire de Toulouse, connaît un grand succès.
10. Les boîtes _____ vous vous intéressez ont un poids moyen de 200 grammes chacune.
11. La publicité de lancement, _____ le but était de faire connaître le produit, a coûté une somme énorme.
12. La compagnie avec _____ vous êtes en concurrence, est le sujet d'une OPA.
13. Les produits chimiques _____ résiste ce métal sont nombreux.
14. Le camion par _____ ont été transporté _ les plaques de verre est tombé _ en panne.

15. Votre facture, au sujet de _____ nous vous avons déjà téléphoné, n'a pas encore été réglé _ .
16. Voilà le chèque _____ votre conseil m'a donné.
17. Le lot _____ est indiqué ici est le vôtre.
18. C'est un mouvement de fond de la part des industriels britanniques_____ veulent travailler avec la France.
19. Elle est directrice d'une firme import-export _____ s'appelle "France-GB".
20. Votre télécopie _____ nous n'avons reçu que la première page a dû s'égarer quelque part.

Answers: *1. que, entreprise; 2. auxquels; 3. lequel; 4. dont; 5. laquelle; 6. laquelle; 7. duquel; 8. qui; 9. duquel; 10. auxquelles; 11. dont; 12. laquelle; 13. auxquels; 14. lequel, transportées, tombé; 15. laquelle, réglée; 16. que; 17. qui; 18. qui; 19. qui; 20. dont.*

B3 Making comparisons

Here is a checklist of useful structures for comparing quantity, quality, and anything from products to regions of a country.

- **Similarity**

La Bretagne | *ressemble à* / *est très semblable à* | la Cornouaille.

Les deux régions | *se ressemblent* / *ont beaucoup en commun.*

Elles ont | *des problèmes pareils/identiques.* / *les mêmes problèmes.*

Cela *ressemble beaucoup à* du cuir.
C'est *une espèce de* plastique.
Mais *on dirait* du cuir.

Ces deux machines ont | *la même* hauteur; / *le même* poids;

l'une est *aussi haute que* l'autre/l'une pèse *autant que* l'autre.

La première se chauffe *aussi* rapidement *que* la deuxième.

- **Difference**

Il ne s'agit pas de la même chose.
Cela varie selon les régions.
Ce n'est pas du tout comparable.

- **More or less**

plus / moins —— que | inférieur / supérieur | à

Cette marque est | *inférieure à* l'autre / *moins performante que*

La compagnie hollandaise paie **plus que** la compagnie britannique.

Le produit est **trop** cher **pour** se vendre facilement
Le tunnelier est **trop** grand **pour** rentrer dans le trou.

Note that for the best/dearest, you use **de**:

C'est le meilleur modèle **de** toute la gamme.
C'est le plus travailleur **de** toute l'équipe.
C'est la meilleure compagnie d'assurances du monde (= in the world).

Note also that in comparisons you have **plus/moins ... que**, but in giving quantities, sums of money etc, you use **plus/moins de**:

Le voyage en avion revient *plus* cher *qu'*en train.
Le billet de chemin de fer vous coûtera *moins de* FF1000.
Le billet d'avion vous coûtera *plus de* FF5000.

- **Contrasting**

Alors que ... } While/but
Tandis que ...

Du côté britannique la craie est propre, | tandis que / alors que du côté français elle est plus difficile à travailler.

| d'une part ... | de l'autre / d'autre part | on one hand ... on the other |

D'une part vous avez l'avantage de la qualité, de l'autre un prix très compétitif.

A vous

Use the above expressions to reply to the questions about the two quotations below:

1. Comparez les frais de transport chez les deux sociétés.

2. Comparez ensuite les frais d'entreposage?

3. Quels sont les avantages et les inconvénients des devis proposés par les deux sociétés?

La Société Porte-à-porte   *La Société Transpartout*

Transport des marchandises	FF30 000	Transport des marchandises	FF25 000
Entreposage (5 jours max)	FF500	Entreposage (pour 24 heures)	FF120
Formalités de douane	FF100		
Livraison au destinataire	FF300		

C Extend your vocabulary (un mot à tout faire)

Faire is sometimes called a **verbe passe-partout**, because it can be used in so many ways. If you are aware of some of these, you can increase your word-power instantly!

THE LANGUAGE OF BUSINESS

C1 **Faire** with measurements, distances and time

You have probably already used **faire** to express dimensions, weight, quantities, prices. Here are some more examples:

La pièce fait 10m de long sur 12m de large.
Ça fait 2 kilos de pommes.
Cela fait 10 kilomètres de l'atelier à l'usine.
Deux bières et un café, ça fait 30F.
Combien fait ce tuyautage? – 95F le mètre.

As well as **depuis**, **il y a** and **voilà**, **cela fait** or, colloquially, **ça fait** can be used to measure time. (Remember to express **time up to now** with the **present**, and a **point in the past** by the **passé composé**.)

A vous

In the following sentences, replace **cela fait** with one of the other expressions.

1. Cela fait bientôt 2 ans que nous attendons une visite de la part de votre représentant.
2. Cela fait 6 mois que nous lui avons écrit.
3. Cela fait déjà longtemps que nous avons décidé de chercher ailleurs.

Answers: *1. Voilà bientôt 2 ans que nous attendons une visite de la part de votre représentant. 2. Nous lui avons écrit il y a 6 mois. 3. Nous avons déjà décidé depuis longtemps de chercher ailleurs.*

C2 'Cela fait hollandais'

Il/cela fait can mean 'he/it looks'

example: ça fait bien = it looks good;
ça fait cher = that seems dear.

(**Il fait** can also mean to 'try to look', 'to pretend', e.g., Il fait l'innocent = he's pretending not to know anything.)

In the following examples, rephrase the sentence using **Il/ça fait**. Bear in mind that using **ça fait** will often make them sound more colloquial, so these are phrases you'll use in an informal setting.

A vous

1. Ce décor me paraît un peu lourd.
2. L'histoire qu'elle raconte me semble un peu bizarre.
3. Ils font vieille Angleterre, ces meubles.
4. Cela va les impressionner si vous montrez tous vos diplômes.
5. Ce film donne très envie d'aller en Californie.
6. Il se prend pour un patron compréhensif.
7. Il fait semblant d'être celui qui a tout perdu.

Answers: *1. Ça fait un peu lourd, ce décor.*
2. Ça fait bizarre, l'histoire qu'elle raconte.
3. Ça fait vieille Angleterre, ces meubles.
4. Cela va faire bien si vous montrez tous vos diplômes.
5. Ça fait très envie d'aller en Californie, ce film.
6. Il fait le patron compréhensif.
7. Il fait celui qui a tout perdu.

C3 Expressions with **faire**.

faire un chèque	to write a cheque
faire la connaissance (de quelqu'un)	to meet, get to know someone
faire le détail	to give a breakdown (in retail it can also mean to detail)
faire exprès	to do something on purpose, to do all one can
faire de son mieux	to do one's best
faire une offre	to make an offer
faire le plein	to fill up (with petrol)
faire peur à	to frighten
faire de la route	to travel

Notice also:

Il se fait tard	it's getting late
Cela ne fait rien	it doesn't matter
Comment se fait-il que (+ subjunctive)	Why, how is it that...

THE LANGUAGE OF BUSINESS

A vous

Try to find the appropriate expressions for the blanks below: sometimes you are asked for a whole expression, sometimes part of one.

1. Ayant reçu une lettre dans laquelle le directeur me fait une belle _____ d'emploi, je suis allée voir sur place avec mon mari.
2. Nous avons fait beaucoup de _____ sans trouver d'hôtel.
3. Le paysage sauvage nous a fait _____ à tous les deux, d'ailleurs il commençait à _____ .
4. Heureusement nous n'étions pas à court d'essence, car nous avons pu _____ à une station-service qui était restée ouverte.
5. Finalement, au bout de trois heures, nous avons trouvé un restaurant qui _____ aussi hôtel.
6. A l'hôtel nous avons _____ d'une personne charmante, qui a fait _____ pour nous mettre à l'aise.
7. Comment se fait-il que vous _____ si tard? a-t-elle demandé.
8. Cela ne _____ . Demain, c'est dimanche, vous pourrez faire la grasse matinée.
9. Le lendemain, elle a demandé si nous avions l'intention de payer en espèces, ou de lui _____ .
10. Je n'ai pas compris pourquoi le montant était si élevé, alors je lui ai demandé de _____ de la facture.

Answers: *1. offre; 2. route; 3. peur, se faire tard; 4. faire le plein; 5. faisait; 6. fait la connaissance, fait de son mieux; 7. arriviez; 8. fait rien; 9. faire un chèque; 10. faire le détail.*

C4 How to get things done (faire faire)

Look at these examples:

Avant de continuer, il a fait faire une étude détaillée.	Before proceeding, he had a detailed survey done.
Elle a fait réparer le toit.	She had the roof repaired.

Now cover up the right-hand column and see if you can think how to say the following in French. Then compare your answers with those on the right.

A vous

1. The company gets its brochure translated into three languages.
2. We got all the old machines replaced.
3. They had a brand new house built.
4. We had the premises inspected/surveyed.
5. You will have to get a market survey done.

La société fait traduire sa plaquette en trois langues.
Nous avons fait remplacer toutes les vieilles machines.
Ils ont fait construire une maison toute neuve.
Nous avons fait inspecter les locaux.
Il vous faudra faire faire une étude du marché.

D Make your language work

D1 Comparisons

Quelle voiture?

Here are details about three cars, the BMW 318, the Peugot 405 and the Renault 21. (Source: *Linéaire auto*). We want you to compare them as regards

- a. their performance;
- b. their fittings and extras;
- c. price and running costs.

First of all look again through the phrases you can use to make comparisons (p 229–31). Then consult the tables below.
   Follow the outline below to make your comparison.

a. Performance

1. Comparez la vitesse maximum des trois voitures.
2. Et en ce qui concerne l'accélération et les reprises, quelle est la voiture la plus performante des trois?
3. Est-ce qu'il y a une différence quant à la consommation?
4. Les trois voitures sont finalement très comparables: où résident les différences principales?

b. *Equipements*

5. Si vous tenez absolument à avoir un ordinateur de bord, quelle voiture choisissez-vous?
6. Une des voitures offre-t-elle la possibilité de programmer la température?
7. Et si votre famille insiste que la voiture ait des appuis-tête à l'arrière pour les grands voyages, que ferez-vous?
8. Pour les mêmes raisons, il serait souhaitable d'avoir un accoudoir central arrière. (soit . . . soit).
9. Du point de vue de la sécurité, quelle est la voiture la mieux équipée (ancrage de ceintures, projecteurs anti-brouillard etc.)?
10. Au niveau du confort (réglage du siège, température, verrouillage centralisé) quelle est la meilleure voiture?
11. Est-ce qu'il y a des choses précises que vous recherchez particulièrement?
12. Au total, est-ce qu'il y a une voiture qui est mieux équipée que les autres?

Quelle voiture?

LES PERFORMANCES	BMW 318iS	PEUGEOT 405 Mi16	RENAULT 21 TXI
VITESSE MAXI (km/h)	206	215	207
ACCELERATIONS			
400 m départ arrêté (s)	16.3	16	16.8
1 000 m (s)	30.1	29.5	31
REPRISES			
Depuis 50 km/h en 4ᵉ : 400 m (s)	17.1	17.1	17
1 000 m (s)	32.3	32	32.1
Depuis 50 km/h en 5ᵉ : 400 m (s)	19.2	19	18.6
1 000 m (s)	37.1	36.7	35.7
De 80 à 140 km/h en 5ᵉ (s)	25.2	24.3	23.6
De 80 à 120 km/h en 5ᵉ (s)	15.6	15.1	14.5
En 4ᵉ (s)	9.9	9.7	10.3
En 3ᵉ (s)	6.9	6.3	7.1
CONSOMMATIONS			
Routière litres aux 100 km	12.7	13	12.7
Autonomie (km)	400	500	450

ESTABLISHING A BRIDGEHEAD

LES PRIX				
		BMW 318is	PEUGEOT 405 Mi16	RENAULT 21 TXI
	(F)	126 900	145 310	121 600
Puissance administrative (CV)		9	10	10
OPTIONS				
Climatiseur		13 284	8 555	9 410
Sièges avant chauffants		2 161	1 289	–
Intérieur cuir		9 171	8 164 (1)	8 380
Peinture métallisée		3 209	1 836	1 740
Toit ouvrant électrique		6 611	3 906	4 430
Antiblocage		7 619	série	9 280
Pont autobloquant		3 381	–	–
Lèves-vitres électriques AR		–	1 719 (2)	1 760 (3)
Lave-projecteurs haute pression		–	1 289	–
Dispositif lave/essuie-phares		2 905	–	–
Rétroviseurs ext. dégivrants		818	–	–

(1) Avec lève-vitres électriques et appuis-tête arrière (2) avec appuis-tête arrière et accoudoir central avant (3) + 2 rétroviseurs électriques et dégivrants.

MAINTENANCE ET PIECES DETACHEES			
	BMW 318is	PEUGEOT 405 Mi16	RENAULT 21 TXI
MAIN-D'OEUVRE (heures)			
Dépose-repose moteur	3.8	7.5	7.2
Dépose-repose boîte de vitesses	1.9	5.0	3.3
Remplacement de l'embrayage	2.3	5.5	3.8
Remplacement plaquettes avant	0.7	0.8	0.6
Remplacement de l'échappement	0.7	1.0	1.3
PRIX (T.T.C.)			
Echange standard moteur	21 539	15 753	12 635
Echange standard boîte	11 123	6 895	5 920
Deux disques de freins avant	1 235	533	1 087
Jeu de plaquettes AV	410	284	190
Deux amortisseurs arrière	1 859	835	688
Echappement complet	5 805	2 106	2 446
Filtre à huile	48	56	46
Alternateur neuf	5 870	1 660	1 708
ENTRETIEN-GARANTIES			
Espacement des vidanges	12 000*	10 000	10 000
1re révision	2 000 km	1 500/2 500	1 000/3 000
Révisions ou contrôles	22 000*	10 000	10 000
Garantie mécanique	1 an	1 an	1 an
Garantie anticorrosion	6 ans	6 ans	6 ans
Nombre de succursales (France)	–	50	62
de concessionnaires (France)	168	404	448
d'agents (France)	42	4 194	8 012

237

THE LANGUAGE OF BUSINESS

EQUIPEMENTS	BMW 318is	PEUGEOT 405 Mi16	RENAULT 21 TXI
Accoudoir central avant	non	non	non
arrière	non	oui	oui
Air conditionné	non	non	non
Allume-cigare arrière	non	non	non
Antenne électrique	oui	non	non
Appuie-tête arrière	option	non	oui
Rétroviseur ext. côté passager	oui	oui	oui
Réglable de l'intérieur	électrique	électrique	électrique
Dossier arrière fractionné	non	non	oui
Eclairage du coffre	oui	oui	oui
du moteur	non	non	non
de la boîte à gants	oui	oui	oui
Eclairage temporisé	non	oui	non
Essuie-glace à deux vitesses + intermittent	oui	oui	oui
à cadencement variable	non	oui	non
Jalousie arrière	non	non	non
Lave-phares	option	option	option
Lève-glaces électriques avant	oui	oui	oui
à fonction aut.	non	non	oui
Miroir de courtoisie	passager	passager	passager
Ordinateur de bord	non	non	oui
Projecteurs antibrouillard	oui	oui	oui
Radio et lecteur de cassette	option	option	option
Réglage des points d'ancrage de ceintures	non	oui	oui
Réglage du siège conducteur en hauteur	oui	oui	oui
en appui dorsal	oui	oui	oui
Réglage radio au/ou sous le volant	non	non	oui
Rhéostat de tableau de bord	oui	oui	oui
Spots de lecture avant et arrière	non	avant	avant
Température programmable	non	oui	oui
Trappe protège-radio	non	oui	non
Verrouillage centralisé des portes	oui	oui	oui
du coffre	oui	oui	oui
commande à distance	non	oui	oui
Vide-poches avant central	oui	oui	oui
de portières	oui	oui	oui

c. *Entretien et prix*

13. Comparez la fréquence des révisions.
14. Faites de meme pour la fréquence et le prix des vidanges.
15. Imaginez qu'il faut remplacer la boîte de vitesse: combien est-ce que cela vous coûterait pour chaque voiture?
16. Selon les prix indiqués, quelle est la voiture la plus chère et combien coûte-elle? Et la moins chère?
17. Compte tenu de tous ces faits, résumez en trois ou quatre phrases quelle voiture vous semble être la meilleure.

Places in prospect

Here is information on two French departments. Read it through carefully and make up as many sentences as you can about the relative size, population, climate and industrial activity of the two departments. Record the sentences on your blank cassette and compare them to the answer on the study cassette.

ISERE (38), dép. du sud-est de la France (région Rhône-Alpes); 7 500 km^2; 768 450 hab. (103 au km^2) [France : 95]. Ch.-l. *Grenoble*.
ADMINISTRATION. 3 arrond. (*Grenoble*. 525 100 hab.; *La Tour-du-Pin*. 110 900 hab.; *Vienne*, 132 500 hab.). / 50 cant, / 538 comm.

Le département s'étend sur deux ensembles bien différents. La partie orientale appartient aux *Alpes* (Préalpes de la Grande-Chartreuse, massif de Belledonne, Oisans, etc.); elle est découpée par les vallées de l'Isère (Grésivaudan en amont) et de ses affluents (Drac et Romanche), seuls secteurs où l'altitude tombe au-dessous de 500 m. L'Ouest est constitué par les plateaux du *bas Dauphiné* dominant la vallée du Rhône. Malgré l'extension de la montagne et un climat souvent rude, la densité de la population est supérieure à la moyenne nationale.

L'*agriculture* n'emploie que le dixième de la population active. L'élevage des bovins est la ressource essentielle de la montagne: les cultures sont médiocres sur les plateaux du bas Dauphiné, plus riches (fruits) dans la vallée du Rhône et le Grésivaudan.

L'*industrie* est beaucoup plus développée (elle intéresse la moitié de la population active). Elle est fondée en majeure partie sur l'électrométallurgie et l'électrochimie, favorisées par la production d'hydro-électricité. Elle est surtout représentée dans l'agglomération de Grenoble, qui regroupe plus de 40 p. 100 de la population totale.

La présence de Grenoble explique en majeure partie la très nette augmentation de la population départementale intervenue récemment, alors que l'émigration se poursuit dans la montagne et dans les «terres froides» du bas Dauphiné.

PAS-DE-CALAIS (62), dép. du nord de la France (région Nord-Pas-de-Calais); 6640 km^2; 1 397 200 hab. (210 au km^2) [France : 95]. Ch.-l. *Arras*.
ADMINISTRATION. 7 arrond. (*Arras*, 289 200 hab.; *Béthune*, 275 800 hab.; *Boulogne-sur-Mer*, 152 600 hab.; *Calais*, 105 400 hab.; *Lens*, 364 500 hab.; *Montreuil*, 87 800 hab.; *Saint-Omer*, 121 900 hab.). / 57 cant. / 907 comm.

Localités Principales	Nombre D'hab.	Localités Principales	Nombre D'hab.
Calais	74 900	Carvin	17 100
Arras	53 600	Berck	16 700
Boulogne-sur-Mer	50 100	Sallaumines	14 800
Lens	42 000	Harnes	14 600
Liévin	35 900	Auchel	14 100
Bruay-en-Artois	28 600	Bully-les-Mines	14 100
Béthune	28 400	Outreau	13 700
Hénin-Beaumont	27 030	Méricourt	13 500
Avion	22 400	Nœux-les-Mines	13 300
Saint-Omer	19 600	Oignies	12 600

Ouvert sur la Manche et la mer du Nord, le département comprend une bande de plaines au N. (partie méridionale de la *Flandre*) et une zone de collines au S. (*collines de l'Artois*) où l'altitude oscille entre 100 et 200 m. Le climat est océanique avec des précipitations assez abondantes, également réparties sur l'ensemble de l'année.

La densité générale d'occupation, très élevée, est due à l'importance de l'*industrie*. Celle-ci emploie pratiquement la moitié de la population active et, plus que le développement du *secteur tertiaire*, explique l'importance de l'urbanisation (25 communes dépassent 10 000 hab.). Au textile de tradition ancienne s'est ajoutée l'extraction houillère dans le quart nord-est du département (d'Auchel à Hénin-Beaumont) donnant naissance à la métallurgie et à la chimie. Aujourd'hui, l'extraction de la houille est en recul et doit même prochainement cesser, ce déclin de l'industrie charbonnière entraînant une certaine stagnation démographique; le textile n'est plus non plus une branche dynamique.

L'*agriculture* occupe moins du septième de la population active (en y englobant la pêche, importante, puisque Boulogne est le premier port français). Le littoral, au S., est animé par le tourisme balnéaire (Le Touquet-Paris-Plage et Berck).

(Source: Larousse *Pluridictionnaire*)

THE LANGUAGE OF BUSINESS

D2 Smooth talking

You will have noticed that the French people who speak in this sequence have at their disposal a range of polite expressions:

Je suis heureux de savoir qu'une nouvelle entreprise anglaise s'installe à Calais.
C'est avec grand plaisir qu'on vous accueille.

They also use a number of 'fillers' to help conversation along:

Eh bien, nous sommes réunis ...
Alors, c'est une vente ...

Here are some others you may wish to use, with explanations where necessary.

Showing agreement or approval

Entendu. D'accord. Parfait. Bien sûr. Absolument. Tout à fait.
Exact/exactement. Voilà. C'est ça. Effectivement, en effet.
Alors là, oui (you're in agreement about a specific point).
Bon alors, bien alors (business well concluded; ready to move on to the next point)

Polyfillers, for the gap when you hesitate or pause to start over again

Disons voyez-vous je veux dire que ... euh, c'est une espèce de ... comme je disais à propos de ...

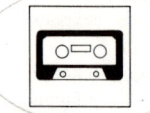

Some of these little words can be used to express a whole range of meanings, according to the intonation. Read the phrases below, and listen to them on the study cassette.
– Ah bon ...? (douteux)
– Ah bon! at last, I understand
– Ah bon! that is it, there is nothing more to be done
– Ah **bon**?! (Est-ce possible?) Is it possible?

– Voilà ... (et vous continuez à donner une explication)
   ex: Voilà ... le seul problème c'est que ...

240

ESTABLISHING A BRIDGEHEAD

- Voilà (= d'accord) alright, O.K.
- Voilà (je vous ai tout expliqué; *voilà* la raison!) I told you everything; that is the reason.

- Enfin! (ouf!) at last!
- Enfin . . . (hesitation)
    ex: Enfin je ne sais pas moi . . .
- Enfin! (ça suffit) = reproach

- Quand même (= come off it, you must be joking!)
- Il faut quand même avouer que . . . (nevertheless; you revise or defend an opinion)
- quand même (after all, despite everything)
    ex: ils ont gagné quand même, malgré les problèmes.

Polite phrases

Je suis très heureux de vous accueillir.
Nous sommes ravis de faire votre connaissance.
Soyez les bienvenus! Merci d'être venu.
Je vous présente ma collègue.
Vous permettez que nous ouvrions la fenêtre?
Je vous en prie!
Excusez-moi, je me suis trompé.
Si vous voulez bien m'excuser, je vais être obligé de vous quitter.
C'est gentil de votre part . . .
Bon voyage/bon retour/ bon appétit.

A vous

Read the dialogue below and see if you can make it run smoothly using some of the expressions listed above. Then listen to the answer on the study tape.

1. A Bonjour! Monsieur X?
   B Oui. Très heureux de vous connaître.
   A _____ (it's nice of him to receive you and sorry you're late)
   B _____ (he asks you to sit down)
   A Merci bien. _____ (you're hot and want to take off your coat)
   B ------

THE LANGUAGE OF BUSINESS

2. Now add fillers in the blanks below and read the text aloud, recording it on a blank cassette. There is again a full answer on the study cassette.

M. Kusmirek montre un échantillon de son travail à M Helliott.

K: Même pour la distribution, qui a parfois beaucoup de texte à mettre, les agences se battent généralement pour dire 'il faut aérer', 'il faut laisser respirer un peu'.

H: Ils sont asssez traditionnels, à ce point de vue, les Anglais encore.

K: Vous connaissez le sujet Green, Verte? _____ cette compagnie a décidé de modifier les voitures pour que l'essence . . .

H: L'essence sans plomb!

K: _____, on a mis des fleurs à l'intérieur, dans le pot d'échappement et on a continué avec ce style qui diffère chaque mois.

H: _____ Il faut avoir de bons yeux! C'est ce qui nous fait rire souvent quand on voit ces annonces, on dit ça c'est anglais! Vous avez l'art de remplir, il n'y a plus de blanc, on trouve pas de blanc.

K: _____ il y a encore de la place, on pourrait mettre une autre abeille là peut-être. _____ c'est parce que le client, il vend des voitures d'occasion et il doit y mettre autant que possible.

H: On a plus de mal en France à faire des choses comme ça.

K: Chaque centimètre carré, ça a une valeur pour lui.

H: Non, _____ ça vous est pas propre, toutes les annonces . . .

E Dialogue

Listen several times to another extract of Anthony Kusmirek's radio interview on the study cassette. The second version has only the interviewer's questions on it: try to reply by paraphrasing Kusmirek's main points in your own words. (Use the pause button when it is your turn to speak.)

I: Concrètement, Anthony, ce séjour à Lille, c'est une amorce de dialogue avec des partenaires? Est-ce que vous pensez que plus ou moins à court terme tout cela, cette rencontre, va se concrétiser par des projets sur le plan économique, sur le plan professionnel?

A: Oui, je vois des échanges où des entreprises françaises voudraient pénétrer le marché anglais et voudraient des conseils, très précis au point de vue marketing, packaging et dessin qui représentent les moeurs tout à fait britanniques et les besoins des consommateurs dans notre pays et de la même façon de l'autre côté, en France, je vois qu'il y a des grandes compagnies anglaises qui voudraient des détails très précis du marché français.

I: On parle de raz de marée britannique à la fois sur le plan économique et sur le plan touristique. Est-ce que vous n'avez pas peur que la France ait une réaction brutale hostile?

A: Non, ce qui m'intéresse c'est que, je me renseigne assez bien au sujet de ce qui se passe en France; chez nous en Angleterre on parle de 1992 comme une étape économique vers l'Europe il y a deux ou trois ans et maintenant ils sont en train de discuter la situation du point de vue éducation, le rapport, de la façon de parler et de s'entendre.

Sketch: Les Anglais

So what do you do with an old barn that has a leaky roof, rotten beams and stinks of cows? In the Nord Pas-de-Calais region of France the answer seems to be to sell it to the English. It is useful to note the discussion between Josianne and Albert about 'old francs'. Although the system changed over 30 years ago, many people still refer to this currency value when talking about large bills or buying houses.

Key words and phrases

le couvreur	roofer
foutre le camp (vulg.)	to disappear, leave, collapse
les poutres	wooden beams

Business notes

Establishing a Bridgehead

With the removal of barriers to trade in the Single European Market, physical distribution is destined to undergo major changes which will affect suppliers, end-users, transport companies and freight-forwarders. As companies move towards achieving greater economies of scale through being able to reach a greater European market, the location of both manufacturing and distribution facilities will become a critical factor in deciding on the best method of flexibly supplying a market, which, whilst being transnational, will still retain discernible differences in preferences, culture and customer service requirements. Industries will no longer be necessarily serviced from local facilities in their own country but in their search for cost reduction, will concentrate on single centres of production to supply the whole European market. This might well be accompanied by focusing distribution on two or three major warehousing facilities.

Also of importance will be:

- *Cabotage*, the ability of a transport company to move goods between points in another country. This will represent a threat for general hauliers but major opportunities will exist for joint ventures between British and French companies.
- Whether large French retailers will continue with their current system of large numbers of regional and more specialised warehouses (*plateformes*) or move towards the centralised dedicated composite warehousing which has been the feature of the UK retail distribution system over the last few years. If and when French retailers become more concentrated, their logistics may well be re-organised along these lines.

ESTABLISHING A BRIDGEHEAD

- Whether French retailers will abandon in-house transport fleets and warehousing and contract out to third-party suppliers as is the case in the UK.
- The increase in goods being transported by rail with the opening of the Channel Tunnel.

Changes in distribution patterns, coupled with the opening of the Channel Tunnel and the construction of the TGV-Nord, are forecast to benefit greatly the Nord Pas-de-Calais Region. Already, over 50 French and British distribution companies have been established in the area and it is anticipated that other manufacturing sites will follow the recent examples of Coca-Cola, Continental Can, Péchiney and Cyanamid in Dunkirk and Peugeot-Fiat in Valenciennes. Certainly, in contrast to the county of Kent, which broadly wishes to remain part of London's Green Belt, there are numerous opportunities for British companies to find the land they seek in vain in South-East England. The region occupies a position of strategic importance. New road axes fan out from Calais towards Belgium, Holland and West Germany and in the North East, Northern and North West France via Dieppe, Boulogne and Rouen and South via the existing links to Paris and ultimately more directly through Troyes.

Centres of particular activity are:

- **The Dunkirk enterprise zone of** 30 hectares at Wormhout where Dialatron (telephones), Jenson (Johnson & Johnson Group) and various other Continental companies are already installed. In the case of Dialatron its research laboratories are situated at Whitstable in Kent, thus within easy access of Dunkirk. A prime move in this company's case was the new mayor of Dunkirk (and also the Minister of Transport!) M. Delabarre, who supported Dialatron's efforts to obtain France Telecom's approval to sell its various telephone products on the French market (Dialatron is to bring initially 100 new jobs, rising eventually to 200, to Dunkirk, in an area where unemployment is well above the national average, largely due to the job losses in the steel and shipbuilding industries).
- **A further 270 hectares in Dunkirk** (managed by Sodiqueque), which after a slow start has began to attract a whole host of overseas investors – particularly from Belgium, a country which has been particularly active in the area as a whole, both in distribution and manufacturing. The site offers exoneration from corporate tax for ten years.

- **Four sites in Calais**
  1. The ZAC at the Fréthun-Coquelles Terminal (see previous chapter).
  2. The Dunes industrial estate covering some 400 acres flanking the sea with a projected link to the A26 motorway.

     It is on this site that the British company Sandhurst, based in Lille, has decided to buy a plot of land from the town of Calais, which is developing the site. The company has one year to apply for building permission (*le permis de construire*) and three years to complete its building. If, at the end of the three year period, the company has not complied with the *cahier des charges*, it may be asked to sell the land back to the council, at the same price as it is paying now. If it wishes to sub-divide the land or resell, it must have the agreement of the Calais council. Such details are laid down in the general conditions (*le cahier des charges*). A building is to be erected on the site which houses offices, a maintenance shop and an exhibition hall, and Sandhurst is at liberty to let any of these premises to third parties, but it must remain owner of the whole section of land. In the event of its being resold, the whole *parcelle* must be sold as a unit. Calais council wishes to avoid speculation and is principally interested in the site being used to create employment (remember that the level of unemployment in the areas, 14 per cent, is one of the highest in France). It is on questions such as these that it is crucial to have expert advice, hence Tim Dean has taken along his lawyer in France, Philip Jenkinson, to explain the exact ramifications of what he is signing.
  3. The Beau-Marais estate, for small and medium-size companies and comprising some 300 acres on the main Calais-Dunkirk road.
  4. The Courtaulds estate; Courtaulds has buildings and land on its site close to the interchange linking the present and future motorway some six miles south west of Calais which it plans to use in industrial co-operation projects with other companies.
  5. The Arlington estate, close to the A26 Motorway.
  6. The commune of Coulogne, just east of the tunnel terminal is also set for development and has full planning permission for light industry and distribution facilities, housing and shops. One British property developer, Piccadilly Securities, has already bought a 90 acre site in Coulogne.

Various grants are available such as the *Prime à l'Aménagement du Territoire*, the *Prime Régionale à l'Emploi*, the *Prime Régionale à la Creation d'Entreprise*.

A useful address is the Calais Economic Development Council (CEADEC), 12 boulevard Clemenceau, Calais, tel: 21 34 66 83.

- **Lille**. The town is pinning all its hopes on the TGV (Brussels will be 35 minutes away, Paris 50 minutes and London, eventually, 90 minutes), the tunnel and 1993 and there are many signs of a revival of its fortunes after recent closures and redundancies in textiles, one of its main industries. Most activity is centred around the business centre to be built above the new TGV station and which is to become another 'La Défense', the business area of Paris, with some 150,000 square metres of offices (many are now built in smart converted textile companies' buildings), hotels, shops and congress halls. In addition, the airport at Lille is to be extended and an international transport centre is to be built in Tourcoing. Hitherto, on the periphery of traffic flows between the UK, Holland and West Germany, Lille sees the new rail and road infrastructure as bringing it right into the heart of the so-called Golden Triangle. In spite of these obvious attractions, however, various doubts are being expressed:

1. The strengths of Roissy airport and Brussels may well outweigh any advantages Lille has to offer.
2. Industry is still contracting in the area with few signs of any new pole of technological speciality emerging.
3. The town, together with the rest of the Nord-Pas-de-Calais region is shunned by French managers (*cadres*) whose main preference is overwhelmingly for Paris and the South. This trend is reinforced by a general exodus of young graduates away from the region.
4. There is a very fragile research base in Lille, compared with other regions of comparable industrial importance.
5. Its young labour force is poorly qualified.

In the video scene, various documents are handed over, one from the surveyor (*le géomètre*) who will have had to draw up a site plan to show the various sections (*parcelles*) and the second to the Land Registry (*le cadastre*), with whom the surveyor will have had to register the site plan. The *cadastre* works together with the *Conservation des Hypothèques* (the local office in this case is in Boulogne) which maintains a register of all mortgages and charges affecting a title. Hence this present contract (*acte*) will be published at the *Conservation*. Another important document to be signed during the proceedings will be a VAT form to show commitment to build on the land.

A few final comments on buying land/property for whatever purpose, commercial or private, in France. The legal function of transferring titles in France, i.e. conveyancing, is performed by a single lawyer, the notaire, who remains impartial and independent of both parties. His function is to make out the contract, witness signatures, collect and disburse the purchase price and register the transfer. Also, there is no completion after initial signing of the contract as in the UK. Completion and signing of the contract are simultaneous in France (but do not forget to ask to see a draft – *un project d'acte*). There is, however, a preliminary agreement (*un compromis de vente*) at which stage a deposit (*des arrhes*) is paid – 5 per cent, in the case of Sandhurst. This represents a firm commitment by both parties to buy (hence gazumping and gazundering are unknown in France!).

Normally, the copy of the contract (*la copie de l'acte*) will be produced and handed over in person at a later date after stamping at the *cadastre* [usually this takes two months but because of a strike (*une grève*) by the tax authorities (*les services fiscaux*), on this occasion it was to take considerably longer – six months].

Finally, a registration tax is payable, calculated according to the value of the land.

In the next sequence, Tim Dean is seen talking to the mayor of Les Attaques, a small village on the road to St Omer, a few miles out of Calais and close to the A26 motorway. As previously explained, mayors are all-powerful in France and his decisions and opinions on what sort of development he wants will be vital. In this instance, for example, the area concerned is a zone de 30NA, an area for residential development, and he is determined to have small shops as well as housing (not council houses – *les HLM*), but no supermarkets or hypermarkets or industrial units. Sandhurst's proposal is for a small shopping mall. The very fact that there are virtually no shops at the moment is the main reason why the mayor wishes the building of houses to be in phases to allow time for appropriate facilities to be developed.

It is essentially through the land development plan (*Plan d'Occupation des Sols – POS*) for the commune, that the mayor holds his crucial and overriding power. The main problem, however, is that in many cases, the POS is used in complete isolation from that of the adjoining communes, a situation which often leads to the impression of facing a gigantic shapeless jigsaw puzzle. Developers should be aware, therefore, of what is happening around them in terms of compatability with their own plans – a difficult task, when it is remembered that there are some 17,000 mayors wielding a POS! In this case, the town of Calais is preparing a master plan for zoning of the whole district and hence the mayor does have this as an overall constraint.

In the last sequence, M. Elliott is typical of small French advertising agencies in that he has a management background, i.e. he went to an *Ecole de Commerce*, a management school. His assistants are essentially those who do the creative and artistic work – his job is more the marketing aspects.

Anthony Kusmirek realises the substantial differences which exist between advertising in the UK and France and is therefore seeking to form an association with Tam-Tam whereby each company could introduce the other to customers and advise on differences in style, tastes, market segments and general approach. For example, M. Elliott noticed during Anthony's presentation that a number of his advertisements were 'fussy' and full of detail, a feature which the French often associate with British advertising. The French require more space and air. Speaking later on of an English company making and supplying kitchen furniture for the French market and for which Tam-Tam had an advertising contract, Anthony suggested stressing the English side of the product. According to M. Elliott, however, this could have a negative connotation in that kitchens are associated with cooking and English cooking has not exactly the best of reputations in France! The final version of the publicity was more Italian in style and colour thus in fact disguising the company's British origins.

In addition, the kitchen furniture market is a replacement market close to saturation in the UK, whereas it is a newish market in France for young couples. Publicity would therefore have to be handled accordingly. Such an understanding of differences is crucial and hence the importance of Anthony's visit. M. Elliott had hitherto only thought of concentrating on his immediate regional market, extended to other adjoining regions as the company grew. But, thanks to Anthony's persuasion he is now realising that to visit Britain is no harder than to go to Paris and he is certainly most interested in Anthony's suggestions of collaboration, which represents yet another way of penetrating the French market.

Business Magazine 6: 'entente cordiale'

For companies setting up in France, the bureaucracy can often appear to be a minefield, and certainly a knowledge of the way the local politics operate is essential. But setting up can often have implications beyond purely doing business. In this magazine programme you can hear the experiences of different companies whose ventures into France have sometimes led to a newly discovered entente cordiale.

Chapter 7

Conducting meetings
'Moitié anglais, moitié français'

Introduction

Meetings are one of the chief tools of communication in any business. It is important to be able to understand what is happening and contribute effectively. This may be difficult in English at times, and will definitely be so in French. Do not assume that you will be able to get away with just English 'because everybody understands English anyway'. As more and more companies develop a European approach, other languages are creeping into the board room.

In this chapter you will:

- see an Anglo-French company, Eurotunnel, as it plans the media coverage of the first underwater breakthrough of the Channel Tunnel
- watch the English branch of a French bank, Crédit Agricole, as they work out how best to help clients referred to them from France.

On the language side you will

- revisit the subjunctive and the perfect tense
- develop your skills in the use of infinitives, and verbs and adjectives and their prepositions
- put your language skills to use in business situations

Now watch the final video sequence (11 35 08). Use the key words and phrases below if you have any problems in understanding the dialogues.

CONDUCTING MEETINGS

Key words and phrases

Réunion au siège social d'Eurotunnel

la couverture	the coverage
nos propres actionnaires (m)	our own shareholders
quotidien	daily
esquisser un budget	to set a budget
susciter	to create
les droits (m) exclusifs	exclusive rights
en tout cas (m)	in any case
manquer	to lack
percer	to pierce, make or drill a hole in
une paroi	a partition, a wall
s'effondrer	to fall down, collapse
au-delà	beyond, further than
ça ne me gêne pas	that does not bother me

Réunion dans les locaux du Crédit Agricole

l'ordre du jour (m)	agenda
je vous les remets	I am handing them over to you
désigner	to choose, nominate
le compte rendu	the minutes
s'en occuper	to deal with something, to undertake to do
aborder	to deal with, tackle, discuss
mener des opérations (f)	to lead operations
Caisses (f) Régionales	regional banks
les gisements (m)	large reserves of business
la concrétisation	materialisation (of a plan, project)
une incompréhension	lack of understanding
des services (m) qui relèvent plus de ...	services which arise more from ...
mal à l'aise (f)	ill at ease
un enjeu	stake
canaliser	to channel

Faux amis (Pitfalls)

la couverture par la presse	press coverage (not: blanket)
un agenda	a diary (not: agenda)

251

THE LANGUAGE OF BUSINESS

un ordre du jour	an agenda
les minutes	very detailed account of legal acts, judgments
le compte rendu	the minutes

Listen and understand

A1 Getting the gist

1. Quel était l'objet de la réunion qui s'est tenue au siège social d'Eurotunnel?

   L'objet de cette réunion était de discuter de la couverture, par les médias différents, de la jonction du tunnel de service.

2. Quels sont les trois points à l'ordre du jour de la réunion qui s'est tenue au Crédit Agricole de Londres?

   Premièrement, le compte rendu de la précédente réunion est approuvé, puis le questionnaire concernant les relations du Crédit Agricole à Londres avec les Caisses régionales en France est étudié et, dernièrement, l'établissement d'une liste de questions à poser au siège social de Paris est établie.

A2 Getting the details

Réunion au siège social d'Eurotunnel

1. Pourquoi le tournage d'un film sous terre pose-t-il des difficultés?

   Parce qu'il faut travailler dans un espace restreint.

2. Pourquoi propose-t-on d'avoir, en plus des équipes de télévision, des équipes de cinéma?

   Parce qu'Eurotunnel veut avoir un document pour ses propres archives.

3. Va-t-on se limiter uniquement à une couverture visuelle?

   Non, on veut inviter des représentants de tous les médias.

4. Quel est l'objectif poursuivi par Eurotunnel en invitant tous les médias à cet événement?

   L'objectif est d'atteindre un public aussi large que possible.

5. Pourquoi l'idée d'accorder des droits exclusifs à une seule chaîne de télévision n'est-elle pas réaliste?

Parce qu'il est difficile de vendre un événement historique.

6. Pourquoi la jonction des tunnels risque de ne pas être aussi spectaculaire que la rencontre de deux tunneliers?

Parce qu'il s'agit de la jonction de deux tunnels l'un à côté de l'autre.

Réunion dans les locaux du Crédit Agricole

1. Qu'est-ce que la présidente de la séance distribue juste avant la réunion?

Elle distribue un ordre du jour et des dossiers.

2. Quel est le rôle du secrétaire de la réunion?

Son rôle est de rédiger un compte rendu à partir des notes qu'il aura prises au cours de la réunion.

THE LANGUAGE OF BUSINESS

3. Est-ce que les exemples de collaboration entre Londres et d'autres implantations du Crédit Agricole à l'étranger sont nombreux?

Non, mais cela dépend des domaines dans lesquels on travaille.

4. Où réside l'origine de certaines difficultés et parfois même de l'incompréhension entre les Caisses Régionales et Londres?

Elle réside dans le fait que la clientèle des Caisses Régionales n'a pas du tout la même structure que la clientèle de Londres.

5. Quel est le type de clientèle en provenance de France qui pose le plus de difficultés au Crédit Agricole de Londres?

Ce sont les petites entreprises.

6. Y a-t-il unanimité sur la question concernant l'évolution de la nature des demandes en provenance des Caisses Régionales?

Non, mais certaines personnes pensent qu'il faut continuer à informer les Caisses Régionales sur la stratégie menée par le Crédit Agricole à Londres afin que ses Caisses puissent mieux canaliser leurs demandes.

CONDUCTING MEETINGS

7. Quelles sont les Caisses Régionales qui sont les mieux informées sur l'activité de Londres?

Ce sont les plus grandes Caisses Régionales.

8. Est-ce que l'objectif du Crédit Agricole de Londres en matière de clientèle est différent de celui des agences françaises?

Oui, il est totalement différent puisque Londres travaille plutôt avec de grandes entreprises alors que les Caisses Régionales travaillent avec des PME.

B Develop your skills

B1 The subjunctive once more! (Il faut que vous fassiez attention)

As the subjunctive is so important in French, and so unfamiliar to English speakers, here is another opportunity to practise for you. You will find a mixture of sentences below. It is up to you to decide whether or not the subjunctive is needed, and in which tense.

A vous

1. Il faut que nous _____ (comprendre) ce qui va être le 'breakthrough'.
2. Il est important que vous _____ (savoir) que le mot 'breakthrough' est plus fort que le mot 'jonction'.
3. Il est essentiel que la réponse _____ (être) positive, sans que nous n' _____ (avoir) besoin de répéter la question.
4. Quand la jonction sera faite, je crois qu'il _____ (être) facile de 'vendre' cet événement historique.
5. Moi, au contraire, je ne pense pas que cela _____ (paraître) si facile que ça.
6. Autrement dit, je crains que nous n' _____ (avoir) du mal à faire la publicité qu'il faudrait.
7. Les directeurs souhaitent qu'une décision définitive _____ (prendre - passive) avant la fin de la réunion.
8. Il est certain que nous _____ (devoir) conserver ces films pour les archives.
9. Il est possible que jusqu'à présent nous n' _____ pas assez (penser) à l'exploitation médiatique.
10. Le gouvernement exige que tout _____ (terminer - passive) à temps.

Answers: *1. comprenions; 2. sachiez; 3. soit, ayons; 4. sera; 5. paraisse; 6. ayons; 7. soit prise; 8. devrons; 9. ayons pensé; 10. soit terminé;*

B2 The conversational past or perfect tense

After the subjunctive, we will now have another look at the conversational past or **passé composé**. We already mentioned in earlier chapters that the past participle has to agree with the subject if the verb takes **être** as auxiliary.

La reine est morte.
(**mourir** is conjugated with **être** and **la reine** is feminine)

Ces opérations qui nous ont été confiées.
(the passive always uses **être** and the past participle therefore has to agree with the feminine plural subject.)

The above examples are, however, not the only situations in which the past participle has to show agreement. In the following phrases you will see that the auxiliary is **avoir** but that the past participle has agreement endings.

La petite difficulté qu'on *a* eu*e*.
Les demandes qu'on *a* reçu*es*.

As you can see, the past participle **eue** agrees with the direct object (D.O.) **la petite difficulté**. Similarly, **reçues** agrees with **les demandes**. The reason for this agreement is because *the direct object precedes the verb!*

In both English and French the direct object frequently follows the verb:

Subject	Verb	Direct Object
He	saw	the comet
Il	a vu	la comète

When the direct object is a pronoun, however, the situation changes in French but not in English:

Subject	Verb	Direct Object
He	saw	it

Subject	Direct Object	Verb
Il	l'	vu*e*

Another possibility where the direct object precedes the verb is:

Direct Object	Subject	Verb
The comet that	he	saw
La comète qu'	il	a vu*e*

This explains why you will hear, for instance, 'La lettre qu'il a écrite.'.

One little word of warning: be careful not to confuse the direct and indirect object (the indirect object pronoun has the sense of to/for you/us etc.).

Direct Object	Subject of verb	Indirect Object	Verb
La lettre qu'	il	nous	a écrite

A vous

In the following exercise, place the direct object before the verb, and make any other necessary changes. Write your answers out, then compare them with the ones in the right-hand column.

Example: Elle nous a écrit une lettre.
La lettre *qu'*elle nous a écrit*e*.

1. Vous nous avez posé une question.

   La question que vous nous avez posée.

2. Ils ont pris une décision hâtive.

   La décision hâtive qu'ils ont prise.

THE LANGUAGE OF BUSINESS

3. Le bureau de Londres a offert une aide financière.   *L'aide financière que le bureau de Londres a offerte.*

4. J'ai vu une évolution rapide.   *L'évolution rapide que j'ai vue.*

5. Il a fait une chose extraordinaire.   *La chose extraordinaire qu'il a faite.*

> **B3 Infinitives in English and French** (Il est important d'apprendre à les utiliser.)
>
> You may have noticed that the English gerund (expressions with the -ing form) are translated by the infinitive in French. In the meetings in this sequence, you hear:
>
> merci beaucoup de nous recevoir   many thanks for having us here
>
> le problème de faire un film   the problem of making a film

A vous

Look at the example below and transform the following sentences in a similar way, using il est – de faire. (in colloquial French you will also hear 'c'est facile de faire'.)

Example: Apprendre le français, c'est facile.   Learning French is easy.

Il est facile d'apprendre le français.   It is easy to learn French.

1. Payer par lettre de crédit, c'est commode.   *Il est commode de payer par lettre de crédit.*

2. Connaître la langue du client, c'est essentiel.   *Il est essentiel de connaître la langue du client.*

3. Avoir un lit escamotable, c'est pratique.   *Il est pratique d'avoir un lit escamotable.*

4. Trouver du bon vin en Angleterre, c'est impossible.

Il est impossible de trouver du bon vin en Angleterre.

5. Regarder un match de cricket, c'est passionnant.

Il est passionnant de regarder un match de cricket.

Answer the following questions along the lines indicated.

Example: Une aide financière? (Say the bank's already promised it to you).

Une aide financière? Mais la banque me l'a déjà promise!

1. Des crédits supplémentaires? (But we've already accorded them to you).

Mais nous vous les avons déjà accordés.

2. Le questionnaire? (We sent it back to them a fortnight ago).

Nous le leur avons envoyé il y a quinze jours.

3. La démarche à suivre? (We (use **on**) have explained it to him over and over again).

On la lui a expliquée à maintes reprises.

4. Des vacances d'hiver? (He had promised them to himself).

Il se les était promises.

5. Des services financiers? (London has offered us some – N.B. No agreement with 'en'.).

Londres nous en a offert.

B4 Verbs, adjectives and their prepositions

We have just seen that the English gerund (-ing form) is often translated with an infinitive in French. Another situation where infinitives are frequently used in French is after prepositions. In French almost all prepositions are followed by an infinitive (the exception that confirms the rule is **en** – e.g. **en faisant**).

Je commence à apprendre l'espagnol.
Je vais aller en Espagne pour me perfectionner.

but
> C'est en parlant beaucoup qu'on apprend une langue étrangère.

It is, of course, important to know when to use a preposition and which preposition a verb takes. Look at the following examples to get an idea of which preposition goes with which verbs.

- A number of verbs never take prepositions. These are, e.g., **devoir, pouvoir, vouloir, savoir, espérer, penser,** as well as combinations like **aller voir, entendre dire,** and **faire faire,** etc.:

  Il | veut / pense / espère | venir à dix heures.

- Some common verbs are followed by **à**. Examples of these are: **commencer à, réussir à, se prêter à** (+noun)

  Je commence à m'ennuyer.

- Other frequently used verbs take **de**, e.g., **essayer de, proposer de, profiter de, dépendre de** (+noun)

  On a essayé de finir les travaux à temps.

- Adjectives can also be followed by a preposition (usually **à** or **de**):

  Ils sont heureux de venir.
  Ils sont prêts à partir.

- The use of a preposition with a verb can even change the meaning of that verb:

Il a assisté à la réunion	He attended the meeting
Il a assisté le jeune ménage	He helped the young couple
Il a pensé aux restrictions	He kept the restrictions in mind
Qu'est-ce que vous pensez de cette affaire?	What is your opinion on that matter?

CONDUCTING MEETINGS

A vous

It is up to you now to fill in the blanks in sentences which you may recognise from this sequence and others.

1. En augmentant nos prix, nous risquerons _____ perdre nos clients.
2. On peut commencer _____ en parler.
3. Nous ressentissons le besoin _____ être un peu plus précis.
4. Je tiens absolument _____ le dire.
5. C'est le problème auquel on vous demande _____ réfléchir.
6. On va essayer _____ aller voir ces escaliers.
7. Le soleil a actuellement du mal _____ raser l'immeuble.
8. Les Caisses Régionales arriveront _____ canaliser leurs demandes.
9. On espère profiter _____ cette situation pour essayer _____ dépenser le moins possible.
10. Cette place se prête facilement _____ une installation sur la terrasse.
11. Cela dépend _____ domaines dans lesquels on travaille.
12. Les éléments qui nous permettront _____ cerner notre cible.
13. Nous nous intéressons surtout _____ petites et moyennes entreprises.
14. Que pensez-vous _____ l'emballage de ce produit, Mesdames?
15. Nous pensons sérieusement _____ la possibilité d'élargir notre marché.
16. En effet, nous avons l'intention _____ vendre en Europe de l'Est.

Answers: *1. de; 2. à; 3. d'; 4. à; 5. de; 6. d', 7. à; 8. à; 9. de, de; 10. à; 11. des; 12. de; 13. aux; 14. de; 15. à; 16. de.*

C Expand your vocabulary

C1 Au niveau des prépositions . . .

The French often use prepositional phrases, sometimes to be more specific than is possible with English 'for', 'with', 'from'. For example, you *can* say 'le train de Paris' meaning 'the Paris train', but that is ambiguous, and it is clearer to say:

le train **à destination de** Paris	=	the train **to** Paris
le train **en provenance de** Paris	=	the train **from** Paris

261

THE LANGUAGE OF BUSINESS

You will have heard a number of the following expressions in the video sequence:

en provenance de; au cours de; en matière de; en collaboration avec; au niveau de; au bénéfice de.

Here are a few more:

de la part de (= from, on behalf of); en faveur de (= for);
au sujet de (= about); à bord de (on, i.e. on board); aux alentours de (= around, round the edge of)

A vous

Fit the best expression from both lists above into the blanks below.

1. Je vous apporte un mémorandum ____ directeur de la société.
2. Il souhaite vous voir ____ l'annonce qui doit paraître prochainement dans les journaux.
3. ____ notre dernière réunion, le comité a décidé qu'il fallait placer l'annonce le plus tôt possible.
4. Tous les représentants ont voté ____ nouveaux règlements.
5. Ceux-ci vont opérer ____ succursales récemment implantées dans la région.
6. Le modèle le plus récent a été mis au point par une équipe européenne, ____ des chercheurs japonais.
7. ____ informatique, ils sont les plus forts du monde.
8. En ce qui concerne le matériel, ils ont une avance sur nous; ____ logiciel, ils ont fait des progrès énormes. (le matériel = hardware, le logiciel = software).
9. Les discussions ont eu lieu ____ un navire sans que personne le sache.
10. Les deux présidents ont parlé ____ problème sans aborder la question centrale.

Answers: *1. de la part du; 2. au sujet de; 3. au cours de; 4. en faveur des; 5. au bénéfice des; 6. en collaboration avec; 7. en matière d'; 8. au niveau du (or dans le domaine du); 9. à bord d'; 10. aux alentours du*

D Make your language work

> Monsieur,
>
> Vous êtes invité à assister à la réunion mensuelle de direction qui aura lieu le jeudi 22 mars 19-- à 9 heures au siège de la société PKL, 15 rue des Pommes Jaunes, 75015 Paris.
>
> Vous trouverez ci-joint le compte rendu de la dernière réunion ainsi que l'ordre du jour et les dossiers pertinents à la prochaine réunion.
>
> Dans le cas où vous ne pourriez pas assister à cette réunion, nous vous prions de bien vouloir en informer le secrétaire.
>
> Vous souhaitant bonne réception de la présente, veuillez agréer, Monsieur, l'expression de nos sentiments distingués.

You have received the above letter inviting you to a meeting. Unfortunately, you have other engagements that day and cannot attend. Read the letter carefully and compose a reply along the outline given below. Then compare your reply to the model reply which is, as always, just one of many solutions.

Paragraph 1
J'ai bien reçu votre . . .

Paragraph 2
Toutefois, j'ai le regret de . . .

Paragraph 3
Je vous prie de . . .

Paragraph 4
Avec mes regrets réitérés, je vous prie de . . .

THE LANGUAGE OF BUSINESS

> Monsieur,
>
> J'ai bien reçu votre convocation pour la réunion du 22 mars 19--, et je vous en remercie.
>
> Toutefois, j'ai le regret de vous faire savoir que, pris par des engagements antérieurs, il ne me sera pas possible de me libérer à cette occasion.
>
> Je vous prie de bien vouloir excuser mon absence.
>
> Avec mes regrets réitérés, je vous prie de croire, Monsieur, à l'expression de mes salutations distinguées.

E Dialogue

As we have seen throughout the last chapters, it is often difficult for a non-French speaker to follow what is said during a meeting, especially when the majority of participants are actually French!

One of the problems in these meetings is knowing how to intervene, how to disagree with people without offending them, how to make your point without being interrupted, how to offer your assistance without imposing, etc.

In the following dialogue you will hear an Englishman asking a Frenchman for advice on how to avoid all these pitfalls. Take the role of the Frenchman, basing your answers on the instructions given in English and using the pause button when it is your turn to speak.

E Comment garder la parole lorsqu'on vous interrompt tout le temps?

F (Suggest some expressions that would allow you to continue).

Vous pouvez dire par exemple: 'Laissez-moi terminer s'il vous plaît' ou 'vous permettez que je termine?'

E Je crois qu'exprimer une opinion, ça doit être plus facile. Je suppose que je peux commencer par: 'Je crois que . . .', 'Je pense que . . .' etc.?

264

CONDUCTING MEETINGS

F (Affirm the above examples and give some alternatives.)

Oui, c'est ça. Mais vous pouvez aussi dire: 'Je trouve que . . .' ou encore 'D'après moi . . .'.

E Ce qui m'ennuie pendant les réunions c'est qu'il y a des gens qui imposent leurs vues et qui insistent. Comment les arrêter?

F (Say that that is not difficult and give some examples.)

Eh bien, ce n'est pas difficile. Vous leur dites: 'Ce n'est pas la peine d'insister' ou 'inutile d'insister'.

E Conseiller quelqu'un peut être, dans certains cas, assez délicat. Certains n'aiment pas trop qu'on leur donne des conseils.

F (You could always try saying what you would do in this situation, or ask if it is alright to give some advice.)

Je sais, mais on peut toujours utiliser des formules du genre: 'Si j'étais à votre place . . .' ou 'Si je peux me permettre de vous donner un conseil . . .'. Ça passe plus facilement.

E Par contre, lorsqu'on veut avertir quelqu'un ou déconseiller à quelqu'un de faire quelque chose, je suppose qu'il n'est pas vraiment acceptable de dire: 'Ne faites pas cela, c'est ridicule!'.

F (Give an example using the word 'intérêt'.)

Non, bien sûr. Dites plutôt: 'Vous n'avez pas intérêt à . . .'.

E Proposer son aide sans vouloir l'imposer peut également s'avérer délicat.

F (This problem can be overcome by offering your services 'if they are of any help'.)

On peut contourner cette difficulté en disant: 'Si cela peut vous rendre service, je veux bien . . .'.

E Lorsqu'il s'agit de demander la permission à quelqu'un de faire quelque chose, j'ai toujours utilisé: 'J'aimerais . . .' ou 'Je voudrais . . .'.

F (Offer some other, perhaps more pompous, solutions.)

Oui, ce sont les formules les plus courantes. Il y a aussi, mais je trouve que ces phrases sont un peu pompeuses: 'Puis-je me permettre de . . .' ou 'Permettez que je . . .'

E Exprimer le désaccord 'faible' peut également poser des difficultés. Personnellement, j'utilise une formule assez simple: 'Je ne suis pas tout à fait d'accord avec . . .'.

F (Suggest a more subtle approach saying that you're not quite convinced.)

Oui, mais si vous voulez être un peu plus subtil, vous pouvez dire: 'Je ne suis pas très convaincu de . . .'.

E Désapprouver les actions d'une autre personne peut être encore plus difficile.

F (When disapproving of something always use 'peut-être' in your answer.)

Sans aucun doute. Vous pouvez nuancer votre désapprobation en disant, sans oublier le 'peut-être': 'Vous n'auriez peut-être pas dû . . .'.

E Tactiquement, durant une réunion, il n'est pas mauvais de pouvoir de temps en temps se reprocher quelque chose.

F (Give some other examples which spring to mind.)

C'est vrai! Ça peut marcher. Les formules qui me viennent à l'esprit: 'J'ai eu tort de . . .', 'J'aurais dû . . .' ou encore 'J'aurais mieux fait de . . .'.

E Comment peut-on exprimer son regret à part: 'Je suis désolé'?

F (Use expressions with 'regretter', or 'dommage'.)

C'est assez simple: 'Je regrette d'avoir dit cela' ou 'Je regrette que . . .', 'C'est dommage que . . . (+ Subj.)'.

E Laissez-moi essayer de faire deux phrases avec le subjonctif parce que ce n'est pas évident pour un Anglais. 'Je regrette qu'il ne soit pas venu', c'est bon?

F (Comment on correctness.)

Oui, c'est correct.

E 'C'est vraiment dommage qu'il ne soit pas venu'.

F (Idem.)

Excellent!

E Pour finir, comment peut-on exprimer son inquiétude?

F (Suggest expressions with 'peur' and 'craindre'.)

Puisque vous maîtrisez bien le subjonctif vous n'aurez pas de problème: 'J'ai peur que . . .', 'je crains que . . .' plus le subjonctif, bien sûr!

Language comment

You may have noticed that one of the participants of the Eurotunnel meeting used the word 'coincé' whereas he should have used 'restreint', 'limité' or 'étroit'. Someone else could not find the verb 'profiter de' and used the English equivalent 'to take advantage'. The same person started a sentence with 'Il faut qu'on soit . . .' and then continued with 'très attention'. He probably wanted to say 'Il faut qu'on soit très attentif', or 'Il faut qu'on fasse attention'.

The above shows that the French themselves can also make little mistakes in the heat of a debate. These little mistakes, however, do not stop them from communicating, and that is the essence.

It is wise to pay attention to the verb 'manquer', which can change meaning depending on whether it is followed by a preposition or not.

Ce matin, il a manqué l'autobus.	This morning he missed the bus.
Il lui manque deux francs pour acheter ce livre.	He is two francs short for buying this book.
Il a manqué à sa parole.	He did not keep his word.

During the meeting at the Crédit Agricole de Londres, some participants used English words. This is a common phenomenon if you happen to live abroad for a number of years. You end up being influenced by the language of the country you live in and assume a certain jargon typical to your profession.

an agenda	=	un ordre du jour, not agenda
the minutes	=	le compte rendu, not les minutes*
the branches	=	nos agences,
		nos succursales, not branches

* 'Minutes' is a word which is also used in French, but only in a legal context, e.g. les minutes des actes notariés, d'un jugement. They are, however, very detailed whereas 'le compte rendu' is limited to the essentials.

Note

In order to be able to follow what is said during the Crédit Agricole meeting in London it is important that you understand the structure of the Crédit Agricole:

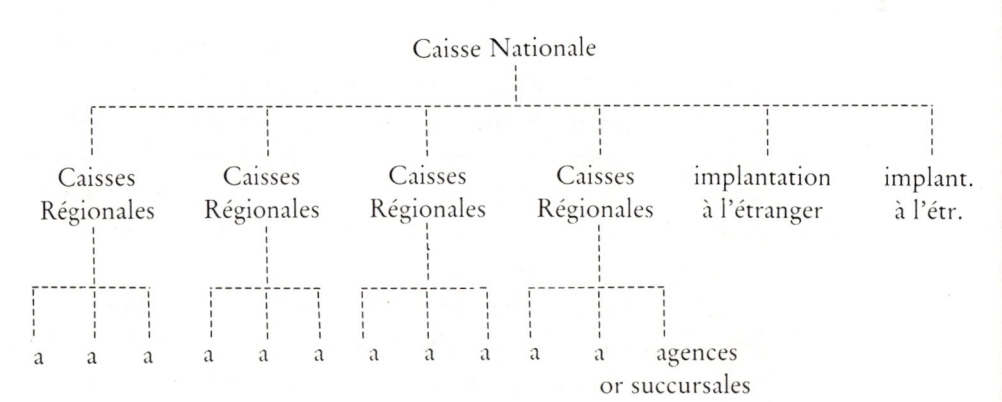

```
                          Caisse Nationale
       ┌──────────┬──────────┬──────────┬──────────┬──────────┐
    Caisses    Caisses    Caisses    Caisses   implantation  implant.
   Régionales Régionales Régionales Régionales  à l'étranger  à l'étr.
    ┌──┬──┐    ┌──┬──┐    ┌──┬──┐    ┌──┬──┐
    a  a  a    a  a  a    a  a  a    a  a  a  agences
                                              or succursales
```

Although the word 'agences' is used in the sentence:

> Le questionnaire qui nous a été envoyé par le siège à Paris concernant nos relations avec nos branches en France, nos agences en France . . .

what is actually meant is 'les Caisses Régionales'. The 'implantations à l'étranger' which are mentioned a bit later, generally have the same status as the 'Caisses Régionales'. These 'Caisses Régionales' are therefore not 'agences' of the Crédit Agricole in London.

Similarly, 'maison mère' should not be translated with 'parent company', rather with 'main office'.

Sketch: La bise

Having two ways of saying 'you' in French can make life a bit complicated for anyone wanting to learn the language. In broad terms, **vous** should be used in all formal situations to be polite, and **tu** only in familiar circumstances. Though, of course, it isn't really that straightforward! A rule of thumb is, if in any doubt, use **vous** to be safe. Also, although we think of the French as always kissing one another, there are actually a lot of unwritten rules regarding who to kiss and when – try shaking hands instead and let your French companion take the lead when it comes to proffering a cheek.

Business notes

The example of Eurotunnel illustrates the way in which transnational and indeed multinational companies will increasingly be staffed. Its board brings together an equal proportion of British and French directors, each one of whom must speak and understand the other's language and, equally as important, the way the business mentality and culture differs in each country. As the impetus of the Single European Market builds up, more and more top teams of this nature will be constituted in the wake of joint ventures, mergers and acquisitions. A new breed of manager is hence emerging – the Euromanager, capable not only of speaking one or two languages other than his own but understanding the economic, social and cultural environment of the EC countries. He will need this background because the nature of his job is changing as pan-European companies emerge. His home country may still be his base but in addition to dealing with his own national staff, he will have to:

- converse, socialise and negotiate with customers and suppliers from other EC countries
- recruit and integrate nationals from other countries into management teams
- supervise the work of groups of people from different countries
- manage a boss of a different nationality
- find business opportunities and make investment and divestment decisions in the EC
- negotiate with trade union representatives, national governments and EC Commission officials.

For those companies which are operating from the UK on continental markets, the acquisition of such skills at senior management level has meant buying in foreign managers with international experience who can operate and think transculturally. Multinationals, once used to having a headquarters in each separate national market, are creating international management teams in a single European headquarters, based in London, Paris, Brussels, etc., as they move to rationalise and standardise production, advertising and distribution across frontiers.

However, the proper supply of multi-cultural and multi-lingual talent is not being left solely to the constitution of Boards of Directors. Much lower down the organisation, many companies are recruiting groups of graduate trainees from different European countries and through job rotation in a range of functions across Europe, the creation of European 'universities' and training programmes (Olivetti, ICL, Otis Elevators, etc.) and individual assignments in other countries, they are getting to grips with the reality of developing a European culture from the bottom up. An important point here, of course, is understanding the higher education qualifications in other EC countries. Mutual recognition of such qualifications is one thing, knowing their level and value in their national context is another and hence, if doing business in France, a company must know the difference between a university and a *Grande Ecole* (and the pecking order!), the meaning of a BTS (*Brevet de Technicien Supérieur*) or a DUT (*Diplôme Universitaire de Technologie*), both technician qualifications, to understand fully how compatible their French staff appointments are with similar recruits both in the UK and in other EC countries.

In this video sequence, there are two meetings, one at Eurotunnel's headquarters and the second at Crédit Agricole's London office. The senior Eurotunnel executives are discussing the publicity arrangements for the final break-through of the tunnel and ensuring that the company obtains maximum exposure for the event. Many proposals are discussed for the British Prime Minister and the French President to participate in the celebrations when the tunnels meet in the middle. There are difficult logistic problems, but these may be worth overcoming for such an historic event. The meeting also discussed how the proceedings would be televised, the special medals the workers will get and the brochures which are to be sent to shareholders. Later on in the meeting (and not appearing on the video) they discussed the TGV and the possibility of inviting more British parliamentarians to experience it at first hand. Eurotunnel believes that a high speed line connecting Folkestone with London and the main lines going North and West is a central part of Britain's infrastructure requirements for the 1990s.

In the second sequence, the proceedings are more formal and much closer to what might be expected from a typical French meeting. But formality goes beyond the mere structure of the meeting. The use of *vous* or *tu* will give an indication of the closeness of relationships and so too will the traditional French handshake. The strength of a handshake (even whether a hand is offered at all!) will give many clues to the various levels of power wielded in a company. A senior manager must always be expected to extend his hand first to a junior – the other way round is pure presumption. A refusal to shake hands may mean displeasure and the briefest touch of the hand could well denote a certain coolness. On the shop-floor it is a sign of solidarity with the workers and goes a long way towards establishing harmonious relationships.

Formality shows itself, too, in the way in which positions in the hierarchy, particularly in large French companies, are all important. Here, qualifications are often crucial in determining whether you are a *cadre* (manager), *agent de maîtrise* (supervisory grade), *technicien* (technician), *employé* (clerical staff) or *ouvrier* (worker). Movement between the *cadre* and *technicien/agent de maîtrise* levels is very difficult in France, the former being largely reserved for engineers and those having been to business school. Technicians are regarded as too specialised to reach managerial grade (whose tasks are considered more 'noble'). Class distinctions are often observed in this way and are a pervasive feature of French society.

French meetings may be more formal, but they are also noisier and the occasion for long discussions of principle and theory. The French love talking concepts and British businessmen must adapt to what seems a much more verbose way of doing things. Banging fists, slanging matches and often very direct speaking are all part of the culture and the rules of the game (and collective decisions are often hard to take!). In their efforts to be diplomatic, the British are often seen as hypocritical so be sure that what you say can be interpreted at its face value. Liking a proposal often means its acceptance in France whereas in the UK it is often one of a range of different possible reactions.

Lastly, an informal, friendly and joking approach to business might well be frowned on in a French context – that is, until you get to know those concerned well. The French may often appear aloof and remote during an initial meeting. Personal relationships are often very important to them and too quick a familiarity can be taboo. They would claim, however, that the British approach is much more superficial – friendship in France, once gained, goes very deep. One important rider must be added here, however – the young *cadres* are beginning to adopt a more informal approach and consider the habits discussed above as being old-fashioned. The basic advice is, then, be aware of a French manager's position, background and age – it could be vital to do your homework!

Crédit Agricole, the bank figuring in the video sequence and probably comparatively unknown in the UK, is not only one of the largest banks in France but also in the world. It owes this position largely to the fact that it has traditionally been the 'farmers' bank and has hence had the savings of the vast rural sector in France at its disposal. Like many of the large deposit banks in France it has had an international network for some years and is now discussing ways of improving its services to its customers now that the Single Market is imminent and French small and medium-sized companies are beginning to do more business abroad. Its customers are increasingly non-agricultural private individuals and companies (more and more in towns, too) since its monopoly of preferential loans to the agricultural sector has ceased and consequently it has had to branch out into other businesses.

It forms part of the mutual banks sector which is only one of a number of different specialist sectors which constitute the banking scene in France. This group also includes the *Banques Populaires, Crédit Coopératif* and *Crédit Mutuel* which all have a co-operative status with members (sociétaires).

Other groups are:

- *Caisses d'Epargne*, the *Ecureuil* (squirrel) group of savings banks, with its traditional tax-free passbook account, Livret "A".
- The high street banks. BNP and Crédit Lyonnais are still nationalised and are major institutional investors, possessing share holdings and seats on boards in many private companies. This can be important to remember in the event of takeover bids as there may be special arrangements whereby banks have the option to issue special subordinated loans which can count as equity. Société Générale was privatised under the previous Chirac government. Paribas and Indosuez are the major merchant and investment banks.
- *Sociétés financières*, comprising finance houses specialising in a wide range of activities including leasing, mortgages and consumer finance.
- *Institutions financières spécialisées* which include Crédit Foncier, Crédit National and the Sociétés *de développement régional* (like venture-capital companies). The principal function of these state-owned institutions is to provide long-term investment funds.

All of the above categories are called *établissements de crédit* and belong to the *Association Française des Banques*. They often cater for different clientèle segments but can broadly offer the same kind of products and services. One particular feature of French banking is the high level of technology used. Within the next two years, for example, the whole system will be using the so-called smart-card (*carte à puce*). Other financial institutions of note are the three nationalised insurance companies GAN, AGF and UAP which, again, are major institutional investors and exert considerable influence on the stock market.

Business Magazine 7: 'The Euro Manager'

Managing in Europe opens up possibilities for co-operation between different companies, which, by working in conjunction with each other can better exploit a particular niche in the European market. In this last business magazine we look at partnerships, acquisitions and mergers as a way of developing market share in France and beyond.

Grammar kit

by Minou Reeves

We saw earlier in this book that grammar is the foundation of a language. In order to speak a language correctly, confidently and flexibly you need to be familiar with the basic rules of grammar.

This section gives an overview of some basic points of grammar which are not treated in detail in the language chapters.

Some of the basic building blocks of language are:

- **A sentence**   A complete utterance conveying a piece of information or an idea. It contains a verb and ends in a full stop.
- **A clause**   A subsection of a sentence, e.g. 'he promised *that the order would arrive in time.*
- **A phrase**   A group of words bound together by their meaning, e.g. James – a noun,
  The Company's Managing Director – a noun phrase.
- **A noun**   Names a being, or a thing.
- **An adjective**   Qualifies the noun.
- **An adverb**   Qualifies an adjective or verb.
- **A pronoun**   Stands in for a noun.
- **A verb**   Says what the subject is doing/not doing.

In the sentence below you will find a number of the 'parts of speech' to which any grammar course will refer.

The	new	manager	called
definite article	adjective	noun	verb
the	whole	team	to
definite article	adjective	noun	preposition
a	meeting	because	he
indefinite article	noun	conjunction	pronoun
wanted	to brief	them	
verb	verb infinitive	pronoun	

Nouns

Nouns are used to name a being (human or non-human)

    la femme   (woman)
    le chien   (dog)

or a thing (concrete or abstract)

    le bâtiment   (building)
    la livraison   (delivery)
    l'efficacité   (efficiency)

Gender

In French, all nouns have a gender. They are either masculine or feminine. When you learn a noun, you should learn its gender at the same time. This is important because the gender determines a great number of other aspects within the sentence. Nouns with the following endings tend to be feminine:

-sion	-ence	-une	-ise
-tion	-ale	-dé	-ée
-aison	-ole	-tié	-ette
-ance	-ure	-ière	-ude

Nouns with the following endings are usually masculine:

-asme	-acle	-oir	-isme
-al	-et	-eau	-oil
-at	-ment	-ail	-age

Plural nouns

In most cases you can make a noun plural by adding an **-s** to the singular form.

    la femme   les femme*s*   (women)
    la pièce   les pièce*s*   (pieces)
    le véhicule   les véhicule*s*   (vehicles)

There are a number of variations to this rule:

1. Nouns ending in **-s**, **-x**, and **-z** do not change in the plural

    la fois   les fois   (times)
    le taux   les taux   (rates)
    le nez   les nez   (noses)

2. Many nouns ending in **-au**, **-eau**, **-eu**, **-oeu**, take an **-x** to become plural.

le tuyau	les tuyaux	(pipes, tubes)
le marteau	les marteaux	(hammers)
le jeu	les jeux	(games)
le voeu	les voeux	(wishes)

3. Nouns ending in **-al**, change to **-aux** in the plural.

| le journal | les journaux | (newspapers) |

Note: The same rules apply to adjectives in the plural

| un beau jour | des beaux jours | (nice days) |

Articles

Definite article = the
Indefinite article = a, an
Partitive article = some, any

The article in French depends on the gender of a noun. The table below provides a few examples.

	definite article	indefinite article	partitive article
Singular	le	un	du
	la	une	de la
	l'	un	de l'
	l'	une	de l'
Plural	les	des	des
	les	des	des
	les	des	des

The partitive

Du, de, de la, des, (the partitive) expresses 'some' or 'any' in English:

Je voudrais **du** café — I'd like some coffee
Il aura **des** problèmes énormes — He'll have enormous problems

Du, de la, des, become **de** in 3 cases

1. After expressions of quantity

| assez de | (enough of) | une boîte de | (a box of) |
| beaucoup de | (a lot/much of) | une bouteille de | (a bottle of) |

277

peu de	(a little of)	un verre de	(a glass of)
trop de	(too much of)	une tasse de	(a cup of)
tant de	(so many of)	un kilo de	(a kilo of)
moins de	(less of)	une douzaine de	(a dozen of)
plus de	(more of)	une tranche de	(a slice of)

Compare the following phrases and spot the different translation.

Je voudrais *du* café	I would like some coffee
but: Je voudrais une tasse *de* café	a cup of ...
J'ai du travail	I have some work
but: J'ai beaucoup *de* travail	I have a lot of work
J'ai assez de travail	I have enough work
Beaucoup *de* nos clients	Many of our customers

La plupart and **plusieurs** form the exceptions to this particular rule. The partitive article after **plusieurs** does, contrary to expectation, not change:

La plupart *du* temps   Most of the time

whereas plusieurs does not take a partitive article at all.

plusieurs produits   several products

2. **Before an adjective *preceding* its noun:**

Il aura des problèmes très graves
but Il aura de très graves problèmes

3. **After a negation** (see also Language Chapter 2, section B6)

Je voudrais du café
but Je ne veux pas de café

The preposition **de** in combination with **le, la, les,** also becomes **du, de la** and **des.**

L'intérieur de la voiture	The interior of the car
La facture du 4 Janvier	The invoice of 4 January
Les désirs des clients	The wishes of the clients

Furthermore: the preposition **de** is needed after certain expressions, such as **avoir besoin de**:

j'ai besoin d'argent   I need money/I need some money

THE GRAMMAR KIT

Pronouns

Words which replace nouns or nominal expressions. They vary in form depending on their case, i.e., whether they are the *subject* of the verb or *direct* or *indirect object*.

Examples:

Je	**vois**	**l'homme**		I see the man
subject	verb	direct object		
Je	**le**	**vois**		I see him
subject	direct object	verb		
il	**me**	**voit**		He sees me
subject	direct object	verb		
Elle	**lui**	**donne**	**la lettre**	She gives him the letter
subject	indirect object	verb	direct object	
Elle	**la**	**lui**	**donne**	She gives it (= the letter) to him
subject	direct object	indirect object	verb	

		Subject	Direct Object	Indirect Object
singular	1st person	je	me, m'	me, m'
	2nd person	tu	te, t'	te, t'
	3rd person	il (m)	le, l'(m)	lui (m)
	3rd person	elle(f)	la, l'(f)	lui (f)
plural	1st person	nous	nous	nous
	2nd person	vous	vous	vous
	3rd person	ils (m)	les (m)	leur (m)
	3rd person	elles (f)	les (f)	leur (f)

For practice of direct object pronouns see Language Chapter 5, B1

For disjunctive ('strong') pronouns (**moi**, etc.) See Language Chapter 4, B3.

The pronoun **on** is used in spoken language to replace **nous** or **ils**, but takes the **il/elle** form of the verb and can mean 'one', 'people', 'you', 'we', or 'they'.

On fabrique des produits de haute qualité.   We manufacture high quality products.

Relative pronouns

Words which are used to introduce clauses giving further information about a noun.

Qui is the relative pronoun as a *subject* of the clause and refers to a person or thing.

> Le monsieur qui *parle avec votre directeur* est notre représentant.
> The gentleman who *is talking to your director* is our representative.

Que works as the *direct object* of a clause and may refer to a person or thing.

> La dame que vous avez vue à l'exposition est mon associée.
> The lady whom you saw at the exhibition is my partner.

In the perfect tense, the past participle agrees with the preceeding relative pronoun which is the direct object. Hence **La dame** *que* j'ai vu*e*.

For practice of **qui/que** see Language Chapter 6, B2

Ce qui Is used as *subject* when there is no preceding noun and refers to things only.

> Savez-vous ce qui est arrivé?
> Do you know what has happened?

Ce que Is used as *direct object* when there is no preceding noun and refers to a thing.

> Il nous a dit ce que nous devons faire.
> He told us what we have to do.

A qui Is used as *indirect object* and refers to persons only

> La personne à qui vous avez donné les documents est notre comptable.
> The person to whom you gave the documents is our accountant.

Tout ce qui, tout ce que Means 'everything that', 'all that'.

> On a vu tout ce qui est dans cette salle d'exposition.
> We have seen everything that is in this exhibition hall.
> Tout ce que vous m'avez montré m'intéresse beaucoup.
> Everything that you showed me interests me very much.

For **celui, ceux, celle** and **celles** – see Language Chapter 4.

Lequel is used after a preposition (**pour lequel, duquel**, etc.) It can refer to persons or things and then agrees with the preceeding noun (**laquelle, lesquels, lesquelles**).

La raison pour laquelle je vous ai téléphoné . . .	The reason for which/that I phoned you . . .
Je n'aime pas les hôtels dans lesquels (*or*: où) il n'y a pas d'ascenseur.	I do not like hotels in which/where there is no elevator.

Please note that after the preposition **à**, you get **auquel, à laquelle, auxquels** and **auxquelles**. After the preposition **de** the forms are: **duquel, de la quelle, desquels, desquelles**.

Le projet auquel nous avons travaillé a fini par être réalisé.	The project on which we worked has finally been realised.
Les réunions auxquelles vous assisterez . . .	The meetings in which you will take part . . .

Dont is used more often than **de qui**, **duquel**, and means 'whose', 'of/about whom', 'which'.

Voici le nouveau modèle **dont** je vous parlais	Here is the new model (**that**) I was talking to you about
L'emballage **dont** nous avons besoin revient très cher	The packaging (**that**) we need works out very expensive

Interrogative pronouns

These are used in questions such as 'Who?' 'What?' 'Whose', 'Whom?' 'To whom?' **Qui** is 'who' when used as a *subject*

Qui êtes-vous?	Who are you?
Qui est ce monsieur?	Who is this gentleman?
Qui sont les directeurs de Brimax?	Who are the directors of Brimax?

Qui is 'whom' when used as an *object*.

Qui avez-vous rencontré à la conférence?	Whom did you meet at the conference?
Qui est-ce que vous avez vu a l'exposition?	Whom did you see at the exhibition?

Que means 'what'. Use **que** when there is already a subject.

Que voulez-vous faire?	What do you want to do?
Qu'est-ce qu'il veut?	What does he want?

A qui means 'whose' or to 'whom'.

A qui sont ces papiers?	Whose papers are these?

Quoi means 'what'. Use **quoi** with pronouns.

 De quoi vous a-t-il parlé?   What did he speak to you about?

Indefinite pronouns and adjectives

These are used when no precise indications are given about the nature of things or people referred to, like 'everybody', 'nobody', 'people', 'someone', 'somebody'.

 Quelqu'un m'a donné   Someone gave me this
 ce nouveau catalogue.   new catalogue.

N'importe qui	– anyone	n'importe où	anywhere
N'importe quoi	– anything	n'importe quand	anytime
N'importe quel(le)	– any	n'importe comment	anyhow

Personne means 'no one', 'nobody'

 Personne ne sait la réponse.   Nobody knows the answer.

Quelques-uns, quelques-unes – means 'some', 'a few'.

 Vous restent-ils des catalogues   Have you still got the catalogues
 de l'année dernière? Oui, nous   from last year? Yes, we still have
 en avons quelques-uns.   some.

Quelques refers to a small number of indefinite items or people and often corresponds to 'a few', 'some'.

 Pourriez-vous me donner   Could you give me some
 quelques renseignements?   information?

Quelque chose	– something
Quelquefois	– sometime
Quelquepart	– somewhere

Plusieurs means several, various.

 Nous avons plusieurs clients   We have several customers in France
 en France

Certains can be 'some', 'a certain number of'. Whereas **quelques** refers to an indefinite number, and **plusieurs** stresses plurality '**certain(s)**' is more definite in that it refers to a subsection within a group.

 Certains de mes amis français   Some of my French friends believe
 pensent que la vie est plus   that life is more expensive in London
 chère à Londres qu'à Paris.   than in Paris.

Chacun (m) **Chacune** (f)   each one, everyone

Chacune de ces machines fait deux tonnes de poids	Each of these machines weighs two tons

Chaque   every or each.

chaque jour	every day
chaque matin	every morning
Chaque échantillon est muni d'une fiche technique.	Each sample comes with a technical index sheet.

L'un, L'autre   These are often used in the same sentence to distinguish between two individual things or persons or between two groups.

Ici vous voyez deux bâtiments; l'un est l'entrepôt, l'autre le garage.	Here, you see two buildings; one is the warehouse, the other the garage.

Other expressions with **l'un** and **l'autre** are

L'un(e) et l'autre	– both
Ni l'un(e) ni l'autre	– neither
L'un(e) ou l'autre	– either

Le même, la même, les mêmes – the same one(s)

C'est le même produit	This is the same product
Ce sont les mêmes articles	These are the same items

Adjectives and adverbs

Adjectives are used to describe the qualities of nouns, and adverbs describe the qualities of verbs and adjectives.

Adjectives

In French adjectives vary according to the gender and number of the noun. Pay attention to the ending as it will affect pronunciation.

Le marché franç*ais* – the French market
La mode franç*aise* – French fashion.

Although most adjectives follow the noun they qualify, some precede the noun. The most common ones are:

beau, bon, joli, jeune, vaste, grand, haut, long, petit, court, mauvais, méchant.

Do realise, however, that the position of an adjective can sometimes change its meaning.

la semaine dernière	last week
la dernière semaine	the last week
un certain changement	a certain change
un changement certain	a definite change
un ancien collègue	a former colleague
une usine ancienne	an ancient factory

Adjective agreement

We already saw that an adjective agrees in gender and number with the noun it qualifies. The general rule is to add **-e** for feminine, **-s** for masculine plural, and **-es** for feminine plural.

Elle est intelligent*e* et très content*e* de son travail.   She is intelligent and very happy with her work.

Feminine endings

Adjectives ending in the masculine form in one of the following letters, or group of letters, follow slightly different rules for feminine agreement.

Masc.	Fem.	
-x	-se	sérieux – sérieuse
-s	-sse	gros – grosse
-ien	-ienne	parisien – parisienne
-l	-lle	manuel – manuelle
-et	-ète	complet – complète
-f	-ve	bref – brève
-er	-ère	premier – première

and here are some common exceptions to the above rules:

doux – douce
vieux – vieille
beau – belle

The feminine agreement for adjectives whose masculine form ends in **-eur** can be one of the following:

protecteur – protectrice
extérieur – extérieure
flatteur – flatteuse

Plural endings

The general rule for plural agreement is to add **-s** for masculine plural and **-es** for feminine plural, but there are again exceptions.

Many of the adjectives ending in -al change to **-aux** in masculine plural; otherwise they follow the normal rules for agreement:

principal – principaux

An example of the exception to this rule is **final – finals**.

Comparative and superlative forms of adjectives

In French the comparative is formed by adding **plus** (more), **moins** (less) or **aussi . . . que** (as . . . as).

Le voyage en voiture est cher	The journey by car is expensive
Le voyage par le train est *plus* cher	The journey by train is more expensive
Le voyage en car est aussi cher que le voyage en voiture	The journey by coach is as expensive as the journey by car

The superlative is formed by adding **le plus** or **le moins**

Le voyage en avion c'est *le plus* cher	The journey by plane is the most expensive

You can use many other adjectives in a similar way:

plus difficile	–	more difficult
plus facile	–	easier
moins cher	–	less expensive
moins commode	–	less comfortable

It is important to realise that in both comparative and superlative the adjective has to agree with the noun.

Comparative:	*Ma* voiture est grande	My car is big
	Sa voiture est *plus* grande	His car is bigger
Superlative:	Votre voiture est *la plus* grande de *toutes*	Your car is the biggest of all

Interrogative adjectives

Interrogative adjectives are used to express queries about the character or identity of the thing or person referred to, e.g. **quel** (what/which).

	sing.	plur.
masc.	quel	quels
Fem.	quelle	quelles

Quelle est votre réponse? — What is your answer?
(**la** réponse(f), therefore **quelle**)
De quel type de produit êtes-vous à la recherche? — What type of product are you looking for?
(**le** type(m), therefore **quel**.)

Possessive adjectives

As with all other adjectives, in French possessive adjectives agree with the noun and not with the person to whom things belong:

> her *book* is *son* livre (le livre)
> his *pen* is *sa* plume (la plume)

So when you say **sa maison** or **son bureau** it could mean both 'her' or 'his' house or 'her' or 'his' office. Equally, you say **mon travail** for 'my work', no matter whether you are a man or a woman. It is the noun that determines the possessive adjective.

The possessive adjectives are:

	feminine		masculine	
English	singular	plural	singular	plural
my	ma	mes	mon	mes
your	ta	tes	ton	tes
his	sa	ses	son	ses
her	sa	ses	son	ses
our	notre	nos	notre	nos
your	votre	vos	votre	vos
their	leur(m)	leurs	leur	leurs
their	leur(f)	leurs	leur	leurs

For use of 'le mien' etc see language Chapter 4, B5

Demonstrative adjectives:

Adjectives which are used to point things out, e.g., 'this', 'that', 'these', 'those', are *demonstrative adjectives*. They *agree with the noun*. The French equivalents are:

	sing.	plur.
masc	ce, cet	ces
fem.	cette	

le secteur: ce secteur — ces secteurs
une organisation: cette organisation — ces organisations

Cet is used before a vowel or mute 'h'
cet après-midi — cet homme

Nationalities as adjectives

It is necessary to learn the endings of the various nationalities and their agreement. Often they end with *ais* or *aise* in the feminine form.

    Il est Franç*ais*   Elle est Franç*aise*

There are also some nationalities that end with *ois* or *oise*

    Il est Suéd*ois*   Elle est Suéd*oise*

Some nationalities end in -ien and ienne

    Il est Italien   Elle est Italienne

Nationalities ending in 'd' take an 'e' in the feminine form:

    Il est Allemand   Elle est Allemande

The following nationalities are invariable:

    Il est Belge   Elle est Belge
    Il est Suisse   Elle est Suisse

Languages are masculine in French; the name for a language often takes the same form as the word for the male inhabitant of that country, but written with a small letter:

    le français/je parle français
    l'anglais/je parle anglais
    l'allemand/je parle allemand

Adverbs

As we have mentioned before, adverbs describe verbs and adjectives. They are formed as follows:

- Most adverbs in French are formed by adding **-ment** to the feminine form of the adjective:

Masc. Adjective	Fem. Adjective	Adverb	English
sérieux	sérieuse	sérieusement	(seriously)
final	finale	finalement	(finally)

Il étudie le français sérieusement	(adverb describes verb)
Elle est sérieusement malade	(adverb describes adjective)

287

- Adverbs derived from adjectives ending in **-ant** and **-ent** in the masculine take the ending **-mment**

Masculine Adjective	Adverb	English
courant	couramment	fluently
constant	constamment	constantly
évident	évidemment	evidently
fréquent	fréquemment	frequently

Comment parle-t-il le français?   How does he speak French?
Il le parle couramment.   He speaks it fluently.

- When the adjective ends in a silent **e** it is usually changed to **é** before adding the **-ment** to form the adverb.

Masculine Adjective	Feminine Adjective	Adverb	English
énorme	énorme	énormément	enormously
profond	profonde	profondément	profoundly, deeply

Je suis profondément touché(e)   (I am deeply touched by your
par votre gentillesse.   kindness).

- If the adjective ends in a vowel, the ending **-ment** is simply added to the masculine form:

Masculine Adjective	Adverb	English
poli	poliment	politely
vrai	vraiment	really, truly

- Some adverbs are identical to the masculine adjective form. Here is a list of these invariable adverbs:

bas	low
cher	expensive
chaud	hot
tard	late
dur	hard

- Some adverbs are entirely different from their adjective form:

Adjective	English	Adverb	English
bon	good	bien	well
mauvais	bad	mal	badly
meilleur	better	mieux	better
petit	small	peu	little, few

Il parle bien le français — He speaks French well (adverb)
Les vins français sont bons — French wines are good (adjective)

Conjunctions and prepositions

(See language Chapter 7, C1 for prepositions)
Conjunctions are the joints in the system, linking sentences and part sentences, and showing relationships between ideas and events. Prepositions show the relations between objects and persons.

Conjuctions a few examples:

où (where)   d'où (from where)
comment (how)   quand (when)
pourquoi (why)   puisque (as)
parce que (because) tandis que (whereas)
lorsque (when, as)

Dites-moi quand vous voulez me voir — Tell me when you want to see me.
Je dois vérifier où se trouve votre facture. — I have to check where your invoice is.

Prepositions a few examples:

à (to, in)   de (from, of)   après (after)
chez (at)   par (by)   sur (on)
avant (before) en (in)
sous (under)   avec (with)

Verbs

Verbs are the heart of a language and enable the speaker to express actions and feelings. The basic form of the verb is the *infinitive*:

parler   to speak
venir   to come

In French the infinitive usually ends in **-er**, **-re**, **-ir**, **-oir**.

The verb operates in two *moods*; the indicative and the subjunctive. *The indicative mood* refers to things of certainty that are happening, have happened or will happen:

Il parle	he speaks
ils vont	they go

The *subjunctive mood* refers to suppositions, things that need to happen, ought to happen. It reveals feelings of uncertainty, fear, doubt, compulsion.

Il veut que j'aille.	He wants me to go.
Je doute que ce soit une bonne idée.	I doubt that this is a good idea.
Il craint qu'ils ne fassent pas le travail.	He fears they might not do the work.
Il faut que je finisse ce projet.	I must finish this project.

Verbs can further be divided into two voices, *active* and *passive*. The voice is active when the subject is the agent.

Nous fabriquons des voitures	We manufacture cars
Nous expédions nos produits en France.	We send our products to France.

The voice is passive when things happen to the subject.

Nos voitures sont fabriquées en Angleterre.	Our cars are manufactured in England.
Nos produits sont expédiés en France	Our products are sent to France

Tenses

Within these two categories, the mood and the voice, verbs can express tense or time – that is *the present* and different types of *past* and *future*. You will find further information about tenses in the following chapters of the book:

The present indicative	language Chapters 1 and 2
The present subjunctive	language Chapters 2, 3 and 7
The future	language Chapters 2
The imperfect	language Chapter 4
The perfect (passé composé)	language Chapter 3
The conditional	language Chapter 6

Conjugation

Within tenses, verbs modify according to their subject: first person, second person, third person, singular or plural.

This modification is called conjugation

Verbs are conjugated in a variety of different ways but mainly fall into four categories according to their ending, **-ir, -er, -re, -oir**. (The conjugation of these four groups is given in the table at end of this section). There are, however some exceptions and peculiarities which you will need to learn. A pocket verb guide would be a very useful investment.

Transitive or intransitive

Apart from mood and voice, verbs can be *transitive* or *intransitive*. The majority of verbs are transitive and *can take an object*. Intransitive verbs *cannot take an object*.

Transitive:	**Il**	**lit**	**la lettre**	He reads the letter.
	subject	verb	object	
Intransitive:	**J'**	**arrive**	**aujourd'hui**	I arrive today.
	subject	verb	adverb	

Affirmative, negative and interrogative

Verbs can be:

Affirmative	Je travaille comme directeur.	I work as a director
Negative	Je ne travaille pas comme directeur.	I do not work as a director.
Interrogative	Travaillez-vous comme directeur? Est-ce que vous travaillez comme directeur?	Do you work as a director.

Spelling changes

The conjugation of some of the verbs undergoes a slight variation in order to preserve their phonetic pattern:

- Because the pronunciation of 'c' can change from 's' to 'k' when it is followed by an 'a', 'o', or 'u', the 'c' is modified to 'ç':

placer	il place	nous placions
but	il plaçait	nous plaçons

- Because the pronunciation of 'g' can change to 'gu' when it is followed by 'a', 'o' or 'u', an 'e' is added to the conjugation ending starting with one of the above vowels.

manger	je mange	nous mangions
but	nous mangeons	je mangeai

- In the conjugation of verbs ending in **-ayer**, **-oyer** and **-uyer** the 'y' changes to 'i' when followed by a mute 'e'.

essayer	nous essayons	vous essayez
but	j'essaie	il essaiera

- The majority of verbs ending in **-eler** and **-eter** double their 'l' or 't' if the letter which follows is a mute 'e'.

jeter	nous jetons	vous jetez
but	il jette	je jetterai

The remainder of these verbs do not double the 'l' or 't' in the circumstances described above, but change the 'e' preceding the consonant into 'è'.

acheter	nous achetons	j'achetais
but	j'achète	nous achèterons

- Verbs ending in **-éder**, **-éger**, **-éler** or **-éter** change their 'é' to 'è' when the syllable they are in is followed by a *final* mute 'e'.

Céder	je cède	Ils cèdent
but	tu céderas	nous céderions

Reflexive verbs

These verbs are mostly connected with personal actions referring to ones self and interacting with others see also language Chapter 2:

Referring to onself	s'installer	to settle
	s'asseoir	to sit down
Interacting	se rencontrer	to meet
	se connaître	to know each other
Impersonal	se passer	to happen
	se trouver	to be located

Reflexive verbs are used in French when the passive voice is used in English.

Ce vin se boit frais	This wine is served chilled
Ces piles se rechargent automatiquement	These batteries recharge automatically

NOTE: When used in the perfect tense, reflexive verbs take the auxiliary **être** (to be).

    Ils se sont installés   They settled

Verb tables

1. **Être**
   - Present participle — étant
   - Past participle — été
   - Present indicative — je suis, tu es, il est, nous sommes, vous êtes, ils sont
   - Present subjunctive — que je sois, que tu sois, qu'il soit, que nous soyons, que vous soyez, qu'ils soient
   - Imperfect — j'étais, tu étais, il était, nous étions, vous étiez, ils étaient
   - Future — je serai, tu seras, il sera, nous serons, vous serez, ils seront
   - Imperative — sois, soyons, soyez.

2. **Avoir**
   - Present participle — ayant
   - Past participle — eu
   - Present indicative — j'ai, tu as, il a, nous avons, vous avez, ils ont
   - Present subjunctive — que j'aie, que tu aies, qu'il ait, que nous ayons, que vous ayez, qu'ils aient
   - Imperfect — j'avais, tu avais, ils avait, nous avions, vous aviez, ils avaient
   - Future — j'aurai, tu auras, il aura, nous aurons, vous aurez, ils auront
   - Imperative — aie, ayons, ayez

Infinitive	parler	finir	partir	répondre	recevoir
Present participle	parlant	finissant	partant	répondant	recevant
Past participle	parlé	fini	parti	répondu	reçu

293

THE LANGUAGE OF BUSINESS

Present indicative	je parle tu parles il parle nous parlons vous parlez ils parlent	je finis tu finis il finit nous finissons vous finissez ils finissent	je pars tu pars il part nous partons vous partez ils partent	je réponds tu réponds il répond nous répondons vous répondez ils répondent	je reçois tu reçois il reçoit nous recevons vous recevez ils reçoivent
Present subjunctive	Que je parle Que tu parles Qu'il parle Que nous parlions Que vous parliez Qu'ils parlent	Que je finisse Que tu finisses Qu'il finisse Que nous finissions Que vouz finissiez Qu'ils finissent	Que je parte Que tu partes Qu'il parte Que nous partions Que vous partiez Qu'ils partent	Que je réponde Que tu répondes Qu'il réponde Que nous répondions Que vous répondiez Qu'ils répondent	Que je reçoive Que tu reçoives Qu'il reçoive Que nous recevions Que vous receviez Qu'ils reçoivent
Imperfect	je parlais tu parlais il parlait nous parlions vous parliez ils parlaient	je finissais tu finissais il finissait nous finissions vous finissiez ils finissaient	je partais tu partais il partait nous partions vous partiez ils partaient	je répondais tu répondais il répondait nous répondions vous répondiez ils répondaient	je recevais tu recevais il recevait nous recevions vous receviez ils recevaient
Future	je parlerai tu parleras il parlera nous parlerons vous parlerez ils parleront	je finirai tu finiras il finira nous finirons vous finirez ils finiront	je partirai tu partiras il partira nous partirons vous partirez ils partiront	je répondrai tu répondras il répondra nous répondrons vous répondrez ils répondront	je recevrai tu recevras il recevra nous recevrons vous recevrez ils recevront
Conditional	Je parlerais tu parlerais il parlerait nous parlerions vous parleriez ils parleraient	je finirais tu finirais il finirait nous finirions vous finiriez ils finiraient	je partirais tu partirais il partirait nous partirions vous partiriez ils partiraient	je répondrais tu répondrais il répondrait nous répondrions vous répondriez ils répondraient	je recevrais tu recevrais il recevrait nous recevrions vous recevriez ils recevraient
Imperative	parle parlons parlez	finis finissons finissez	pars partons partez	réponds répondons répondez	reçois recevons recevez
Conversational past (Passé composé)	j'ai parlé tu as parlé il a parlé nous avons parlé vous avez parlé ils ont parlé	j'ai fini tu as fini il a fini nous avons fini vous avez fini ils ont fini	je suis parti(e) tu es parti(e) il est parti nous sommes parti(e)s vous êtes parti(e)s ils sont partis	j'ai répondu tu as répondu il a répondu nous avons répondu vous avez répondu ils ont répondu	j'ai reçu tu as reçu il a reçu nous avons reçu vous avez reçu ils ont reçu

Vocabulary list

à moins que	unless
abîmé	damaged
abordable	approachable, accessible
aborder	to deal with, tackle, discuss
accueil (m)	welcome
acheter	to buy
acide	acid
acquérir	to acquire, obtain
actionnaires (m)	share-holders
affaire (f)	business
agrandir	to enlarge
agréable	agreeable, pleasant
améliorer	to improve
aménager	to fit out
appareil (m)	machine
approvisionnement (m)	supplies, stock
appui-tête (m)	head rest
argile (f)	clay, shale
arriver à s'implanter	to succeed in establishing oneself
assemblage (m)	assembly
atelier (m)	workshop
attirer	to attract
attrayant(e)	attractive, alluring
au delà	beyond
avant que	before
avantage (m)	advantage
avoir à faire à	to have to do with
bail (m)	lease
bailleur (m)	lessor
balai essuie-glace (m)	windscreen wiper
barbouiller (se)	to plaster, daub oneself
basculer	to swivel, to tip up
besoin (m)	need
bien que	although
boîte (f) de vitesse	gear-box
boîte (f)	tin
boucher	to block
brevet (m)	patent
breveté	patented
bricoler	to tinker with, patch up
cacher	to hide
cadastre (m)	the land register
cadeau (m)	present
caisses (f) regionales	regional banks
cambrioler	to burgle
canaliser	to channel
carte (f) d'accès gratuit	a free entry card
cerveau (m)	brain
chantier (m)	building-site
charger	to load, fill
chauffer	to heat
chèque (m)	cheque
chiffre (m)	figure, number
chômage (m)	unemployment
circuler	to circulate
cloisonnement (m)	partitioning
commande (f)	order
commercial	commercial
commercialisation (f)	marketing
comptabilité (f)	accounts, books
compte rendu (m)	the minutes
compte tenu de nos problèmes	considering our problems
compter sur (quelqu'un)	to count on (someone)
concrétisation (f)	materialisation
concurrent (m)	competitor
connaître	to know
consacrer du temps	to spend time
conseil (m)	advice
consigne (f)	instruction(s), order(s)
constater	to establish, ascertain
convenir	to suit, fit
concevoir	to conceive, devise
coque (f)	shell
couche (f)	layer

295

THE LANGUAGE OF BUSINESS

couverture (f)	1. coverage 2. blanket, cover	embarquer	to embark, to ship
craie (f)	chalk	emboîter	to encase
croire (se) (fort(e))	to think oneself strong	embrayage (m)	the clutch
cuir (m)	leather	empêcher	to prevent, hinder, impede
		emploi (m)	job
débit (m)	(retail) sale, delivery (of orator)	employer	to employ, use
		emprunter	to enter
débrayage (m)	disconnection, uncoupling	encastrer	to embed, to set in
décoller	to take off (in aeroplane)	engager (quelqu'un)	to hire someone
découper	to cut up	engin (m)	machine
défaire	to undo	enjeux (mpl)	stakes
défectif	defective	entreposage (m)	warehousing, storage
dégâts (mpl)	damage	entreprise (f)	undertaking or company, business
dégeler	to defrost		
dégraissage	removal of grease	entrer en concurrence (f)	to compete
délai (m)	delay, respite, time allowed (for completion of job)	envisager	to envisage
		équilibrage (m)	counter balancing
délégué (m)	delegate	esquisser	to sketch
demande (f)	enquiry	essayer d'éclairer	to try to shed light on
démarrer	to set off, to start	établir	to establish
démissionner	to resign	étain (m)	pewter
démodé	old fashioned	étanche	sealed
démolir	to demolish	être en cours	to be taking place
démonter	to take apart	être élevé	to be high (expensive)
dénoncer	to declare, proclaim	exécuter	to carry out
départ (m)	start	exigeant	demanding
dépasser	to overspend	expédier	to dispatch, expediate
déplier	to unfold	exploiter	to exploit, to work (of mine)
désigner	to appoint, choose, nominate	exporter	to export
dessus-de-lit (m)	the bedspread		
détecter	to detect	fabrication (f)	manufacture, production
développement (m)	development	fabriquer	to make
devis (m)	quote	facture (f)	a bill
directeur (m)	manager	faire marche (f) arrière	to go backwards
disparition (f)	disappearance	fait (m)	the fact
distribution (f)	the supply	falloir	to need, to have to
dresser	to erect, to prepare, draw up (contract etc)	ferroviaire	pertaining to a railway
		filiale (f)	a subsidiary
droits (m) exclusifs	exclusive rights	financier (-ière)	financial
ductile	ductile	fisc (m)	inland revenue, the tax department
dupliquer	to copy		
		fiable	reliable, dependable
échantillons (m)	samples	flasque (f)	flask
échéance (f)	date (of payment) falling due of bill	flexible	flexible
		fonctionnement (m)	functioning
écrou (m)	(screw) nut	fond (m)	bottom
effectivement	indeed	forage (m)	drilling, boring
effectuer	to effect, carry out	forer	to drill
efficace	effective, adequate	fournir	to supply, furnish, provide
effondrer (se)	to fall down, collapse	fournisseur (m)	supplier
égard (m)	consideration, respect	frais (m)	cost
éjecter	to eject	fréquemment	frequently
élargir	to enlarge	fret (m)	freight
élastique	elastic	frontière (f)	border
emballer	to pack, wrap up	fureur (f)	fury, rage, wrath

296

VOCABULARY LIST

gainer	to sheath, hem	mal à l'aise	ill at ease, uneasy
gamme (f)	range	malgré	in spite of
gars (m. fam)	the chap	malléable	malleable
gens (mpl.) terre-à-terre	down to earth people	manière (f)	way
géomètre (m)	surveyor	manque (m)	a lack
gêner	to bother, hamper	manquer	to lack, to miss
ça ne me gêne pas	it doesn't bother me	maquette (f) animée	working model
gestion (f)	management (of business), administration	marchandise (f)	merchandise, goods
		ça marche bien	that is popular, successful
gicleur (m)	jet	marge (f) bénéficiaire	profit margin
gonfler	to inflate, pump up	marque (f)	a make, a brand name
gravats (mpl)	rubbish (from demolitions)	matelas (m)	mattress
		matériel (m)	equipment, materials
d'habitude	usually	mener des opérations (f)	to lead operations
haut de gamme (de)	up-market	métier (m)	profession, occupation
HLM (habitation à loyer modéré)	council flat	micro-ordinateur (m)	micro computer, pc
		modifier	to modify
homologue (m)	counterpart	montage (m)	installation
honte (f) nationale	a national disgrace	monter	to set up
huile (f) de vidange	sump oil	morceler (un terrain)	to divide up
hypothèque (f)	mortgage	mouler	to cast, to mould
		mouvement (m) de fond	a groundswell
il est important de	it is better		
il est impossible de	it is possible/may be that	navette (f)	shuttle
il se peut que	it is important to	n'importe comment	anyhow
il vaut mieux que	it is impossible to	n'importe où	anywhere
immeuble (m)	building	n'importe quand	anytime
impayé	unpaid	n'importe quel(le)	any
implantation (m)	an overseas branch	n'importe qui	anyone
implanter	to set up	n'importe quoi	anything
importateur (m)	importer		
impôt (m)	back tax	occuper de (se)	to attend to
incompréhension (f)	a misunderstanding	OPA (offre (f) publique d'achat)	takeover bid
industrie (f)	industry		
industrie agro-alimentaire	agribusiness	opportunité (f)	opportunity
informatique (f)	information technology	ordre (m) du jour	an agenda
inoxydable	non-corrodible, rustproof		
		panne (être en)	to be broken down
je vous les remets	I am handing them to you	parcelle (f)	a plot
jeu (m) de lumière	lighting effects	paroi (f)	a partition
jonction (f)	junction	passer une commande	to place an order
jusqu'à ce que	until	péage (m)	toll
		percer	to bore
lancer (se)	to launch (a product/company)	permis (m) de construire	building permit
		personnel (m)	staff
lave-voitures (m)	car wash	pièce (f) de rechange	a spare part
lit escamotable (m)	foldaway bed	place (f)	square
livraison (f)	delivery	plafond (m)	ceiling
livrer	to deliver	plaque (f)	plate, sheet (of metal)
local (m)	premises	plaquette (f)	brochure
lot (m)	subdivision	poids (m) lourds	heavy goods
lotissement (m) industriel	land for industrial development	portage (m)	cost
		poste (m)	post
loyer (m)	rent	pot d'échappement (m)	exhaust pipe
		pour que	so that
mail (m)	the mall	pourvu que	provided that
maître (m) d'oeuvre	the project supervisor	preneur (m)	tenant, candidate

297

présentation (f)	service, performance
prêter à (se)	to lend itself to
prix de revient (m)	the cost price
produit (m) laitier	dairy product
profiter de	take advantage of
propre	1. clean 2. own
propre à	peculiar to
propreté	cleanliness, tidiness
protéger	to protect
province (f) profonde	the country
puits (m)	shaft
qualité (f)	quality
quartier (m)	area
quelquefois	sometimes
qui aura lieu	which will take place
quotidien(ne)	daily
rabattable	that can be folded back
raccrocher (se)	to fit in with
ranger	to put away, store
rappel	recall
rayon (m)	department (of a shop), a shelf
réalisation (f)	fulfilment
réceptionner	to take delivery of
reconditionner	to recondition
reçu (m)	the receipt
redressement (m)	adjustment
réduire les délais	to reduce the time span
réglage (m)	regulating, adjusting
régler	rule or regulate
régulièrement	regularly
remettre	to put back, to set back
remise (f)	discount
remplir	to fill up
remplissage (m)	filling
renseignement (m)	information
rentable	profitable
ressentir	to feel
résultat à perte (f)	a loss result
retirer	to take off
réunion (f)	meeting
rinçage (m)	rinsing
risque (m)	risk
roulettes (fpl)	castors
rupture (f)	break (in supply)
saisir	to seize
salle d'exposition (f)	the exhibition room
sangle (f)	strap
sans que	without
scinder	to divide, split up (of proposition or political party)
séchage	drying
secteur (m)	area
service après-vente (m)	after sales service
services (mpl.) qui relèvent plus de . . .	services which arise more from . . .
siège (m)	headquarters
sol (m)	soil
soleil (m)	sun
de sorte que	in order that
soupaper (f)	valve
suivi (m)	the follow-up
susciter	to instigate
table (f)	the table
tablette (f)	the flap
technopole (f)	business park
télécopie (f)	fax
tenir à dire	to insist on saying
tenir compte	to take into consideration
terminal (m)	terminal
terrain (m)	land, piece of land
toujours	always
traiter	to process
treuil (m)	winch, windlass
trimestriel (elle)	quarterly
trou (m)	hole
trouver	to find
tunnel (m)	tunnel
tunnelier (m)	tunnel boring machine
tuyau (m)	a tube, pipe
usine (f)	factory
vedette (f)	star
vendre	to sell
vente (f)	sale
verrière (f)	atrium
vis (f)	screw
visage (m)	face
visser	to screw, screw in, screw down
voire même	even going as far as
vraisemblablement	probably, very likely

Where to go

Sources of information and advice

The **French team** in the **Exports to Europe Branch** of the BOTB will be pleased to answer your queries on all aspects of exporting, specifically to France. Contact points are the Head of French Section, Exports to Europe, 071-215 5303.

FOR GENERAL ENQUIRIES about selling to France you can ring the following numbers:

CAPITAL GOODS – 071-215 5197/5451
CONSUMER GOODS SECTOR A – 071-215 4762
CONSUMER GOODS SECTOR B – 071-215 4761

If you prefer you can write to the French Desk, BOTB Room 350, 1 Victoria Street, London SW1H 0ET.

BOTB regional offices

For information on BOTB services for exporters and guidance on general export matters you should, in the first instance, contact your nearest Regional Office. Where appropriate the Director (Exports) or one of the staff will gladly arrange to meet you.

South Eastern Regional Office
Bridge Place
88–89 Eccleston Square
London SW1V 1PT
Tel: 071-215 5000
Telex: 297124 a/b SEREX G

South Eastern Regional Office
Reading Area Office
40 Caversham Road
Reading
Berkshire RG1 7EB
Tel: 0734 395600
Tlx: 847799

South Eastern Regional Office
Reigate Area Office
Douglas House
London Road

Reigate
Surrey RH2 9QP
Tel: 0737 226900
Tlx: 918364 a/b DTI RGT G

Eastern Regional Office
Building A
Westbrook Research Centre
Milton Road
Cambridge CB1 1YG
Tel: 0223 461939
Tlx: 81582 a/b DTI EAO G

North Eastern Regional Office
Stanegate House
2 Groat Market
Newcastle-upon-Tyne NE1 1YN
Tel: 091-232 4722
Telex: 53178 DOT TYN G

Yorkshire and Humberside Regional Office
Priestly House
Park Row
Leeds LS1 5LF
Tel: 0532 443171
Telex: 557925 DTI LDS G

West Midlands Regional Office
Ladywood House
Stephenson Street
Birmingham B2 4DT
Tel: 021-632 4111
Telex: 337919 DTI BHM

East Midlands Regional Office
Severns House
20 Middle Pavement
Nottingham NG1 7DW
Tel: 0602 506181
Telex: 37413 DTI NOT G

North West Regional Office
Sunley Tower
Piccadilly Plaza
Manchester M1 4BA
Tel: 061-236 2171
Telex: 667104 DTI MCHR

South West Regional Office
The Pithay
Bristol BS1 2PB
Tel: 0272 272666
Telex: 44214 DTI BTL G

Welsh Office
New Crown Building
Cathays Park
Cardiff CF1 3NQ
Tel: 0222 825111
Telex: 498228 WOCARD G

Scottish Office
Industry Department for Scotland
Alhambra House
45 Waterloo Street
Glasgow G2 6AT
Tel: 041-248 2855
Telex: 777833 SEPD G

Industrial Development Board for Northern Ireland
IDB House
64 Chichester Street
Belfast BT1 4JX
Tel: 0232 233233
Telex: 747025 IDB NI G

Specialist help available

Export credits guarantee department

The Export Credit Guarantee Department, a separate government department, provides UK suppliers of goods and services with insurance cover against the major financial risks of exporting and may enable its policy holders to obtain access to export finance.

Export Credit Guarantee Department
Export House
50 Ludgate Hill
London EC4M 7AY
Tel: 071-382 7000
Telex: 883601 ECGD DHQW (A-C)LDN

Simplification of international trade procedures board (SITPRO)

SITPRO is an independent organisation set up by the BOTB to simplify export/import trade procedures and documents and ensure that British trade interests are aware of, and get full benefit from, such improvements. SITPRO provides a number of specialist services to exporters and can provide advice about the new Harmonised System (HS) of customs classification and the Single Administrative Document (SAD) form for customs clearance.

Further information can be obtained from:

SITPRO
Almack House
26 King Street
London SW1W 6QW
Tel: 071-287 3525
Telex: 919130 SITPRO G

Science and technology officers

There are Science and Technology Sections in many British Embassies abroad, including Paris. They keep abreast of scientific and technological developments in their countries and can give advice to UK exporters seeking to plan ahead and remain in the forefront of technology. You should contact, in the first instance:

Overseas Technology Information Unit
Room 230
RTP4
Department of Trade and Industry
Ashdown House
123 Victoria Street
London SW1E 6RB
Tel: 071-212 0356

Small firms centres

Operated by the Department of Employment Small Firms Service, these provide free informtion on a wide range of subjects, from sources of supply to government legislation. For further details, including the free booklet *How to Start Exporting: a Guide for Small Firms*, dial 100 and ask for Freephone Enterprise or, if you prefer, write to:

Small Firms and Tourism Division
Department of Employment
Steel House
Tothill Street
London SW1H 9NF

The BOTB also publishes a booklet *Exporting for the Smaller Firm*, available free from any BOTB Regional Office or the French Desk.

Design aspects

The Design Council
28 Haymarket
London SW1Y 4SU
Tel: 071-839 8000
Telex: 8812963

Vehicle regulations

Society of Motor Manufacturers and Traders
Forbes House
Halkin Street
London SW1X 7DS
Tel: 071-235 7000

Exporting medical products and hospital equipment

British Health-Care Export Council
5th Floor
2 Harewood Place
London W1R 9HN
Tel: 071-493 6699

Advice on the export of animals, animal products and fish

Animal Health Division
Ministry of Agriculture, Fisheries and Food
Government Buildings
Hook Rise South
Tolworth
Surbiton
Surrey KT6 7NF
Tel: 081-337 6611

Food regulations

Leatherhead Food Research Association
Randalls Road
Leatherhead
Surrey KT22 7RY
Tel: 0372 376761

British Industrial Biological Research Association (BIBRA)
Woodmansterne Road
Carshalton
Surrey SM5 4DS
Tel: 081-643 4411

Food From Britain
Franco-British Centre
8 rue Cimarosa
75008 Paris
Tel: (1) 45 05 13 08
Telex: 614806

Textile marking

British Knitting and Clothing Export Council
British Apparel Centre
7 Swallow Place
Oxford Circus
London W1R 7AA
Tel: 071-493 6622

Technical requirements

Technical help to Exporters
Linford Wood
Milton Keynes
Bucks MK14 6LE
Tel: 0908 220022
Telex: 825777

Drugs regulations

Proprietary Association of Great Britain
Vernon House
Sicilian Avenue
London WC1A 21QH
Tel: 071-242 8331

Pharmaceutical Society of Great Britain
1 Lambeth High Street
London SE1 7JN
Tel: 071-735 9141

General transport

International aspects of vehicle safety, construction and use regulations and copies of *Your Lorry Abroad* from:

Department of Transport
International Road Freight Office
Westgate House
Westgate Road
Newcastle-upon-Tyne NE1 1TW
Tel: 091-2610031

Carriage of dangerous goods

Carriage by air:

Civil Aviation Authority
Aviation House
129 Kingsway
London WC2B 6NN
Tel: 071-379 7311

Carriage by sea

Department of Transport
Marine Directorate
Sunley House
90 High Holborn
London WC1V 6LP
Tel: 071-405 6911

ADR/RID carriage by road or rail

Department of Transport
FRH2
2 Marsham Street
London SW1P 3EB
Tel: 071-212 8167

Carriage of radio-active goods by road or rail

Department of Transport
Radio-Active Materials Transport Div.
2 Marsham Street
London SW1P 3EB
Tel: 071-212 7249

Goods covered by the Common Agricultural Policy of the EC

The Common Agricultural Policy (CAP) affects essentially the following products: beef and veal, cereals and rice, fish, eggs and poultry, milk, dairy produce, certain oils and fats, pigs and pigmeat, sheepmeat, sugar and products derived from these (including processed fruit and vegetables) and products involving sugar wine and grape musts. Exporters dealing with such commodities must register with:

The Intervention Board for Agricultural Produce
PO Box 69
Fountain House
2 Queens Walk
Reading
Berks RG1 7QW
Tel: 0734 583626

To remedy the market disturbances that would result from the constant fluctuations of the rates of exchange of floating national currencies, a system of Monetary Compensatory Amounts (MCAs) has been introduced. Details on the current rates for your goods can be obtained from the Intervention Board at the above address.

For all these goods, the following information must be entered on the appropriate SAD documents:

1. HS Number
2. Net weight, or the quantity expressed in the unit of measurement to be used in calculating the MCA

This need not be included for shipments of a net weight of less than 1000 kg.

Language services

Translation

Institute of Linguistics
24a Highbury Grove
London N5 2EA
Tel: 071-359 7445/6386

The Institute can recommend one of their members for translation services but does not, itself, undertake translation work.

Institute of Translation & Interpreting
318a Finchley Road
London NW3 5HT
Tel: 071-794 9931

WHERE-TO-GO GUIDE

Language tuition

The government has supported the setting up of a number of 'language export centres' (LX Centres) throughout the country to support language learning for business users. These LX Centres bring together the skills of local providers to offer tailor-made courses of study for individual clients. For information about your nearest LX Centre, contact:

The National LX Office
CILT
Inner Circle
Regents Park
London NW1
Tel: 071-224 3748

Publicity

Central Office of Information

Publicity services for UK exporters can often be obtained through the services of the Central Office of Information who are concerned with the collection from industry of items suitable for dissemination abroad via the Government information services. The COI are interested in news items, feature articles, tape recordings for broadcasting and films for television and other screenings. They are particularly interested in items relating to the development and launch of new products manufactured in the UK.

Further information can be obtained from the Head Office at:

Hercules House
Westminster Bridge Road
London SE1 7DU
Tel: 071-261 8718
Telex: 915444 CENTROFORM LDN

BBC external services

The BBC External Services broadcast throughout the world in English and 36 other languages. An important part of their own output deals with developments in British industry, science and technology. New ideas developed by firms in this country are featured prominently in news and other broadcasts, with the name of the manufacturer mentioned where appropriate. All enquiries reaching the BBC as a result of these programmes are passed on to the firms concerned.

The BBC welcome as much information as possible from industry. They are interested in new processes and products, export successes, contracts and exhibits at trade fairs abroad. You should send information to:

Export Liaison
BBC External Services
Bush House
Strand
London WC2B 4PH
Tel: 071-257 2039/2321
Telex: 265781 BBC HQ G

The French Embassy

The French Embassy
58 Knightsbridge
London SW1
Tel: 071-235 8080

Commercial Section
21 Grosvenor Place
London SW1X 7HU
Tel: 071-235 7080

Consulates:

24 Rutland Gate
London SW7 1BD
Tel: 071-581 5292

11 Randolph Crescent
Edinburgh EH3 7TT
Tel: 031-225 7951

Cunard Building
Whiter Street
Liverpool L3 1ET
Tel: 051-236 8685 includes responsibility for N. Ireland.

La Motte Street
St. Helier
Jersey C.I.
Tel: 0534 26256

The French Chamber of commerce in the UK

The French Chamber is mainly concerned with the promotion of French exports but can sometimes provide useful information. It publishes a list of trade fairs in France. It is located at:

Knightsbridge House (2nd Floor)
197 Knightsbridge
London SW7 1RB
Tel: 071-225 5250

Useful addresses and organisations in France

British commercial representation in France

Business visitors to France are invited to telephone the British Embassy in Paris or the nearest Consulate-General on arrival and arrange an appointment so that they are seen as soon as possible by the officer concerned. It is helpful if some form of advance warning can be given, either via your Regional Office, the French Desk or direct by letter or telex. British commercial representatives in France are as follows:

Paris: Commercial Department
British Embassy
35 rue du Faubourg Saint-Honoré
75383 Paris Cedex 08
Tel: (331) 42 66 91 42
Telex: 65024 INFORM 65024 F

Bordeaux: British Consulate-General
Commercial Section
353 boulevard du President-Wilson
B.P. 91
33020 BORDEAUX CEDEX
Tel: 56.42.34.13
Telex: 570440 F

Lille: Commercial Section
British Consulate-General
11 Square Dutilleul
59800 Lille
Tel: (20) 57 87 90
Telex: 120169 Britain LILLE F

Lyon: Commercial Section
British Consulate-General
24 rue Childebert
69002 Lyon Cedex 1, Rhône
Tel: (7) 837 5967
Telex: 330254 BRITLYO F

Marseille: Commercial Section
British Consulate-General
24 avenue du Prado
13006 Marseille
Tel: (91) 534332
Telex: 420307 Britain MARSL F

The Franco-British Chamber of Commerce and Industry

The Chamber's prime duty is to promote Anglo-French trade and investment and to develop and build contact between itself and the British and French Authorities in order to keep abreast of important developments and, where desirable, to influence the course of events.

It possesses a reference library which Members visiting the Chamber can study on the spot, and offers an information and advice service to Members on a wide variety of commercial problems.

The Chamber can also provide a range of services and has office and presentational accommodation which can be hired for even a few hours. Contacts can be provided for Members with both the Authorities and other businessmen either on an individual basis or by means of functions, debates, receptions, seminars etc.

The Chamber has pooled the experience and expertise of its business and professional Members and other authoritative sources to publish a document entitled *Doing Business in France* designed to help companies to enter the French market. Copies can be bought directly from the Chamber.

The Chamber operates a discount scheme to Members covering car hire, travel and accommodation. Their journal *Cross Channel Trade* contains news/,articles and features of interest to the Anglo-French business community and is sent free to Members. Regional branches of the Chamber also exist throughout France, and often organise social gatherings where business people from both France and the UK can develop useful contacts.

Executives of Member firms who are under the age of forty are eligible to join the Junior Chamber, which is part of the parent body, but which has its own individual programme of functions.

Membership is open to all firms interested in Anglo-French trade, and application forms together with full details on the range of services can be obtained from the Chamber at:

Franco-British Chamber of Commerce
8 rue Cimarosa
75116 Paris
Tel: (1) 45 05 13 08
Telex: 614806 BRCOMPA F

Banks

The major British banks are all represented in France:

Midland Bank (France) SA operate through a variety of subsidiaries – enquiries should be addressed in the first instance to:

Midland Bank (France) SA
6 rue Piccini
75116 Paris
Tel: (331) 45 02 80 80
Telex: 648022 MIDFRA

Barclays Bank SA

Paris Main branch:	33 rue du Quatre Septembre 75002 Paris Tel: 42 96 65 65
Paris, Others	6 Rond Point de Champs Elysées 75008 Paris Tel: 43 59 15 26
	24 avenue Kleber 75116 Paris Tel: 45 00 86 86
	157 boulevard Saint Germain 75006 Paris Tel: 42 22 28 63
	106bis rue St. Lazare 75008 Paris Tel: 45 22 97 72
	56/58 avenue de Suffren 75015 Paris Tel: 47 83 82 82
Greater Paris Area	135 avenue Achille Peretti 92200 Neuilly sur Seine Tel: 624 48 88
	1 rue de la Corderie Centra 340 94150 Rungis Tel: 687 33 72

Other branches at: Aix les Bains, Antibes, Bayonne, Biarritz, Bordeaux, Boulogne, Cagnes sur Mer (subbranch to Nice), Calais, Cannes, Dunkerque, Le Cannet (sub to Cannes), Le Havre, Libourne, Lille, Lyon, Marseille, Menton, Nice, Orleans, Roubaix, Rouen, Saint-Avoid (sub to Sarreguemines), Sarreguemines, Strasbourg, Vence and Monte Carlo, and Monaco.

Lloyds Bank International (France) plc
43 boulevard des Capucines
75083 Paris
Tel: 42 61 51 25
Telex: 210097 INTLOYD Paris

Lloyds also have main offices in Cannes and Monte Carlo

National Westminster Bank sa
18 place Vendome
75021 Paris Cedex 01
Tel: 42 60 37 40

National Westminster Bank have branches at Bordeaux, Lille, Lyon, Marseille, Nantes, Strasbourg, Toulouse, Nice and in Monaco.

Organisation responsible for ensuring goods comply with French and EC regulations (mainly consumer items)

Service de la Repression des Fraudes et du Contrôle de la Qualité
44 bd de Grenelles (15e)
75732 Paris Cedex 15

French customs

Centre des Renseignements de Douanes
Direction Generale des Douanes et des Droits Indirects
8 rue de la Tour des Dames
75436 Paris Cedex 09

Information on VAT (TVA)

Centre des Renseignements TVA
Direction Generale des Douanes et des Droits Indirects
8 rue de la Tour des Dames
75436 Paris Cedex 09

French equivalent of BOTB

CFCE (Centre Français du Commerce Exterieur)
Service des Reglementations
5 rue Pierre de Serbie
75383 Paris Cedex 16

Useful publications

Hints to Exporters – France: a complementary pocket-sized booklet to this profile, containing essential information for business people visiting France, obtainable from your local Regional BOTB Office or from The French Desk BOTB.

British Business: weekly news from the Department of Trade and Industry including articles and information on exporting and overseas markets, exhibitions and fairs, customs regulations and tariff changes. Statistics on industrial production, trade and investment are also published. Available from news-stands or by subscription:

HMSO
PO Box 569
London SE1 9NH
Tel: 071-928 6977 Ext. 472

Marketing Consumer Goods in France: Information on the marketing methods and distribution patterns for consumer goods in France plus details of the major retail outlets, stores, super- and hypermarkets. Obtainable from your local Regional BOTB Office or the French Desk of BOTB.

Mail Order Houses in France: Methods of selling to the French Mail Order Houses and details of the various companies involved in this means of trading. Obtainable from your local Regional BOTB Office or the French Desk of BOTB).

Register of French Companies Involved in Third Country Projects: Available from the French Desk of BOTB.

Abecor Country Report: France
Barclays Bank Group
Economic Intelligence Unit
54 Lombard Street
London EC3P 3AH

Economic Report: France
Lloyds Bank Group Economics Department
71 Lombard Street
London EC3P 3BS

Spotlight France
Midland Bank International
110 Cannon Street
London EC4N 6AA

France: Overseas Economic Report
National Westminster Bank Ltd
41 Lothbury
London EC2P 2BP

OECD Economic Surveys: France
The Organisation for Economic Co-operation and Development, Paris.
Available from HMSO.

Other information

A wide range of handouts and reports on various sectors of the French market and on French regulations is freely available from the French Desk of BOTB.